THE POETRY OF
GEOFFREY HILL

HENRY HART

Introduction by Donald Hall

Southern Illinois University Press • Carbondale / Edwardsville

Copyright © 1986 by the Board of Trustees, Southern Illinois University
All rights reserved
Printed in the United States of America
Edited by Yvonne D. Mattson
Designed by David Ford
Production supervised by Kathleen Giencke

Permission to quote from the following copyright sources is gratefully acknowledged: Geoffrey Hill, *For the Unfallen: Poems 1952–1958* (London: André Deutsch, 1959); *King Log* (André Deutsch, 1968); *Mercian Hymns* (André Deutsch, 1971); *Tenebrae* (André Deutsch, 1978). Reprinted by permission of André Deutsch, Ltd. *The Lords of Limit, Essays on Literature and Ideas* (New York: Oxford University Press, 1984) and *The Mystery of the Charity of Charles Péguy* (Oxford, 1984) reprinted by permission of Oxford University Press.
 Portions of an interview with Geoffrey Hill are reprinted by permission of Faber and Faber Ltd from *Viewpoints: Poets in Conversation*, by John Haffenden (London: Faber and Faber, 1981).

Library of Congress Cataloging in Publication Data
Hart, Henry, 1954–
    The poetry of Geoffrey Hill.

    Bibliography: p.
    Includes index.
    1. Hill, Geoffrey—Criticism and interpretation.
I. Title.
PR6015.I4735Z68   1985   821'.914   85-2122
ISBN 0-8093-1236-0

90 89 88 87 86   5 4 3 2 1

CONTENTS

Acknowledgments   vii

Introduction by Donald Hall   ix

I. Journeys, Meditations, and Elegies: *Early Poems*   1

II. The Embattled Poet and His Tradition: *For the Unfallen*   25

    1. Grammar, Syntax, and the Romantic Tradition   25
    2. History and Judgment   40
    3. Judaeo-Christianity Revised   53
    4. Modernist Sequences   62

III. Power and Authority: *King Log*   81

    1. Continuities   81
    2. The Poetry of *Poesis*   86
    3. The Nightmare of History   102
    4. Doctor Faustus and the Poetry Banquet   118
    5. "Funeral Music"   126
    6. "The Songbook of Sebastian Arrurruz"   140

IV. The Anglo-Saxon Heritage: *Mercian Hymns*   153

    1. Precedents   153
    2. Offa Revealed   161
    3. On Cultured Ground   164
    4. Offa, the Political Artificer   180

CONTENTS

V. Passion Ritualized: *Tenebrae* 193

1. "The Pentecost Castle": Ritual and Romance 195
2. The Journey to Love 199
3. Love, Death, and the Mystical Marriage 207
4. "Lachrimae" 212
5. Rituals of Meditation 216
6. Recreation and Decreation 222
7. "An Apology for the Revival of Christian Architecture in England" 227
8. East and West 234
9. Autumnal Elegies 238
10. Privacies 246
11. "Tenebrae" 249

VI. Spiritual Biography: *The Mystery of the Charity of Charles Péguy* 255

Notes 283

Selected Bibliography 291

Index 295

ACKNOWLEDGMENTS

I would like to thank my parents, grandparents, and Dartmouth College for financial assistance which enabled me to write this book. I am indebted to Anne Stevenson, who read some of my preliminary essays, and to Anthony Thwaite and Carl Schmidt, who examined my Oxford D. Phil. thesis on Geoffrey Hill's poetry and suggested several alterations. I would like to thank Peter Robinson, who pointed out necessary changes in an earlier version of the first chapter; Stephen Wall, who provided editorial assistance on the last chapter; Tina Alvaro, her assistants, and the English Department at The Citadel, who all helped prepare the final manuscript; and Jennie Summerall for her assistance with proofreading. I am indebted to Geoffrey Hill for kindly answering bibliographical questions about his poems. Above all I must thank Richard Ellmann, whose kindness and critical judgment were a continual source of inspiration as I worked on the thesis at Oxford, and Donald Hall, who encouraged me during my first years at Oxford, directed me toward publishers in America, and provided the introduction for the book.

Permission to quote from the following copyright sources is gratefully acknowledged: Geoffrey Hill, *For the Unfallen: Poems 1952–1958* (London: André Deutsch, 1959); *King Log* (André Deutsch, 1968); *Mercian Hymns* (André Deutsch, 1971); *Tenebrae*

ACKNOWLEDGMENTS

(André Deutsch, 1978). Reprinted by permission of André Deutsch, Ltd. *The Lords of Limit, Essays on Literature and Ideas* (New York: Oxford University Press, 1984) and *The Mystery of the Charity of Charles Péguy* (Oxford, 1984) Reprinted by permission of Oxford University Press.

Portions of an interview with Geoffrey Hill are reprinted by permission of Faber and Faber Ltd. from *Viewpoints: Poets in Conversation*, by John Haffenden (London: Faber and Faber, 1981).

The last chapter of this book appeared (in a slightly different form) in *Essays in Criticism* (Oct. 1983). It is reprinted here by permission of the editors of *Essays in Criticism*. The first chapter, also in slightly different form, appeared in *Geoffrey Hill, Essays on his Work* (Milton Keynes, England: Open University Press, 1985) and is reprinted by kind permission of the publishers.

INTRODUCTION
Donald Hall

Geoffrey Hill was born in 1932, in "a small market town" in Worcestershire, as he puts it with characteristic reticence. Both parents had left school at thirteen, and his father became a village constable; his mother's people had been "artisans in the traditional cottage-industry of nail-making." An only child, Hill attended the village school, then traveled to study at a grammar school (public in the American sense) from which he won a scholarship to Keble College at Oxford. For some years he taught at Leeds University; most recently he has tutored and lectured at Cambridge. He was married and has four children.

When he was at Oxford he published a remarkable pamphlet of poems in the Fantasy Poets series. In 1959, André Deutsch in London published *For the Unfallen*, distributed in the United States a year later by Dufour Editions; Deutsch has remained Hill's English publisher, with *King Log* in 1968 and *Mercian Hymns* in 1971, as well as the more recent volumes. The first three books were gathered into one volume in the United States by Houghton Mifflin, *Somewhere is Such a Kingdom*, in 1975; the same publisher issued *Tenebrae* in 1979. Most recently, Hill has published a long poem, *The Mystery of the Charity of Charles Péguy*, and a collection of essays, *Lords of Limit*; for these books, his American publisher is the Oxford University Press in New York (1984).

When he was seven, Hill began to sing in the choir of the Church of England in his village. Poetry may have found its beginning in the choirloft. The structure of Hill's poetry may be approached by musical analogy, and in a sense the Church hovers at the center of his work: His language is Christian but his spirit is never unequivocally redeemed—to begin the contradictions by which one speaks of Hill's work. This poetry is suffused with religion but it is not a hymn of belief; it is a lyric of struggle and pain, obsessed with the Christianity from which it takes little comfort or solace. The Church is power, doctrine, institution, and history. Of all major modern poets Hill is the most suffused with history, which layers his language. History is England first, from the half-mythical Mercia through Shakespeare's England to nineteenth century industrial architecture and twentieth century motorways. Behind this England is a Europe which is Roman or Holy Roman, local tribes speaking their Frankish and Anglian dialects; Old English prevails; toward the end of the *Mercian Hymns*, he tells of a grandmother "whose childhood and prime womanhood were spent in the nailer's darg."

Hill's martyrs include Sebastian, Southwell, and Dietrich Bonhoeffer, and they are not only Christian. The overwhelming event of modern history is Hitler's Germany. As C.H. Sisson says in an essay about Hill, both history and myth are "repositories of the common experience which gives meaning to what we feel as individuals." Although the poems are strongly emotional, they are general rather than personal. When Hill doubts his martyrs, we understand that his skepticism is self-directed, but we do not hear details of the life suspected. Mistrust makes the slogan on his shield: he entertains no subject without suspecting his own entertainment. His Southwell wrote that a "poet, a lover and a liar are by many reckoned but three things with one signification." If Hill takes poetry as seriously as anyone alive, he doubts in particular that part of himself that takes poetry seriously: "The tongue's atrocities." In his early "Orpheus and Eurydice," Hill's Orpheus approached the "still moist dead," "to be judged/ For his song. . . ." —and the poem ended with Orpheus "serene even to a fault."

INTRODUCTION

The eroticism of Hill's language is as noteworthy as his self-doubt. The natural world in these poems is fecund and thick with the blood of sex, wounds, and sexual wounds, attractive and repellant together, "an earth of sickly richness" as one critic called it. No recent poetry belongs more to the body, in the texture of its mouthy rhythm and in its fleshy imagery. Because one speaks of Geoffrey Hill, one must add: It is also a poetry repelled by body. With his thrust and retraction, eros and thanatos, sexual desire intertwines with suffering and suspicion—but this remains a poetry of extraordinary sensuousness.

A poet of Hill's difficulty inspires criticism, good and bad together. Christopher Ricks, in two essays collected in *The Force of Poetry* (1984), has been Hill's foremost critic. (It is typical of both men that Ricks works at Hill's punctuation with an excitement that most critics could not muster for incest in the royal family.) I will not discuss Hill's critics here, but I must quote Seamus Heaney as he imagines Hill at work: "Hill addresses the language . . . like a mason addressing a block. . . . Words in his poetry fall slowly and singly, like molten solder, and accumulate to a dull glowing nub. I imagine Hill as indulging in a morose linguistic delectation, dwelling on the potential of each word with much the same slow relish as Leopold Bloom dwells on the thought of his kidney."

One must not belittle Hill's difficulty, but one does not praise him because he is hard to read. One praises him because his poetry is beautiful. It is only imperative, for the quality of his beauty, that he achieve it by a complex means. When an art endures past innocence, the artist who will not merely repeat and corrupt old simplicities must undertake greater and greater complexity, unless or until some historical, national, or linguistic revolution wipe the old landscape clear. Footprints in the snow, around the castle of English poetry, trample each other down.

If I have named a theme or two, I hope I don't appear to speak of "Hill's ideas." If poetry were merely ideas it would be pointless to write poetry; if ideas, in their abstract expression, embodied a spiritual and emotional wholeness, we would need no vowels or line-breaks. Hill's quick alternations of tone, his sudden and frequent reverses, work to prevent paraphrase; no sooner does the reader think he has accomplished paraphrase than he realizes that he has allowed a counter-thrust to escape notation. We may as well summarize a Beethoven quartet. It helps to consider music's structure—the way music in its articulated motion continually abolishes itself, sketching the way by traveling, rubbing itself out as it travels. If in the end Hill has contradicted everything he has said, including his own contradictions, he has created and articulated the structure of a mind unable to find rest, defeated and beautiful in stillness, resolved in a perfection of irresolution. These poems of course include the idea, its antithesis, and the emotions engendered by oscillation to and fro; but they do not, because they are great poems, include ideas as a suitcase includes clothes: they embody or enact a wholeness. This resolved manyness, this complexity reaching stasis, this diversity and multiplicity may rest only in the form of poetry: *Hill's poems reveal again what poetry is for.*

Geoffrey Hill's intense Englishness leaches back into the bones of the legionaries tangled with the bones of their shaggy foes. He is roughly as distant from American literature—from Robert Frost *or* Robert Creeley—as Gerard Manley Hopkins from *Gilgamesh*. Therefore it is an American critic, struck by the alien, who introduces us to Hill. Henry Hart has read what Hill has read, supplies background to allow us access to multiple sources, and suggests connections that develop over the years of Hill's work. Hart is our guide to the splendor and difficulty of Hill's construction, image by image, allusion by allusion, but Hart finally reads poems not sources and ideas; this critic attends to poetry's body.

INTRODUCTION

There are poets we do best to read without anyone's voice in our ears, but there are other writers, like Pound and Joyce, for whom critical exegesis can clear away difficulties of structure and allusion, so that the serious reader can focus upon the proper difficulties of just response. Henry Hart's study introduces us to the arduous, intense pleasure of the poetry of Geoffrey Hill.

A Note on the Texts

Page references to quotations for Geoffrey Hill's books and from John Haffenden's *Viewpoints, Poets in Conversation* are taken from the British editions listed in the bibliography. I have used the following abbreviations:

FU   *For the Unfallen*
KL   *King Log*
MH   *Mercian Hymns*
T   *Tenebrae*
MC   *The Mystery of the Charity of Charles Péguy*
LL   *The Lords of Limit, Essays on Literature and Ideas*
VP   *Viewpoints, Poets in Conversation*

1 / JOURNEYS, MEDITATIONS, AND ELEGIES

Early Poems

In 1954, as a young poet about to leave Oxford for a lecturing post at Leeds, Hill defined his poetic program in an open letter published in the *London Magazine*. "There does seem to be quite general agreement," he said, "that each artist, young or old, must work out his own salvation, must cut his own path; and that only those with the most strength and the most courage are likely to get to the end."[1] This combination of qualification and tough assertiveness is either the boast of a young graduate still unsure of his principles or the pledge of a poet who will remain committed to his vision no matter what his peers might say or do.

In fact, Hill's pronouncement reveals much about his work done at Oxford and prophesies the direction it would take afterwards. From "An Ark on the Flood" to *The Mystery of the Charity of Charles Péguy*, his poems depict combatants who pursue salvation with a tenacity which often brings destruction to victor and victim alike. Early and late, Hill offers up for judgment many examples of "heroic" enterprise and, in the ambiguities and paradoxes of his lines, poses an ambivalent response. His is a poetry of irresolution before inflexible resolution, which struggles towards action but only to win Pyrrhic victories. The guilty collusion of poet with politician and saint with soldier in inflicting great harm in service to noble causes, is Hill's most lasting theme. The poet's task, he argues, is to atone for mistakes and crimes, both past and present, personal and public.

His triumphs, when they come, are in the judicious poems themselves—in their wary articulations of defeat.

Hill's poems move in parallel trajectories from a common source. They can be meditative or elegiac, lyric or epic in scope, but they all dramatize some aspect of the devoted man's (and normally the devoted poet's) effort to unite his life or art with his vision of perfection. Hill declared in his "Letter from Oxford" that "the poet . . . hunched in his mackintosh on the top of a bus in the Banbury Road, sits apart from the crowd. Or he follows in the wake of a vision of life that goes before him and which he cannot grasp, a cloud by day and a pillar of fire by night."[2] Moses, in this fanciful collocation, is also Tantalus doomed to grasp for promised fruits he cannot have. Hill's view of the poet changes little over the years. In a later essay, he says: "The poet will occasionally, in the act of writing a poem experience a sense of pure fulfilment," but this should not be "misconstrued as the attainment of objective perfection." No matter how much "a poem is shaped and finished, it remains to some extent within the 'imprisoning marble' of a quotidian shapelessness and imperfection" (*LL*, p. 2). Twenty years later, he is still Tantalus unrequited in his pool.

Most noticeable in the early poems is Hill's uneasy alliance with traditional spiritual exercises. The poems are obsessed, as he says of Robert Lowell's early works, with the "rich European . . . legacies of revelation and self-revelation."[3] But unlike Christian meditation, which directs the mind away from the world towards "at-one-ment" with God, Hill's meditations return to earth to examine its imperfections with scrupulous vigor. In "Genesis," for example, his persona begins beside the ocean, "crying the miracles of God," withdraws into a mythical order beyond creation's violence, and then, after some vacillation, returns "to flesh and blood and the blood's pain." "Genesis" contains aspects of the poetic journey, meditation, and elegy, but casts them in a new and powerful way. Written when Hill was only nineteen, the poem sketches his "genesis" as a young man and points toward the major preoccupations of his work. The poem's most obvious model is the Book of Genesis, but Hill versifies the Bible in his own way, just as Christopher Smart versified the Book of Psalms in his own way in "Song to David." In fact, when "Genesis" first appeared in an Oxford poetry journal, it was dedicated to Smart. Hill changes the Bible's six day scheme of creation into a story of a six day journey, in which the poet responds to the original creation in various moods of love, hate, and stoical resolve.

"Genesis" is also Hill's song of innocence and experience, an imitation of Blake, as Hill said of all his early poems. As an undergraduate Hill was steeped in Blake. He wrote a review of Blake's long prophetic book, *Jerusalem*, although in it he stated his preference for the earlier *Songs*. In Blake's mythic world the archetypal poet works in Eden, where contraries are creative. Hill's poet in "Genesis" begins in a place where body and wind, mind and spirit, sea and land, salt water and fresh water violently but productively conflict. The poem begins with an ecstatic flourish:

> Against the burly air I strode,
> Where the tight ocean heaves its load,
> Crying the miracles of God.
>
> And first I brought the sea to bear
> Upon the dead weight of the land;
> And the waves flourished at my prayer,
> The rivers spawned their sand.

The artist-god striding by the ocean breathes in the wind or *spiritus*, the divine breath which is the afflatus of inspiration, and shores the sea's fragments and its fertile waters against "the dead weight of the land." Like Blake's prophets, Hill envisions himself as a creative spirit struggling to shape a dead chaos into vigorous order which, like God's miraculous creation, is also his word or poem.

After their exertions, Blake's poets retire to Beulah, the married land where contraries peacefully rest. Hill's protagonist also retires to the "steady hills" above the toils of creation. Hill records the departure symbolically:

> And where the streams were salt and full
> The tough pig-headed salmon strove,
> Curbing the ebb and the tide's pull,
> To reach the steady hills above.

But with this ascent comes a fall into a new and disturbing knowledge. Symbolic birds in section II reveal a ferocity which the poet, enchanted by nature's beauty and his work, had failed to perceive. The owl is "soft-voiced"; the ferret "smiles." But none of these predators is innocent. Like the crows of Ted Hughes's poems, their business is tearing off heads. In a clever conceit Hill transforms them into bombers, a common worry for anyone growing up in England during the Second World War. The osprey "plunge[s] with triggered claw," as if commandeering a machine gun in an airplane (and may recall Eliot's similar bird-like bomber—the "dark dove with the flickering tongue" in "Little Gidding"). The other birds "hooped in steel" (like a plane's fuselage) seek to destroy and bloody England's shore as well. Hill recalls:

> The second day I stood and saw
> The osprey plunge with triggered claw,
> Feathering blood along the shore,
> To lay the living sinew bare.
>
> And the third day I cried: 'Beware
> The soft-voiced owl, the ferret's smile,
> The hawk's deliberate stoop in air,
> Cold eyes, and bodies hooped in steel,
> Forever bent upon the kill.'

From the land of violence the young poet flees to compose a "myth," which will not evade the horror but truthfully embody it.

Early Poems

Even as a young man Hill did not veil the real world's troubles behind glossy fictions of Elysian fields and starry heavens. If violence, past and present, prompted him to become a poet, it also became the substance of his major poems. Jehovah's Leviathan and Adam's sinful flesh were his metaphors for a world he would react to with a combination of ascetic withdrawal and furious confrontation:

> And I renounced, on the fourth day,
> This fierce and unregenerate clay,
>
> Building as a huge myth for man
> The watery Leviathan,
>
> And made the glove-winged albatross
> Scour the ashes of the sea
> Where Capricorn and Zero cross,
> A brooding immortality—
> Such as the charmed phoenix has
> In the unwithering tree.

This, of course, is very different from God's blessing of the great whales and winged fowls in Genesis What God pronounces good, Hill finds evil. He refers to the Book of Job, where the Leviathan, "the king of all the children of pride" (41.34), is an emblem of human recalcitrance and imperfection. At this stage in the poem an albatross, reminiscent of Coleridge's bird, comes to symbolize the guilty conscience. Hill's bird scours an apocalyptic sea in its quest for a last judgment, just as it pursues the crew in "The Rime of the Ancient Mariner" and afflicts them with penitential ordeals. Hill, however, lightens his moral seriousness with some straight-faced clowning. The albatross is as much a phantasmal bird as a gloved hand scouring an ashen sink.

The conscience kills, Hill decides in his third section, almost as terribly as the hawks and ferrets in the second. For this reason his protagonist returns from his agonized soul-searching, his "agenbite of inwit," to the world of flesh and blood. His "brooding immortality" resembles the "death-in-life" of Coleridge's poem, a stagnant sea of menacing beasts and ghosts. For Coleridge the moral crisis occurs at the equator, at the center of the world. For Hill it occurs at another center, where the constellation Capricorn and Zero longitude cross: Capricorn, the goat, suggests worldly lust, and the zero-cross suggests Christ's cross on which passion, sacred and profane, is reduced to zero degree. In his meditative withdrawal Hill's poet imitates Christ, since he dies from the world only to return in a second coming. He is also the phoenix, whose "unwithering tree" is a type of cross emblematic of eternal cycles of ashen deaths and fiery resurrections.

Hill diagnoses the isolated, brooding imagination as an inferno of fire and ice, filled with pointless madness rather than principled energy:

> The phoenix burns as cold as frost;
> And, like a legendary ghost,
> The phantom bird goes wild and lost,
> Upon a pointless ocean tossed.
>
> So, the fifth day, I turned again
> To flesh and blood and the blood's pain.

The phoenix could represent all natural cycles, but here refers specifically to intense imaginative experience which, like Yeats's paradoxical "agony of flame that cannot singe a sleeve," burns most fiercely when the mind is withdrawn, frozen, dead to the world. It is from this introspective "death-in-life," however, that Hill turns. His ghosts need blood to live; his spirits need bodies. His journey is cyclical; it departs from the body's violence and pain, but then it returns to accept the flesh and move toward redemption.

Hill traces a similar journey in "An Ark on the Flood," where Ishmael and Ahab depart from a world where "barns remained unfilled and everywhere / The orchards blackened and began to rot." His Melvillean characters sail to a visionary mountain associated with a transcendent God, but from there fall back into their original state of decay. At the mid-point of their quest,

> the shadowing breeze
> Lifts its dark head above the waves of grass;
> Wringing from rough such calm
> That, as on mountains once, so we upon
> The stiff crest of the waves could walk dry-shod,
> Drowning the sea in surf of timbrels loud,
> Nor pass that peak, nor find our vision gone.

This sublime moment, however, recalls the "Calenture" of John Donne's "The Calme"—the tropical disease in which delirious sailors believe that the sea is a green field. After the storm has passed in Donne's poem,

> Onely the Calenture together drawes
> Deare friends, which meet dead in great fishes jawes:
> And on the hatches as on Altars lyes
> Each one, his owne Priest, and owne Sacrifice.

(In Hill's poem too, "the priest is fettered to the sacrifice.") Convinced he can walk on "the waves of grass" (like Christ), Ahab drowns. Ishmael, similarly credulous, dies on earth where, in a parody of the vegetation gods Demeter and Dionysus, he becomes a corn stalk entangled in vines. Both return to earth after pursuing delusions of transcendence. "The Revelation," "Prospero and Ariel," "Gideon at the Well," "To William Dunbar," and "Saint Cuthbert on Farne Island" all record passing moments of revelation in which the hero finds his apocalyptic expectations painfully rebuffed by mundane facts.

By making his outward journeys symbolic of inner ones, Hill fuses the spiritual exercise with the myth of the heroic quest, altering both in the process. The goal of meditation is to die from the world and, through an intensification of memory and imagination (composition of place), prepare the soul for a colloquy with God. Hill's quests aim to awaken moral perception and to recreate, linguistically, the world as it is. Because these quests so often terminate in death or silence, Hill turns to the pastoral elegy for consolation. But here, too, he takes what he needs. When his heroes die and the pastures wither (as is customary in pastoral elegies), the dead are not transmogrified into stars, or geniuses of the shore, or Platonic forms. They are resurrected as vegetation or the poet's words. Journey, meditation, and elegy all trace a rhythm of death and renewal. Hill draws on their traditions and criticizes them at the same time.

While insisting on the "inner light" of perception, Hill seeks rituals to embody it. With Blake, he revered (and feared) the imagination as a type of Christ who revealed, remade, and judged the world. Because Christ's passion for reformation was bloody as well as Utopian, Hill's attitude towards communion vacillated. At the end of "Genesis," it is embraced with qualifications:

> By blood we live, the hot, the cold,
> To ravage and redeem the world:
> There is no bloodless myth will hold.
>
> And by Christ's blood are men made free
> Though in close shrouds their bodies lie
> Under the rough pelt of the sea;
>
> Though Earth has rolled beneath her weight
> The bones that cannot bear the light.

In these powerfully rhythmic lines, Hill affirms the corporeality of the imagination, but also elegizes those (the metaphorical and literal "dead") whose bodies cannot abide its "light." Christ atones for the weak, but it is not certain whether the weak rise to "bear the light," or whether they even want to.

Early Poems

Years later, Hill defined this "blood myth" and "blood consciousness" in less exclamatory terms, in a gloss on Coleridge's primary and secondary imaginations. The first, he said, "represents an ideal democratic birthright, a light that ought to light every person coming into the world. In the event, the majority is deprived of this birthright in exchange for a mess of euphoric trivia and, if half-aware of its loss, is instructed to look for freedom in an isolated and competitive search for possessions and opportunity." The dead under the world's "rough pelt" (its bestial fur and battering waves) are those who have sunk into blindness. "Therefore the secondary imagination, the formal creative faculty, must awaken the minds of men to their lost heritage, not of possession but of perception" (*LL*, pp. 96–97). Christ in "Genesis" is a "secondary imagination," as are his militant apostles who, after communion, seek to "ravage and redeem the world" and, like John, "to bear witness of the Light, that all men through him might believe" (St. John, 1.7).

In these early poems, the mind's divine light cuts and scars as much as it cures. It can "ravage" the world, which is why in "An Ark on the Flood"—whose epigraph asserts that "the imagination of man's heart is evil from his youth" (Genesis, 8.21)—the journey aims to salvage an original, innocent vision on Ararat. Or it can bring the pain of responsibility and guilt. A brief lyric from Hill's second year at Oxford (1951), written in neat, rhyming quatrains, identifies both the light from the star of Bethlehem and the spear that pierced Christ's side with the "light that ought to light every person coming into the world":

> When the sharp star was seen
> That pierced each naked eye
> And left its scar between
> The thin ribs of the sky
>
> Some men could not forget
> What had so touched the mind;

> But, for all that, the threat
> Took thirty years to find
>
> Its execution here . . .

The light inflicts a spiritual wound (in sky and mind) and calls for a redemption that never comes:

> He had no quick release,
> And, when the others died,
> Still cried out for the peace
> That had been prophesied.

"Good Friday" demonstrates Hill's early skill with mythopoesis, with taking a traditional story and fashioning from it another whose implications are overtly psychological.

From the start, Hill took a stand against spontaneous confessionalism in favor of stately, impersonal formality. He wanted to build durable poems out of ephemeral experiences rather than to "applaud each broken or complacent confession" as it came. "Yet that does not alter the fact that, as a person, I am perpetually engrossed in my own dogged and nuzzling neuroses. . . . I should feel justified in putting into print a poem in which I speak of all these, provided that I had spent myself in tracking down to a point, to a purpose, that purpose being to try to make a poem of enduring worth."[4] Hill agreed with Yeats that "the passion of the verse comes from . . . holding down violence or madness—'down Hysterica passio'. All depends on the completeness of the holding down, on the stirring of the beast underneath."[5]

The characters in his early poems often choose sleep, violence, and death as the "quick release" from mental turmoil, and only Christ-like martyrs persist. The "contemplative way" impels fiery passions and icy withdrawals, mountain climbs "at the Pitch that is near Madness" (in a phrase of Richard Eberhart, a poet Hill imitated at the time), and often tragic falls. Defeat, as a result, can come as partial relief:

Early Poems

> Now Ahab is himself. Though lost and drowned,
> Pitting his bones against the chalky tide,
> He holds his peace . . .

To "rise to a discovery of true personality," Hill claims in an essay, is to make oneself vulnerable to the "moral ideal," and "the effect on us of the moral ideal is not simply admiration; it is confusion; it is accusation; it is judgment" (*LL*, p. 17). Hill's graveyards are full of lapsed idealists who have found peace from moral anguish in death.

Symbols of fire and ice (and clusters of images associated with them) abound in these poems. Many derive from *The Waste Land* and *Four Quartets*, as well as Yeats's "Byzantium," so many, in fact, that Hill did not collect most of these early poems in his first volume. Eliot's "pentecostal fire," which blazes in "midwinter spring," and his remembered world, which burgeons from April's "dead land" of "broken images," rise in different guise among the blossoming hedgerows and icy pools of Hill's "Pentecost" and "The Bidden Guest." Yeats's imaginary flame "that no faggot feeds" and which "cannot singe a sleeve" appears in nearly every poem. "Pentecost," published in 1952, is a good example of Hill's early meditative style, and a rare one since it depicts a reconciliation between antagonisms. Hill envisages the Apostles transposed to an English landscape:

> As hedge-root, though unpromising,
> Flowers powerfully, so, when men heard
> The night around them strangely spring
> Into a quick of blossoming,
> The bramble-flame, the crooked feet of the bird,
>
> They turned to revelation based
> Upon the stolid bone and brain.

The "bramble-flame" cleverly unites Christ's painful dying (crowned with thorns) and the Holy Ghost's utterance at Pentecost. It reveals a paradox of the imagination: that it often thrives when it renounces the world. But there is nothing otherworldly about the experience. Hill describes Pentecost in terms of blossoming hawthorns and growing hedge-roots. The Holy Ghost is corporeal, a vegetal efflorescence. "An Ark on the Flood" develops Hobbes's manifesto "Every Part of the Universe is Body"[6] to the limit by making everything bodily: autumn has a mouth, a vine has udders and knuckles, a river skin and jaws, the ocean a belly and back, a fire hands, and a well lips.

Hill rejects ascetic withdrawal as a permanent condition, but not without first being tempted by it. In "To William Dunbar," he expresses fondness for the Scottish Chaucerian and his timeless world of symbolic swans and fictionalized lovers but consigns them to a "world forgotten", "remote / . . . From the thin trammels of mortality." In lucid, rhythmic lines, he states his differences with the medieval Christianty of his precursor:

> To such a mercy few of us attain:
> Swans dwell apart like Troilus in his sphere,
> And not by sufferings, even, do we gain
> Power, such as theirs, to bring the heavens near,
> But win our faith from all who knew the clear
> Fulness of vision. Here, on Bewdley Bridge,
> I think of you, as of my heritage.

Pondering on a bridge near his hometown in Worcestershire, the poet decides that the otherworldly life is an enchantment to be resisted.

In another of his early poems, "Saint Cuthbert on Farne Island," Hill again expresses ambivalence towards ascetic contemplation and towards its alternative (also saintly and ascetic) of worldly evangelism. The poem opens with an expansion of vision in a dark night, but focuses on personal destiny. Rhyming quatrains, now fused into octets, draw the conflicting contraries into a suave music:

> And so he studied, seeking his own way,
> And found a rough sea-bitten island. There
> He meditated deeply night and day

Early Poems

> Upon the image of his own despair . . .
> To keep the soul, not body, in repair . . .

The retreat "for the spirit's good," however, convinces him that working in society is preferable. He resolves his dialogue between soul and body ambiguously:

> So, knowing now for certain that there could
> Be no new way without its new remorse,
> He drew his mind beneath a solemn hood
> And stopped the stars in their unthinking course.

After the monkish withdrawal, the meditation continues. The stars are extinguished or, paradoxically, internalized where their "unthinking course" illuminates the mind's perplexities.

Cuthbert is a typical hero in that he remains "in uncertainties, Mysteries, doubts," but, unlike Keats's hero of "negative capability," he is always "reaching after fact and reason."[7] Although resolutions occur in these early poems, it is more common for opposites to be suspended in an air of irresolution. As a poet, Hill tries to heal the "diremption between perception and utterance, energy and effect" (*LL*, p. 96). "The Bidden Guest" perhaps best summarizes Hill's sense of diremption, of the failure by the meditator to communicate his private vision (the heart's Pentecost) to those committed (or pretending to be committed) to traditional symbols of the church. Hill's "candles", or churchgoers, seem inflexibly opposed to the inspiration (the wind) of new revelations, although they are moved by the presence of old ones:

> The starched unbending candles stir
> As though a wind had caught their hair,
> As though the surging of a host
> Had charged the air of Pentecost.
> And I believe in the spurred flame,
> Those racing tongues, but cannot come
> Out of my heart's unbroken room;

> Nor feel the lips of fire among
> The cold light and the chilling song . . .

After communion, Hill confesses, "the heart's tough shell is still to crack." Withdrawn in the heart's "interior castle" (as St. Teresa described it), the meditator struggles to return gracefully, but fails. Instead of communing with Christ or his community, he communes with his failure.

The alienated communicant reappears in "Prospero and Ariel" and "Gideon at the Well," but in different guise. In the former poem, spring's efflorescence only accentuates the meditator's wintry confinement:

> Now the beaked crocus breaks its shell;
> The frost has eased out of the ground,
> Out of the rigid pines. But still
> In stubborn seams the light is bound
>
> That striking out from its chill lair
> Blazed high about me.

Icy withdrawal has brought with it an inner Pentecostal blaze, represented by Ariel, as if to compensate for the lack of light outside. If the fields are no longer "appareled in celestial light," as Wordsworth declared in his famous "Ode," Hill still celebrates the "visionary gleam" that flares in the darkness.

> Ariel shrills and beats the air;
> I shall not quench his light. For though
> Half-choked in Lethe, he'd still flare,
> Tarring that dark flood's undertow.

While Prospero frees Ariel in *The Tempest*, Hill puts him to work paving a road to hell. He is another Lucifer, exiled from heaven, who will build over the "dark flood" of pain, lethargy, forgetfulness, and death a Pandemonium where he and his phantasmal comrades must endure.

Hill repeatedly accosts those who fail to base revelation "upon the stolid bone and brain." Gideon craves miracles but fails to achieve the much more modest miracle of leaving winter's barrenness behind and accepting spring's abundance. Seasonal change occurs without any corresponding change in "Gideon at the Well." Like Prospero (or Eliot's persona at the beginning of *The Waste Land*), he is "sealed" in a private hell while flowers bloom menacingly around him. The passionate eloquence he associates with Pentecost has dried up, as has his ability to establish contact with others: "still my tongued heart, rough and dry, / Can find no respite from its thirst." But Hill's afflicted hero is not wholly defeated:

> Being sealed and chosen,
> I raise my staff: the armies move,
> As out of rock, as floods unfrozen.

Gideon battles the demons within, rather than the Midianites without, and partly conquers them.

Hill's visionary warriors, on their many forays into the world, struggle to give up their apocalyptic hopes but never quite manage to. In "The Revelation," for example, the narrator, prompted by St. John of the Cross's *Dark Night*, departs from his "blind" "house of the senses" to obtain grace,[8] but he expects the world to be transformed as it is in the other St. John's revelation. He cannot possibly be satisfied and concludes, bitterly, that the inner nightmare is merely a reflection of the outer one:

> once beyond those walls I did not doubt
> My heart would quicken and my tongue renew.
>
> And it was true I trod accustomed ground,
> My eyes no longer blinded by the glare
> Out of that kiln of darkness. Yet I found
> The world was not transfigured nor laid bare,
>
> Nor pierced with singing voices. I who had come
> Strenuous through fire stood, now, against the light,
> Encountered shapes and shadows that were dumb.
> My heart, though it died not, lay cold and quiet.

Communion on "accustomed ground" again fails. The world is as it was, a silent shadow play at the back of Plato's cave. In "The Revelation," orthodox Christian transfigurations and apocalypses are purged. Emptied of its old beliefs, the mind lapses into a quiet disillusionment, where, with a cold eye, it gazes upon "things as they are."

Elegies were a natural choice for a poet whose meditations struggled to make the past present. But Hill remained iconoclastic, condensing the traditional patterns of pastoral elegy into a few quatrains and satirizing all forms of memorial in doing so. Rather than lament the deaths of people he knew, he elegized literary heroes (Ahab, Ishmael, Hamlet, Merlin, King Arthur), other poets (Isaac Rosenberg, William Dunbar), fictitious characters (Jane, John, and Captain Richard Fraser), and past symbols, both sacred and profane. In these poems, tradition or culture is a field, graveyard, or museum full of cultivated dead things. To interpret the present, the mind must be rooted in the past:

> As the firm emphasis of Spring
> Falls on old stems that have begun
> Fresh growth, so these new graces cling
> Close to the root, interpreting
> The silence of the seed and of the sun.
>   ("Pentecost")

The "stems" (language users, whether readers, critics, poets, or ordinary speakers) derive from roots (linguistic, historical) the energies and materials necessary for new growths. Hill's lines enact what they profess. They gracefully transform lines from Yeats's "Sailing to Byzantium," which, in turn, authorize such appropriations: "Nor is there singing school but studying / Monuments of its own magnificence."

Since "not only the best but the most individual parts of his work may be those in which the dead poets . . . assert their immortality most vigorously," the new poet, as Eliot argued, must cultivate a knowledge of the past. Poetry, from this point

Early Poems

of view, is naturally elegiac and demands "great difficulties and responsibilities."[9] Hill's attitude towards the dead, however, was not always reverential. Tradition, as he explained in his "Letter from Oxford," was full of grand, humiliating ghosts whose monuments made young poets' imitations seem superfluous:

> One might think that the great strength and appeal of Oxford lay in its tradition; that an awareness of this would grant a sense of peace and security. But one has found tradition as cold a shadow here as in Westminster Abbey. There is small comfort in being crowded out by ghosts. Under the chill salty-smelling stone of the great Tudor gatehouses, beneath the high rows of portraits in the halls, thin-lipped prelates, all evil-looking old men, you are brow-beaten by the past.[10]

Hill was later to write that in Jonathan Swift "a sense of tradition and community is challenged by a strong feeling for the anarchic and the predatory" (*LL*, p. 68), an aperçu which could apply to him with equal relevance. These tensions find exemplary expression in "An Ark on the Flood," which imitates (and lampoons) great elegies of the past (Milton's "Lycidas," Robert Lowell's "Quaker Graveyard in Nantucket") but which also diagnoses the crippling influence which such poems can exert. In "An Ark on the Flood," Ishmael passes by many Sirens (the elegiac voices of the past—Virgil, Donne, Milton, Melville, Shelley, Lowell) but without the craftiness of a Ulysses to avert them. The acoustics of past elegies menace him at all points, "drowning the sea in surf of timbrels loud," and, to a certain extent, drowning his poem:

> Old bones are brought to light and, where we dwell,
> The echoes have not died
> Of those who went beneath the clamouring sea.
> But Ishmael's ears are crippled to that sound,
> (O starry mouths amid the oozes drowned)
> The harp hangs silent from the windless tree.

This is elegiac magniloquence which, ironically, regards the dependence on magniloquence as paralyzing. Nevertheless, Hill writes a visionary romance about the death of romantic vision. The first fifty lines trace the heroes' journey towards the visionary mountain and the last fifty their descent from it. Although his heroes struggle to sustain poetic power, they resign to poetic impotence in the end.

Milton's grand style and its gestures of transcendence, however, appear in purified form. Hill articulates his temptations in order to exorcise them. He calls Milton's transcendentalism hollow and sleepy:

> And the ark
> Rises, now, to the rimmed and hollow calm
>
> That is the sleeping crater of the storm;
> Grazing this mountain-valley of the seas
> Where whales and herds of billowy narwhal pass
> In silence . . .

The lines recall Milton's apotheosis in "Lycidas," where the deceased rises to become a "Genius of the Shore":

> So Lycidas sunk low, but mounted high,
> Through the dear might of him that walked the waves,
> Where, other groves and other streams along,
> With nectar pure his oozy locks he laves,
> And hears the unexpressive nuptial song
> In the blest kingdoms meek of joy and love.
>
> (11.172–77)

Hill associates this with the "Grand Armada" chapter of *Moby Dick*, where the whale hunters, experiencing a moment of Platonic vision, find the water "to a considerable depth exceedingly transparent" and gaze at infant whales "still spiritually feasting upon some unearthly reminiscence." The visionary rhetoric of Milton and Melville, however, exerts a negative influence, a vocal in-flowing from stars which Hill finds deadening. The line "(O starry mouths amid the oozes drowned)," with its "straddled adjectives" echoes Milton's "blind mouths" (1. 119) and "oozy locks" (1. 175) but fails to invigorate them. No *spiritus* or creative wind moves through the Aeolian harp at the end. The elegy is nevertheless ambiguously triumphant; it buries elegiac assumptions (heavenly marriages, starry apotheoses) while memorializing the styles in which they were previously embalmed. The final silence represents a temporary truce in the young poet's battle with the mighty dead.

Hill's heroes attack the dead and their splendid artifice because, like the Gorgon's snakes, they threaten to turn them to stone. A poem written two years before "An Ark on the Flood," "God's Little Mountain," again shows how mystical perception, when its idols and ideals are the "stars" of tradition, can paralyze rather than liberate. Simple, declarative sentences, metered quatrains (in which all four lines rhyme or half-rhyme), and a mythical narrative of mountain ascent, however, counterpoise the visionary defeat with a poetic success:

> I waited for the word that was not given,
>
> Pent up into a region of pure force,
> Made subject to the pressure of the stars;
> I saw the angels lifted like pale straws;
> I could not stand before those winnowing eyes
>
> And fell, until I found the world again.
> Now I lack grace to tell what I have seen;
> For though the head frames words the tongue has none
> And who will prove the surgeon to this stone?

Moses on Horeb (the "mountain of God," Exodus, 3. 1) envisaged God speaking to him from a burning bush; Hill's climber, similarly expectant, observes the heavens dismantled in silence. The voices of past "gods" are dead, their angelic images reaped like wheat. The poetic "stars" ("gods whose knees we clutch"[11]), from whom a Pentecostal influx is anticipated, exert a destructive pressure. The heavens—the wheat fields—winnow him, rather than the opposite. In this version of the Last Judgment, dead poets and their angelic images judge the living poet and humble him. A partial healing of the "diremption between perception and utterance" is effected by the poem itself, through its eloquent diagnosis of failure, but still a surgeon is beckoned at the end.

Part of Hill's ambivalence toward the dead must have derived from his immersion in traditional Oxford course work and his simultaneous effort to write new poetry. *The University of Oxford Examination Statutes* of 1950 decreed that students of English Literature prepare to translate Books IV and VI of *The Aeneid* (Aeneas's meeting with the Sibyl appears in "After Cumae" and later in "Offa's Journey to Rome") and passages from *The Anglo-Saxon Chronicles, Aelfric's Homilies, Beowulf,* and *Sweet's Anglo-Saxon Reader* (the latter two provided Hill with events and a title for *Mercian Hymns*). Hill chose a course in tragedy, which began with Aristotle's *Poetics* (the tragic plot, with its peripety and catharsis, provided a blueprint for many of Hill's poems). From the Middle English period, Hill read Chaucer, Langland, and Gower. Texts were taken from Shakespeare, Spenser, and Milton (and adapted in "Prospero and Ariel," "For Isaac Rosenberg," "An Ark on the Flood," and "Genesis"). From the beginning, scholarship posed enchantments and perils for Hill the poet. When he says that "it's at least to the credit of Oxford that it didn't kill [my] . . . devotion to modern poetry" (*VP*, p. 78), he acknowledges a menace struggled with and overcome.

While Hill reacted passionately for or against the dead, he remained remarkably dispassionate toward most of his immediate contemporaries, many of whom he could read in Oscar Mellor's Fantasy Press pamphlets.[12] "They were either Empsonian in the most arid sense, writing cerebral conundrums" or "they were narrating amorous adventures and travel anecdotes in language that was the equivalent of painting-by-numbers." He told his interviewer that he "really cared for neither of those alternatives." Instead, he sought the "fusion of intellectual strength with simple, sensuous and passionate immediacy" in the metaphysical poets (*VP*, pp. 78–80) and in the Americans Allen Tate, Robert

Lowell, and Richard Eberhart. He wanted a "richness of language" in which "history and politics and religion speak for themselves."[13] When he wrote of "amorous adventure" or "travel," it was with tradition pressing on every line.

But when tradition was not attacked or mourned, it was frequently lampooned. The elegy "For Isaac Rosenberg" mocks traditional memorials while employing them to commemorate the hero. With a series of sardonic smiles and half-smiles, Hill surveys sentimental rites of remembrance and grandiose public funerals—" . . . men who mourn their hero's fall, / Laying him in tradition's bed,"—and notes how his two princes succumb to the formalities they denounce:

> When probing Hamlet was aware
> That Death in a worn body lay
> Cramped beneath the lobby-stair—
> (Whose mystery was burnt away
> Through the intensity of decay)—
>
> It followed, with ironic sense,
> That he himself, who ever saw
> Beneath the skin of all pretence,
> Should have been carried from the floor
> With shocked, tip-toeing drums before.
>
> With ceremony thin as this
> We tidy death; make life as neat
> As an unquiet chrysalis
> That is a symbol of defeat:
> A worm in its own winding sheet . . .

Hill, it would seem, also succumbs to tradition—to Richard Eberhart's elegy "The Groundhog," which describes how the poet "seeing nature ferocious" in the dead animal probes its mystery in the "seething cauldron of his being," and to Dylan Thomas's "force that through the green fuse drives the flower," which ends: "And I am dumb to tell the lover's tomb / How at my sheet goes the same crooked worm." But Hill's elegy, more than those of his predecessors, reflects on elegy with witty sarcasm. It concludes that, like all formal ceremonies, the elegy provides a way of ordering and giving shape to events which might otherwise be chaotic, like the chrysalis which wraps the "dead" worm in a "thin" silken gloss and insures its metamorphosis into a butterfly.

One of the best early elegies, "Merlin," again takes an ironic look at rituals of remembrance, this time in the context of Arthurian heroes. Hill shrinks the traditional pastoral elegy into two quatrains, with each of the four lines assiduously rhymed or half-rhymed, and emphasizes the vegetal ontogeny of the dead, who are "the husks of what was rich seed" and who, transformed, become the "pinnacled corn." That the locusts have covered the "long barrows of Logres" like a tide suggests their apocalyptic destruction, but the dead, as in "The Distant Fury of Battle," remain more alive and rapacious than the living. Their ghosts, which traditionally feed on blood, come back to prey on the bloodthirsty predators (the locusts), who are in fact bloodless. Predator and prey reverse roles. The corn to be harvested feeds on the corpses of those who are supposed to harvest it. The new heaven and new earth is no holy city of church spires but the "pinnacled" corn field. The knights, who traditionally restored fertility to the king's domain by killing dragons, now fertilize the soil with their own deaths. Culture (in the museum's "raftered galleries of bone") is dead unless plowed back into the loam.

Not all of Hill's early elegies end with such vigorous vegetal resurrections, but most reflect on conventions of elegy with similar irony. A trilogy of short poems on a fictitious Fraser family, "In Memory of Jane Fraser," "The Tower Window," and "Captain Richard Fraser, Aged 24 Years," confronts death in a mood of sardonic gloom. The pastor's sheepfold, in the first, has turned into a snowy wasteland. The whole landscape resembles a beggar's corpse, "blue with cold" and wrapped in "a

Early Poems

cold shroud." Against this personification of death, Jane Fraser remains vigilant ("Like a strong bird above its prey"), but to no avail. She tries to kill death, like Donne in his "Holy Sonnets," but inevitably submits to it. Predator and prey reverse roles and reverse again when the deceased preys on the living with grief: "Her body froze / As if to freeze us all, and chain / Creation to a stunned repose." Spring arrives in the end, but only minimally, and fails to alter winter's "stunned repose."

"The Tower Window," a memorial to John Fraser, encourages similar expectations of timeless permanence and recalls the customary ways of achieving them, but only to parody them.

> Some men have flowered on death.
> Before the guns, at the fire's mouth,
> Having grown big with faith,
> They have cried all at a breath.
>
> Of these are symbols made,
> As Honour; Love; and faiths decreed.
> Old bones are shelved; old ghosts laid;
> Still the transfigured words abide.
>
> But Fraser, at his death, was dumb.
> Now, where few men come,
> He has an unquestioned claim,
> Like furniture in a room.

Fraser possesses the right of any man to be remembered, but few, besides Hill, remember him. Unlike Arthur, Merlin, and Rosenberg, he has not been transfigured into those august symbols laid "in tradition's bed." Nevertheless, he persists in a room of his own.

Captain Richard Fraser, in a companion piece, suffers a less ambiguous fate. In contrast, he has "flowered . . . / Before the guns." A gravestone transfigures him, but mainly "to point the irony of grief" and mock the ineffectuality of funerals:

> Jane Fraser, now, take back your son
> To Bentley Grange where he was born,
> And see him huddled among clay
> With every due observance done.
>
> There is a stone where deeds still show
> Old scars above, the new below,
> Though where his limbs lie trodden down
> No sun can ever come or go.

The carved gravestone mimes Fraser's scarred body but offers a bleak reward besides the "pinnacled corn" of "Merlin."

Early and late, Hill reflects on elegiac dispensations in poems rich in irony and ambiguity. He courts formality but simultaneously mocks it. Like Allen Tate, Hill seeks to pattern chaotic energies rather than pretend they do not exist. He pits cherished Christian beliefs against biological and geological facts and remarks on their relation. He supplicates earth's energies, and the dead to direct them, but resists them in the act of transforming them. Hill's obsession with the dead is really his obsession with tradition and history, whose organic and seasonal cycles he ritualistically observes in nearly every poem. Meditations, often disguised as mythical quests, follow the natural rhythms of withdrawal and return, rising to intense perception and passionate articulation, then falling back to the silent, recalcitrant earth. When moral perception fails, and when the vanity of the artist's attempt to act as conscience and unacknowledged legislator of his race predominates, Hill rises to challenge these defeats by writing of them winningly. After Oxford, he continued to dismantle ceremony ceremoniously, and, as in "For Isaac Rosenberg," with new energy "make life as neat / As an unquiet chrysalis / That is a symbol of defeat."

2 / THE EMBATTLED POET AND HIS TRADITION

For the Unfallen

Grammar, Syntax, and the Romantic Tradition

Of the poems published at Oxford between 1950 and 1954, Hill kept only six in *For the Unfallen*. The poems written in the middle and the late 1950s are no less agonized and problematic, but now he sets his personal conflicts against the larger backdrop of political and social history. He regards private thoughts and emotions like a spectator, as if they belonged to another person or to all people, and dramatizes their significance with greater rhetorical subtlety. "An Ark on the Flood," "God's Little Mountain," and several of the short elegies brought him to a dead end. Disillusioned with the quest for ecstatic moments of vision and perfect fulfillment, he could accept the world of brutal reality, fall silent, or strike out in a new direction.

In 1954, after beginning the Bachelor of Letters course in English Literature at Oxford and passing the qualifying exams, Hill took his position as a lecturer in English Literature and, shortly after, in 1956, married Nancy Whittaker. At Oxford, he liked to imagine himself "hunched in his mackintosh on top of a bus in the Banbury Road" or on a mountain peak, pursuing ideals with single-minded purpose. With his new responsibilities, he was forced to climb down from the sublime heights, breathe a less rarefied air, and struggle to adapt to communal arts. Three poems written in 1955, "Solomon's Mines," "The Distant Fury of Battle," and "Asmodeus" describe the struggle to escape the obsessions which threatened to silence his poetry at Oxford. In these poems, he imagines himself trapped in a mine, graveyard, or house, battling to get free.

Hill reacts to heroic societies of the past, such as Solomon's kingdom in Israel during the tenth century B.C., social relations of the present, and traditional uses of grammar and syntax with the same mixture of impassioned devotion and principled rebellion. If he preserves the romantic poet's grammatical syntax, which accords with "the conscious mind's intelligible structure," he also shatters it with ungrammatical exclamations, bitter cries for release, and groans of despair. In his essay "The Conscious Mind's Intelligible Structure," which discusses romantic assumptions about mind and language in terms of grammar and syntax, he claims that "it may sometimes be necessary to mimic a dilemma,"[1] and with common and distorted syntax, exact and off-rhymes, regular and irregular meter, ambiguous and straightforward diction, he mimes two contradictory views of world and mind: the one inherited from classical thought, which declares that the material universe is bounded by definite, knowable limits of space and time, and the other given impetus by contemporary scientific thought, which suggests that the universe is a relative, indeterminate, ongoing process. Torn between rational ideals of order and empirical recognitions of chaos, Hill formulates his doubts and anxieties in the very texture of his verse.

While Hill was conducting his assault against the destructive passions of the romantic, as well as the traditional ways of bottling them up, Donald Davie and the Movement were taking a more antiseptic approach which sought rigid allegiance to "purified" or "chaste" diction, grammatically proper syntax, and conventional urbanity. Davie's manifestoes were important to Hill's development in that they served as catalysts for his reaction against them. Although Hill, like Davie, felt a deep affinity for Yeats and the romantic tradition—for their examples of social and linguistic order—he found "romanticism" much more complex and problematic than his contemporary. He questioned, first of all, whether a romantic tradition even existed. "Yeats recognized himself, though not without irony, to be an artist in the nineteenth century Romantic tradition. This is a self-limiting truism which requires prompt qualification since, on investigation, no such simple entity as the Romantic tradition can be discovered."[2] If romanticism existed, it was elusive, and only masks could convey (and partly conceal) its numinous presence, its *Zeitgeist*:

To make a distinction based on Yeats's . . . terminology in *A Vision*, one might suggest that Romanticism had (and has) both false and true masks. The false mask is formed from what Jacques Maritain admirably summarized as the two unnatural principles: the fecundity of money and the finality of the useful. . . . The false mask either gleams amid the fecundity of money or utters, in terms of the finality of the useful, the wrong kind of moral answer. . . . the "true mask" could be shaped in one of two ways, each of which is in accord with "the conscious mind's intelligible structure." The first way presupposes a grammar of assent. The second way is available if the first is not; and is the way of syntax. Syntax could be understood as Donald Davie presents it in his book *Articulate Energy* (1955) or it could be extended to accommodate Simone Weil's "law of artistic creation," as defined in *The Need for Roots*.[3]

The romantic quest can aim for capitalist and utilitarian felicities or for the "traditional sanctity and loveliness" of art, which may or may not be useful or lucrative. The capitalist races after his ideas of power by piling up money. The poet, in accordance with romanticism's true mask, "ex-planes" the "conscious mind's intelligible order" through conventional grammar and syntax. In another essay, Hill associated the "unnatural" principles of romanticism with "the sin . . . which Maritain termed 'angelism', the refusal of the creature to submit to or be ruled by any of the exigencies of the created natural order," and added that "such a refusal to submit to these exigencies has itself been seen as the crime of capitalism, imperialism, modern technology and technological warfare" (*LL*, p. 4). Hill's ideal demands a rapprochement between transcendence and nature. It presupposes a grammar, a set of laws which organize and conventionalize ways of using language, of apprehending the world, and of acting within it. Davie early on identified grammatical with civilized orders and therefore rejected the modernists. Hill made room for Simone Weil's definition of syntax as a "simultaneous composition on several planes at once,"[4] which suggests that the modernists were not simply voicing the mind's confusions and biases but its multifaceted complexity. In the heyday of the Movement, Hill wanted to write poems somewhere between the traditional syntax of Yeats and the dislocated syntax of Pound, the purified diction of Wordsworth and the linguistic density of Joyce. If he questioned or even undermined intelligible structures, he did so intelligibly and ceremoniously, using formal devices of rhyme, meter, and stanza, and plots in line with biblical and Aristotelian paradigms. Nevertheless, he would distort grammar and syntax so that they expressed some of the mind's irrational outbursts.

"Solomon's Mines," written in 1955 (the same year Davie's *Articulate Energy* appeared, and three years after *Purity of Diction*), demonstrates Hill's new syntactical techniques. The poem is a sentence fragment, three quatrains long, without proper subject and verb, hooked together by an exclamation point, parentheses, commas, and semicolons. It expresses the poet's ambivalence towards romantic tradition, and towards the famous and supposedly civilized kingdoms of history. Hill resurrects the heroic dead in order to interrogate them and their heroic deeds and, at the end, after he has discovered their motives and means, announces that he would just as soon abandon them. They are "best" dead, he remarks, punning on "best." Out of his equivocation Hill makes an exquisite, ambiguous music which possesses the immediacy of a colloquial exclamation of fascination and disgust and the formality of a laboriously pondered response:

> Anything to have done!
> (The eagle flagged to the sun)

For the Unfallen

> To have discovered and disclosed
> The buried thrones, the means used;
>
> Spadework and symbol; each deed
> Resurrecting those best dead
> Priests, soldiers and kings;
> Blazed-out, stripped-out things;
>
> Anything to get up and go
> (Let the hewn gates clash to)
> Without looking round
> Out of that strong land.

Like the protagonist in H. Rider Haggard's book *King Solomon's Mines*, Hill discovers and then abandons Solomon's treasures, but he is not so much a treasure hunter as an archaeologist burdened with a historical conscience. He digs up relics from Solomon's time and then—like God in Revelation—judges the dead according to their works. His journey of descent and ascent is ultimately disillusioning. Even though at first he covets fame like the eagle, he changes his mind when he discovers "the means used" to achieve fame. Like Eliot in "Ash Wednesday," he wants to say but never quite manages to:

> I no longer strive to strive towards such things
> (Why should the agèd eagle stretch its wings?)
> Why should I mourn
> The vanished power of the usual reign?

As Hill mines the buried past, he asserts that he wants "to have done" with history's "best dead." Like Orpheus, however, he will always look around on his way back from the underworld and, like Eurydice, return there.

His battle with grammar and syntax, as well as with other customary social forms, continues in "The Distant Fury of Battle," where he depicts an outright war between the individual talent and his linguistic tradition. Grass and other living organisms symbolize the living poet, and a graveyard of stone sculpture the dead and their legacy of artifice. The two camps pair off, fight, negotiate peace, and then, with great ardor, return to creative coexistence. Unlike "Solomon's Mines," his new poem retains traditional grammar and syntax but forces them to the breaking point. The poem enacts what it describes. Its tortuous syntax, winding around commas, dashes, and semicolons, mimes an individual's desperate struggle to leave tradition in the grave but also to resurrect it and make it new.

Hill begins with a murderous gesture as he tries to depose the angelic masks and images of romantic tradition:

> Grass resurrects to mask, to strangle,
> Words glossed on stone, lopped stone-angel;
> But the dead maintain their ground—
> That there's no getting round—
>
> Who in places vitally rest,
> Named, anonymous; who test
> Alike the endurance of yews
> Laurels, moonshine, stone, all tissues;
>
> With whom, under licence and duress,
> There are pacts made, if not peace.

In this emblematic satire, the dead seem more vital than the living, and when the poet attacks them, they prove as unkillable as angels. As in "God's Little Mountain," when Hill declares "I saw the angels lifted like pale straws" and falls as if wounded, to earth, he fights, in "The Distant Fury of Battle," against enchantments with transcendental "essences," as Allen Tate does at the beginning of "Ode to the Confederate Dead." The dead "test" the living in an apocalyptic war and judgment which now is poetic. Yews and laurels (famous dead poets), moonshine (luminous imaginations and their spirited distillations or poems), sculpted stone artifice, and tissues (strong poets) all compete in an endurance test to see whose artifacts will survive.

For the Unfallen

Hill continues his meditation on the poet and his tradition (has he developed by nature or nurture?) to the end. "There's naught to kill but the animated dead," Tate declared in "The Oath," but Hill tries to make peace with the ghosts that haunt and enchant him:

> Union with the stone-wearing dead
> Claims the born leader, the prepared
>
> Leader, the devourers and all lean men.
> Some, finally, learn to begin.
> Some keep to the arrangement of love
> (Or similar trust) under whose auspices move
>
> Most subjects, toward the profits of this
> Combine of doves and witnesses.
> Some, dug out of hot-beds, are brought bare,
> Not past conceiving but past care.

All those who "worship images," whether they be born with talent or whether they acquire it through great labor, to Hill's catholic sensibility are members of a community which memorializes the word. Students "devour" words as their Catholic counterparts "devour" communion wafers. The professors, the new priests, supervise. Poets "finally learn to begin" when they learn Eliot's lesson: that not only the best but the most individual parts of their work are those in which the dead poets may assert their immortality most vigorously. The servants of language (its "subjects") become the masters or guardians "under whose auspices" literary tradition is passed on.

For Hill, tradition is a "trust," those who guard it trustees, and those who benefit from it beneficiaries. It is also a trust in the sense that it is a big business, a "combine" of firms, a monopoly, whose managers fix the prices by dictating which subjects will and will not be taught. A "combine" can also be a wheat thresher (Hill compared the dead to winnowers in "God's Little Mountain"), but, on a more mundane level, it is a group of devotees competing to "profit" from the past. As "doves" and "witnesses," they parody holy spirits and martyrs as much as they emulate them. At the poem's end, the plant dug from the hotbed of cultivated soil (the ground of tradition) offers a radical, and perhaps necessary, alternative to the culture-bound poet.

Hill wrote his poem in his first year as a lecturer at Leeds and, it would seem, in direct response to Eliot's claim that the poet must sacrifice himself to the perpetuation of tradition. At first, he flatly denies Eliot and portrays the youthful talent as a bellicose strangler who does anything but surrender. As the poem progresses, however, he moves closer to Eliot's position, before, at the end, attacking it once again. While fighting to free himself from tradition's angelic images and glossy words, Hill, ironically, does not hesitate to requisition supplies of images and words from other poets. The poem, in fact, owes a good deal to Tate's "Ode to the Confederate Dead," which depicts a similar elemental war in a graveyard of angelic monuments. Tate wrote that he intended his poem to celebrate "the theme of heroism, not merely moral heroism, but heroism in the grand style, elevating even death from mere physical dissolution into a formal ritual."[5] Tate wanted to restore the chivalric agrarian past of the South, but admonished: "Leave now / The shut gate and the decomposing wall," as at the end of "Solomon's Mines," Hill exclaims: "Anything to get up and go / (Let the hewn gates clash to)." If Hill finds in Tate's poem an attractive ambivalence towards tradition, he finds in Richard Eberhart's "The Fury of Aerial Bombardment" a germinal title and in the older poet's passionate graveyard meditations precedents for his own.

In "Asmodeus" (1955), Hill's graveyard and battlefield are transposed to his house (Tate in his "Ode" asked, "Shall we . . . set up the grave / In the house?"), a place where he confronts demons from the past as well as a lover in the present. He strives to remain faithful to "the conscious mind's intelligible structure," symbolized by the house, but concedes his exasperation by wrenching his syntax until it is nearly unintelligible. The ro-

For the Unfallen

mantic poet, Hill asserts (quoting Keith Sagar), "sees the poet's vocation as a 'searching for a way of reconciling human vision with the energies, powers, presences, of the non-human cosmos' " (*LL*, p. 15). Here, he tries to reconcile the demons of destruction with the muses of creation. Asmodeus is the spirit of anger in Jewish demonology (in the apocryphal Book of Tobit, he destroys seven of Sarah's marriages by killing her bridegrooms on their wedding nights). For Hill, he represents all those powers and presences, in himself and nature, which he must "at-one" with in order to purge. He is a Promethean figure who summons all his strength to wrestle manic energies to the ground, where he can civilize them or at least express them in a poem of grammatical and syntactical order.

In the second sonnet of "Asmodeus," Hill finds himself evicted from his house of patterned energies and from the rest of his compatriots (the Movement poets perhaps), who surround themselves with cosy rumors and easy truths. They inhabit the sunlit world of common-day reality. Hill raves and burns among the angels of a starlit night:

> The night, then, bravely stiffen; you are one
> Whom stars could burn more deeply than the sun,
> Guide-book martyr. You, doubtless, hear wings,
> Too sheer for cover, swift; the scattered noise
> Of darkness looming with propitious things;
> And nests of rumour clustered in the world.
> So drummed, so shadowed, your mere trudging voice
> Might rave at large while easy truths were told,
> Bad perjurable stuff, to be forgiven
> Because of this lame journey out of mind.
> A tax on men to seventy-times-seven,
> A busy vigilance of goose and hound,
> Keeps up all guards. Since you are outside, go,
> Closing the doors of the house and the head also.

In his characteristic tone of half-serious mockery, Hill disparages, but also partly justifies, the ways of his contemporaries. If he is nakedly exposed to the influx from the stars (angel wings are too sheer to cover him), like Plato, he recognizes the madness caused by such exposures. Although his peers are fledglings protected in nests from "the energies, powers, presences, of the non-human cosmos," their avoidance of demonic energies seems prudent. He, however, is one who eagerly pursues the sacrificial life of taxing vigilance and demonic combat. He leaves contemporary literary fashion and gossip, as well as his lover (and even his sanity), behind and strikes out into the dark night.

A man against the crowd, Hill's Asmodeus commences a journey which parallels and parodies St. John of the Cross's dark night of the soul. In his famous meditation, St. John traces the soul's departure from the house of "serious lust and indoor sin" along a purgative way to meditative calm and union with God:

> It was a sheer grace for this soul that God in this night put to sleep all the members of its household, that is: all the faculties, passions, affections, and appetites which live in its sensory and spiritual parts. God put them to sleep to enable the soul to go out to the spiritual union of the perfect love of God without being seen, that is, without the hindrance of the affections, etc. For these members of the household are put to sleep and mortified in this night, which leaves them in darkness, that they may not be able to observe or experience anything in their lowly, natural way which would impede the soul's departure from itself and the house of the senses.[6]

Hill reshapes St. John's motifs of night vigil, burning desire, sheer grace, and house leaving into a sardonic portrait of the embattled mystic, exacerbated by lovers and compatriots, who closes his "house of the senses" in order to pursue his ideals.

In these transitional poems (written between 1954 and 1955), Hill goes a long way beyond traditional romantic notions of order. In short, he becomes a modernist who gathers his fragments into new wholes. A poem which demonstrates the extent of Hill's shift towards modernist conceptions of language and reality and which is specifically about his changing attitude to romanticism is "Elegiac Stanzas," composed in 1957, "On a Visit to Dove Cottage." Both title and cottage belong to Wordsworth. Unlike Donald Davie, who, in *Articulate Energy*, exalted Wordsworth for his intelligible syntax which "mimes something outside itself and outside the world of its poem, something that smells of the human,"[7] as if his type of poetry could still be written, Hill, on his visit to Dove Cottage, elegizes Wordsworth and everything he represents.

In his poem, Hill upholds the principle of T. E. Hulme that in order to mime or "ex-plane" the world's metamorphoses, the poet must adopt fragmentary, open-ended forms. His elegy, in fact, is one long ungrammatical line which begins *in medias res* without proper subject or verb and extends over six quatrains, ending ambiguously with diction and syntax that echoes its beginning. It is an impressive valediction to the idea of an orderly universe, which Davie and Wordsworth still find intact outside the formal boundaries of their poems. Without discarding symmetrical stanza, meter, and rhyme entirely, Hill depicts a continuum of shifting forms, one of which is Wordsworthian romanticism.

Wordsworth, in his own "Elegiac Stanzas," mourned the loss of his childhood imagination and the advent of a more mature acceptance of custom and civilized control:

> I have submitted to a new control:
> A power is gone, which nothing can restore;
> A deep distress hath humanized my Soul.

Hill, going one step beyond Wordsworth, mourns the loss of the "new control." Both as twentieth-century tourist and literary historian, Hill gazes at Wordsworth's relics and records the eclipse of romantic ideals and visionary gleams: the romantic assent to formal, customary grammar; the belief in the permanence of natural and artistic monuments; the devotion to readily intelligible poetry fashioned from "incidents and situations from common life . . . in a selection of language really used by men";[8] the happy marriage between sublime ideas and mundane realities, whereby "the discerning intellect of man" is "wedded to this goodly universe"; and the faith in a spiritual economy in which profits will compensate losses—all these are romantic skeletons shelved by the modernists. Hill's poem is a cinematic progression, like an old film full of abrupt transitions, which traces the history of romanticism's masks and images, in his own work if in nobody else's. Hill begins with a panoramic shot of its natural and unnatural forms, and those forces which break them up:

> Mountains, monuments, all forms
> Inured to processes and storms
> (And they are many); the fashions
> Of intercourse between nations:
>
> Customs through which many come
> To sink their eyes into a room
> Filled with the unused and unworn . . .

Like Wordsworth meditating on George Beaumont's picture of Peele Castle in a storm, which he takes to be an emblem of "the Poet's dream / . . . cased in the unfeeling armour of old time," inured to "the lightning, the fierce wind, and trampling waves," Hill thinks of similar "forms / Inured to processes and storms." But he mocks Wordsworth by declaring that it is worldly fashion and petty customs that are the eternal forms now, rather than sublime portraits of paintings and poets. Wordsworth warned in his "Intimations of Immortality":

> Full soon thy Soul shall have her earthly freight,
> And custom lie upon thee with a weight,
> Heavy as frost, and deep almost as life!

Hill puns on customs, making them both the cultural ways of international tourists (including their "fashions" of syntax and diction) as well as the stations at ports where "earthly freight" is checked. He identifies the tourists as the new romantics, the literary pilgrims, who, by witnessing Wordsworth's relics, slough off their "freight" of custom and commune with a universal spirit. What they find in Dove Cottage are the authentic death masks of romanticism, which are distinct, as Hill said in his essay, from those modeled from the "fecundity of money" or "finality of the useful." They are "unused and unworn." From them come intimations of immortality.

Confronted by Wordsworth's effects, Hill's characters relish the thought of devouring them eucharistically. Romantic artists, Blake and the symbolists affirmed, are the new Christs; their images are materials for rituals in a poetic church. Their original inspirations emanate from their sacrifices (artifices) like holy spirits. What the tourists or readers eat is literally "nothing," a sign for a thing but not the thing itself, which, as Hill points out in his poem, possesses the power to redeem past acts and facts. The purpose of the poem, ultimately, is a catharsis in which love and charity displace boredom, confusion, fear, and hatred. As Hill's meditation on artifice proceeds, the tourists approach Wordsworth's relics:

> To bite nothings to the bone:
>
> And the daylight between facts;
> And the daylight between acts;
> Groping of custom towards love;
> Past loving, the custom to approve . . .

Somewhat like Eliot's cultural gossipers in "Prufrock" ("in the room the women come and go / Talking of Michelangelo"), Hill's fashionable tourists peep into famous places and pretend to commune with sacred spirits. Hill satirizes them, as he satirizes himself, since he is one of the voyeurs as well. They resemble the hollow men, who congregate in that grey area

>   Between the idea
> And the reality
> Between the motion
> And the act . . .

They inhabit the sunlight between facts and acts, an imaginary place with real spirits in it, and consume a mess of shadows for their meat. Hill's poetic pilgrims are essentially common people who try to learn from Wordsworth (as Hill does):

> A use of words; a rhetoric
> As plain as spitting on a stick;
> Speech from the ice, the clear-obscure;
> The tongue broody in the jaw . . .

Wordsworth is not only their mentor, he is a type of Christ, who instructs them by example to brood in icy withdrawal and then to return to speak the *lingua franca* of the people.

At the end of Hill's poem, there is a rhythmical surge which imitates the spiritual apotheosis of a traditional elegy. The *genius loci*, which is Wordsworth's spirit, appears to the communing travelers as a king on a throne or coronation stone:

> Greatly-aloof, alert, rare
> Spirit, conditioned to appear
> At the authentic stone or seat:
> O near-human spouse and poet . . .

This is the extraordinary ordinary man, the supernatural naturalist who redeems "the conscious mind's intelligible structure" by being able, as Wordsworth said in his "Preface," "to choose incidents and situations from common life" and, "in a selection of language really used by men," wed them to the intellect. The purpose of Hill's poem is to transfigure mundane customs, the syntax and diction of common language, the landscape of the Lake District, and Wordsworth's rural cottage into a lasting (profitable) poem full of

> Mountains, rivers, and grand storms,
> Continuous profit, grand customs
> (And many of them): O Lakes, Lakes!
> O Sentiment upon the rocks!

Hill's symmetries recall Beaumont's picture of the castle built "upon the rocks." But while Hill resurrects the romantic spirit and places it on firm foundation, he simultaneously exclaims that romantic "sentiment," like the Christian spirit from which it partly derives, is "on the rocks," irrevocably shattered.

In his oblique way, Hill manages to suspend all masks of romanticism at the end of his poem without affirming any. The Christian desire to win spiritual profits from worldly losses is placed alongside the capitalist desire to gain continuous profits from the losses of others. Embittered perhaps by his own meagre financial rewards from poetry, which hardly compensate for the labor expended, Hill implies, sardonically, that artists must be dead, like Wordsworth, to earn a decent wage.

The passion Hill elegizes in his poem is for a "grammar of assent" which would prescribe ways to affirm the intelligible orders represented by both Wordsworth and Christianity. If Wordsworth in his long life moved from one grammar to another—from romanticism to Christianity—Hill, at the age of twenty-three, had already moved from a relatively orderly grammar and syntax to a perplexingly dislocated one. "Failing a grammar of assent, syntax may serve," he writes, borrowing Cardinal Newman's phrase, and, in his poem, he replaces grammatical proprieties with syntactical idiosyncrasies. Wordsworth, in gaining a secure faith, lost imaginative power. Sceptical of all grammars and the air-tight worlds they induce us to believe in, Hill represents the upheaval of both in the upheaval of his lines.

Joyce once claimed, to justify *Finnegans Wake*, that "one great part of every human existence is passed in a state which cannot be rendered sensible by the use of wideawake language, cutanddry grammar and goahead plot."[9] In language that undercuts conventional grammar and plot, Hill, like Joyce, continually recalls the old forms but only to revoke or distort them. To sacrifice intelligibility (the kind Wordsworth is famous for) is not easy for Hill. To do so requires "a burnt offering of a powerful and decent desire . . . to be immediately understood by 'a common, well-educated, thoughtful man, of ordinary talents' " (*LL*, p. 94). His attitude toward romantic ideals is close to Yeats's in "Easter 1916," which remains "distrustful yet envious, mistrusting the abstraction, mistrusting its own mistrust, drawn half-against its will into the chanting refrain that is both paean and threnos."[10] But Hill is more convinced than Yeats that the old romantic notions of order are wrong. Through tortuous syntax that makes Yeats's poetry seem simple, Hill dramatizes his debate between a commitment to traditional laws, whether of natural science, language, or courts, and his recognition of their perpetual breakdown before a disturbing, partially indeterminate, shape-shifting reality.

History and Judgment

In "Little Gidding," written a little over a decade before Hill departed from Oxford, Eliot affirmed that "history is now and England" and sought to witness all times, past and future, in a pattern of timeless moments. In "The Dry Salvages" he took part of his message from Krishna, part of it from Revelation:

> O voyagers, O seamen,
> You who come to port, and you whose bodies
> Will suffer the trial and judgement of the sea
> Or whatever event, this is your real destination.

Hill's poems return obsessively to trials and judgments of the sea. Eliot's object was to make history present so that the failures and accomplishments of the past could act as beacons for the future. Although Hill distrusts all talk of "timeless moments" and envisions history as a repetitive struggle, "red in tooth and claw," like Eliot, he resurrects the dead for contemporary edification. In his interview with Blake Morrison, he said:

I think that it is a tragedy for a nation or a people to lose the sense of history, not because I think that the people is thereby necessarily losing some mystical private possession, but because . . . it is losing some vital dimension of intelligence. I'm entirely in sympathy with those who would argue that in order to control the present one needs to be steeped in the past. I think my sense of history is in itself anything but nostalgic, but I accept nostalgia as part of the *psychological* experience of a society and of an ancient and troubled nation.[11]

The sea, the damned, and the dead, as in the Book of Revelation, predominate in Hill's history poems, but so do efforts to judge and learn from them.

If Hill regards the past as a protracted cataclysm, he is also critical of myths of cataclysmic revelation and judgment. He would agree with Frank Kermode in *The Sense of an Ending*, who said that 'the most terrible element in apocalyptic thinking is its certainty that there must be universal bloodshed. . . . Thus the world is changed to conform with a fiction, as by the murder of the Jews."[12] Aware of the danger of apocalyptic fictions when imposed on society, Hill attacks apocalypse, with its neatly organized beginning and end, by fracturing his narratives. He sides with D. H. Lawrence, who scorned the biblical Apocalypse for what he saw as its hatred of the natural world, and points to the collusion between apocalypse and holocaust, artifice and sacrifice.

Although Hill has been linked to the poets of the Great War—Owen, Gurney, Rosenberg, and Sassoon—and to Keith Douglas of the Second World War, he differs from the war poets in fundamental ways. His war poems are characteristically about the survivors and those who did not fight, rather than about the actual combatants. They express uncertainty and difficulty in speaking about and for the victims. "Two Formal Elegies, For the Jews in Europe" (1955–56) contains many of the themes which characterize Hill's history poems. The two sonnets affirm the Old Testament quality of the Holocaust and question the reasonableness of shocking the living with memories of atrocities. Hill's poetic martyrs, however, sacrifice all forms of comfort in the attempt, so often futile, to bear witness (martyr from the Greek *martus* originally meant "witness") to historical sins and sufferings.

Hill's first sonnet begins, forebodingly, with a grotesque parody of judgment. While the poet acknowledges the Jews "disposed" of during the Holocaust, he berates all those with prejudiced or indifferent dispositions for whom the Jews continue to be, even in death, "unyielding" and "tight-fisted" ("clenched") with "their abused bodies and bonds." Hill plumbs the depths of every word and edges towards blasphemy when he writes:

> Knowing the dead, and how some are disposed:
> Subdued under rubble, water, in sand graves,
> In clenched cinders not yielding their abused
> Bodies and bonds to those whom war's chance saves
> Without the law . . .

Hill echoes Homer, who said in *The Iliad*, that "the chance of war / Is equal and the slayer oft is slain," but he gives the lines his own twist. The dead are subdued and buried by Germans but also by the ignorance and repression of contemporary minds that refuse to remember them. The living who abandon the Mosaic law, which prohibits killing as well as bearing false witness (they kill and refuse to bear any witness), sacrifice nothing because they remember nothing.

If Hill followed Moses' pillar of fire and cloud in his Oxford poems, now he embraces Moses' laws of sacrifice and atonement with the ardor of a zealot. Sacrifice and atonement, he declares, are misunderstood, forgotten, or dismissed by modern society. If the Mosaic law guided people through the wilderness and allowed civilization to flourish there, now

> The wilderness revives,
>
> Deceives with sweetness harshness. Still beneath
> Live skin stone breathes, about which fires but play,
> Fierce heart that is the iced brain's to command
> To judgment—(studied reflex, contained breath)—
> Their best of worlds since, on the ordained day,
> This world went spinning from Jehovah's hand.

Here, Hill alters Yeats's statement that "too long a sacrifice / Can make a stone of the heart" ("Easter 1916") and proposes that the heart should be made a stone on which sacrifices are performed. To distinguish painful sacrifice from murderous holocaust, Hill emphasizes that, in the former, the "fires but play," as in Yeats's "Byzantium," where the initiates die into "an agony of flame that cannot singe a sleeve." The imagination's fires do not actually burn like the Nazis' crematoriums. They remember rather than dismember the past. The cathartic purge of tragic fiction is affirming rather than genocidal. For the Jewish victims of the Holocaust, the world of fiction is the best of worlds. There, they live on as witnesses of the past and guides for the future, rather than the "subdued" victims of the "best of all possible worlds" heedlessly celebrated by Voltaire's Pangloss and governed by the jealous, angry god, Jehovah.

Kermode states in his discussion of apocalyptic fictions and their influence on history, that "if *King Lear* is an image of the promised end, so is Buchenwald; and both stand under the accusation of being horrible, rootless fantasies, the one no more true or more false than the other, so that the best you say is that *King Lear* does less harm."[13] Hill, on the other hand, notes the obvious difference between a tragic image and a tragic event. To make the tragic image communicate the full horror of the fact so that it avoids decaying into a bland image is the poet's task. "The burden which the writer's conscience must bear is that the horror might become that hideously outrageous thing, a cliché. This is the nightmare, the really blasphemous thing: that those camps could become a mere 'subject'."[14] In his poem he observes with sober bitterness:

> For all that must be gone through, their long death
> Documented and safe, we have enough
> Witnesses (our world being witness-proof).

The "long death" of the Jews is their history of persecution, "safe" because it is now contained in literature. After World War II, six million Jews, and the countless who memorialized them, "witnessed" by deed or word the afflictions of the Nazis. If the contemporary world is "witness-proof," as an umbrella is waterproof, it is because it resists these historical facts. The frequency of atrocities and the multitudes of books which record them, Hill points out with gloomy irony, threaten to make them ordinary and acceptable.

Hill ends his poem with a satirical sketch of his fellow midlanders, who are also "mediterraneans" (their heritage is rooted in Mediterranean culture) but who are now simply vacationers *from* rather than martyrs *to* their past. If the ocean is the destructive element—history's purgatorial nightmare flickering like a gigantic crematorium—they lie on the beach and let their bodies build up insulation (fat) against its ghastliness.

> Here, yearly, the pushing midlanders stand
> To warm themselves; men, brawny with life,
> Women who expect life. They relieve
> Their thickening bodies, settle on scraped sand.
>
> Is it good to remind them, on a brief screen,
> Of what they have witnessed and not seen?
> (Deaths of the city that persistently dies . . . ?)
> To put up stones ensures some sacrifice.
> Sufficient men confer, carry their weight.
> (At whose door does the sacrifice stand or start?)

Although Hill asks many questions about witness and sacrifice, he concludes that, with the death of civilization ("the city") always at hand, "sufficient men" (in number and responsibility) must devote their lives to remembering the past. As Christopher Ricks has observed, the line "without the law" and the last line of the second sonnet transform Kipling's "Recessional" as well as Tennyson's line "The guilt of blood is at your door."[15] But Hill is less affirmative than Kipling or Tennyson. Although he stands for a Christ-like vigilance, an act of witness and sacrifice, he ends with a question rather than an answer.

In his self-critical debate, Hill wants to judge historical events as if for the first time, in an unmediated way, rather than depend on the accounts of past writers. He shows an archaeologist's care for evidence (guns, wounds), as in "Requiem for the Plantagenet Kings," where the English Channel becomes his principal exhibit. Here, the sea, "possessed" by demons of victors and victims, ruinous armaments and ruined bodies, offers up its dead for judgment:

> For whom the possessed sea littered, on both shores,
> Ruinous arms; being fired, and for good,
> To sound the constitution of just wars,
> Men, in their eloquent fashion, understood.

For whom or to whom does history speak? To the students of politics interested in the constitutionality of wars? To the poets like Shakespeare who can transform the slaughters into eloquent plays? Tate declares:

> Turn your eyes to the immoderate past,
> Turn to the inscrutable infantry rising
> Demons out of the earth—they will not last.

Hill summons the moody, promiscuous, blood-thirsty Plantagenet kings into his house for closer evaluation:

> Relieved of soul, the dropping-back of dust,
> Their usage, pride, admitted within doors;
> At home, under caved chantries, set in trust,
> With well-dressed alabaster and proved spurs
> They lie; they lie; secure in the decay
> Of blood, blood-marks, crowns hacked and coveted,
> Before the scouring fires of trial-day
> Alight on men; before sleeked groin, gored head,
> Budge through the clay and gravel, and the sea
> Across daubed rock evacuates its dead.

Tyrannical king and butchered soldier lie (and "lie" to those who behold them) in their "well-dressed" tombs. The offenders perjure themselves. The specimens to be considered (blood-marks, hacked crowns) have decayed, like once vigorous words (marks) into clichés. The poet must rejuvenate language in order to rejuvenate the dead. Myths that distort past events must be cleared away for precise revelation. Only then can there be a final judgment.

Myth and history clash in "The White Ship," a poem about the wreck of Henry I's "White Ship" in 1120 (caused by the crew's drunkenness),[16] in which his son William drowned ("seaman / And king's son also"). Hill finds in the catastrophe an archetypal myth of sin, fall, and resurrection but uses myth only to arouse expectations which he can then purge. He alludes to *The Tempest* (where Ferdinand, a "king's son also," imagines he has drowned), St. John's "sea full of dead," and Dante Gabriel Rossetti's "White Ship," a 271-line poem about the incident, in which the narrator is miraculously saved by God and a Christlike fisherman. There are no miracles, however, in Hill's poem. The dead are dead, and for ascertainable reasons. No matter who intervenes, they will not be resurrected into any other world outside the poem. The poem is a quiet but moving lyric on death's finality:

> Where the living with effort go,
> Or with expense, the drowned wander
> Easily: seaman
> And king's son also
>
> Who, by gross error lost,
> Drift, now, in salt crushed
> Polyp- and mackerel-fleshed
> Tides between coast and coast,
>
> Submerge or half-appear.
> This does not much matter.
> They are put down as dead. Water
> Silences all who would interfere;
>
> Retains, still, what it might give
> As casually as it took away:

> Creatures passed through the wet sieve
> Without enrichment or decay.

The sea, a mundane sieve rather than mythical transmogrifier, passes the dead on as they are, unaltered. Its purpose is didactic, to school the historical intelligence in harsh facts rather than their sugared substitutes. Although there is no "enrichment" for the dead, there may be enrichment for the living.

Against those who erect mythical abstractions to assuage history's violence and death Hill aims his sombre, satirical wit. In "The Guardians," he again attacks venerated idols, this time Plato's program of education in *The Republic*, which aims at protecting Athenian youths from both the realities and fictions of violence so that they may remain blissfully ingenuous. The poem addresses the issue of innocence and experience, as Socrates once spoke of it to Adeimantus:

Neither, if we mean our future guardians to regard the habit of quarrelling among themselves as of all things the basest, should any word be said to them of the wars in heaven, and of the plots and fightings of the gods against one another, for they are not true. No, we shall never mention the battles of the giants, or let them be embroidered on garments; and we shall be silent about the innumerable other quarrels of gods and heroes with their friends and relatives. If they would only believe us we would tell them that quarrelling is unholy, and that never up to this time has there been any quarrel between citizens; that is what old men and old women should begin by telling children.[17]

In Hill's poem, the young guardians depart from the older guardians into a world that they know nothing about. Their educations in the Republic have been worthless. Ignorant of both historical and mythical brutalities, they are vulnerable to them. The stormy ocean, symbol of worldly cruelty, destroys them. Hill offers a knowing lament:

> The young, having risen early, had gone,
> Some with excursions beyond the bay-mouth,

Some toward lakes, a fragile reflected sun.
Thunder-heads drift, awkwardly, from the south;

The old watch them. They have watched the safe
Packed harbours topple under sudden gales,
Great tides irrupt, yachts burn at the wharf
That on clean seas pitched their effective sails.

There are silences. These, too, they endure:
Soft comings-on; soft after-shocks of calm.
Quietly they wade the disturbed shore;
Gather the dead as the first dead scrape home.

Quietism is not Hill's way, however, even though his tone is quiet. He means to implicate the elders in the deaths of the young. The sea again demands judgment.

Similarly, in "Wreaths," another succinct elegy written in the same year as "The White Ship" (1956), an apocalyptic sea evacuates its dead in order to reveal mistaken judgments, appoint responsibility, and point towards wiser actions. The poem mocks those who evade past crimes and deaths to protect sentimental notions of love. "Altered in eyes and skin," these new visionaries are "saint[s] of the wrong religion,"[18] as Yvor Winters said of Hart Crane and his "visionary company of love." To ignore the harsh facts, like Hill's boisterous beach combers, is suicidal. With obvious sarcasm, the poet lampoons the holiday makers who mistake the sea's battlefield for a handsome paradise:

I
Each day the tide withdraws; chills us; pastes
The sand with dead gulls, oranges, dead men.
Uttering love, that outlasts or outwastes
Time's attrition, exiles appear again,
But faintly altered in eyes and skin.

II
Into what understanding all have grown!
(Setting aside a few things, the still faces,

Climbing the phosphorus tide, that none will own)
What paradises and watering-places,
What hurts appeased by the sea's handsomeness!

Both living and dead (who seem interchangeable) have undergone a sea change into something rich and strange but now refuse to "own up" or take responsibility for their heritage of error and terror.

Hill wants to approach history as doubting Thomas approached Christ, with a scepticism that will penetrate hearsay, sentimental abstractions, and fanciful myths and search out actual wounds. In "After Cumae," Hill traces the perilous course of Aeneas from the Sibyl's cave at Cumae (the first Greek city in Italy) to the founding of Rome and Western civilization, and he does so by touching the wound Aeneas has left on the map. His poem is a despondent, satirical, splendidly-wrought judgment of civilization. Like the Sibyl, who speaks to Aeneas of his future, the poet knows that history's mansions are founded on war's ruins. In the sixth book of *The Aeneid*, which Hill had to translate as an Oxford undergraduate, the Sibyl prophesies:

My son, you have passed all perils of the sea,
but ashore still worse await. To Latium's land
the sons of Troy shall come (this care dismiss),
but coming shall find no joy. War, terror, war,
I see, and Tiber flowing red with blood.
(VI, 83–87)

Later, Aeneas's father, Anchises, predicts his son's fame and the grandeur of Roman imperialism. As a twentieth-century man, Hill sees Rome's grandeur arising from ruins and bloodshed. The Sibyl's "mouthy cave," or oracle, is perennially obscured by new heroes seeking laurels of fame:

The sun again unearthed, colours come up fresh,
The perennials; and the laurels'

> Washable leaves, that seem never to perish,
> Obscure the mouthy cave, the dumb grottoes.

The new heroes are lusty bulls charging at bright colors. The Sibyl's grottoes are dumb because nobody listens to them. The sea, full of wreckage and corpses, testifies to modern and ancient debacles:

> From the beginning, in the known world, slide
> Drawn echoing hulls, axes grate, and waves
> Deposit in their shallow margins varied
> Fragments of marine decay and waftage . . .

Those "in the known world" (Aeneas's Mediterranean and Plato's knowable shadow world in the cave) perceive that the voyage to civilization (Plato's Republic in the sunlit world of ideal truth and beauty) leaves a wasteland of fragments in its wake. Following Aeneas's voyage on a book's "spread-out" pages, Hill offers a skillful parody of the hero pursuing, or letting himself be pursued by, his destiny.

> And the sometimes-abandoned gods confuse
> With immortal essences men's brief lives,
> Frequenting the exposed and pious: those
> Who stray, as designed, under applied perils,
>
> Whose doom is easy, venturing so far
> Without need, other than to freeze or burn,
> Their wake, on spread-out oceans, a healed scar
> Fingered, themselves the curios of voyage.

Unlike Thomas, who had the benefit of immediate and unmediated contact with the resurrected Christ (Hill's personification of history), Hill can only investigate the past through its artifacts. The heroes and victims have become "curios," their despair and ecstasy matters of historical curiosity.

For the Unfallen

Culture, in Hill's view, seems divided into two camps. The first, as "A Pastoral" demonstrates, is an Eden of forgetfulness and spiritual drifting, the second a place of rigorous vigilance, anxiety, and sacrifice. The pastoral form, William Empson once pointed out, makes "simple people express strong feelings (felt as the most universal subject, something fundamentally true about everybody) in learned and fashionable language."[19] Hill's "Pastoral" expresses universal desires of love and hate in the learned language of intellectuals, war poets, historians, and psychoanalysts.

Hill imagines them, rather fancifully, as an efficient ambulance force of "Pities" (with a glance at Wilfred Owen's "poetry is in the pity"), who seem to indulge in suffering as much as they seek to cure it. Like Blake and Yeats, who saw pity as an ignoble emotion, Hill mocks them but also partly identifies with them. Of Owen's romantic agonies and solemnities Hill has said that "one is free to question how much of this music comes from the realized experience of 1917–18 and how much from a residual yet haunting echo of the nineteenth century rhetoric that Owen fought so hard to overcome."[20] Do the war poets pity the dead or do the dead simply provide subjects to launch their high-flying rhetoric? Hill continues to debate the discrepancy between eloquence and authentic witness. He not only judges the dead but also judges the poetry that commemorates the dead. He sounds like Lowell in his satirical assault:

> Mobile, immaculate and austere,
> The Pities, their fingers in every wound,
> Assess the injured on the obscured frontier;
> Cleanse with a kind of artistry the ground
> Shared by War. Consultants in new tongues
> Prove synonymous our separated wrongs.

Are the modern Thomases (war poets, confessional poets) morbid voyeurs or conscientious historians? The consultants (the psychoanalysts), who base their theories on the premise that "the imagination of man's heart is evil from his youth" (and transform it into the new language of id and anxiety), concur that all are guilty.

Against the Confessionals' hypochondria, Hill is also against the Movement's antiseptic evasion of battlefields and hospitals. Hill speaks for the bourgeois Englishman of the 1950s who manicures his civilized pose and specious fluency with the passion he devotes to his car ("painted and re-aligned"), but only to ridicule him. Hill is a poet driven by "traditional furies," who sacrifices social ease in order to communicate the difficult lessons of history.

> We celebrate, fluently and at ease.
> Traditional Furies, having thrust, hovered,
> Now decently enough sustain Peace.
> The unedifying nude dead are soon covered.
> Survivors, still given to wandering, find
> Their old loves, painted and re-aligned—
>
> Queer, familiar, fostered by superb graft
> On treasured foundations, these ideal features!
> Men can move with purpose again, or drift,
> According to direction.

Having confessed their "separated wrongs," Hill's survivors return to the wayward currents of bourgeois society, where they drift or strike out with renewed purpose. For the drifters, the past is forgotten, a graveyard darkened by vegetation, impervious, unedifying:

> Here are statues
> Darkened by laurel; and evergreen names;
> Evidently-veiled griefs; impervious tombs.

For Hill, man is emphatically a historical and linguistic animal who continually veils the pain of his heritage. The names of past heroes, villains, and victims (the "ever-green names") are everpresent, however, to the mind which recollects them. Hill's history poems bear witness to that intensity of consciousness (and its burden of anxiety) which illuminates the shadowed statues and opens the tombs. Like Joyce, Hill intends to create, or at least resurrect, the conscience of his race by holding up the past in all its bewildering complexity.

Judaeo-Christianity Revised

As with most modern "religious poets," Hill's attitudes towards orthodox belief are perplexed. Rather than affirm traditional doctrines unconditionally, which would indicate the mind's subservience to them, Hill affirms the mind's freedom to alter its postures: to become enchanted, sceptical, devotional, iconoclastic, and revisionary by turn. Poetry, Hill asserts, should be a theatre with many planes, on which diverse beliefs and disbeliefs challenge each other. "If poetry has any value," he told an interviewer, "that value must presuppose the absolute freedom of poetry to encompass the maximum range of belief or unbelief" (*VP*, p. 88).

This is not to say that Hill does not possess strong religious beliefs of his own. "I would not wish to describe myself as an agnostic" (*VP*, p. 98), he says plainly in an interview. Obsessed with the problem of belief, he seeks to reinterpret traditional Judaeo-Christian doctrines and to dramatize them in ways that account for contemporary experience and, especially, for poetic experience. His poetry contains a strange mixture of traditional Christian symbols and a modern man's distrust of all symbols. It is, he says, "a heretic's dream of salvation expressed in the images of the orthodoxy from which he is excommunicate" (*VP*, p. 98).

The notion that art is a substitute for religion, a ritual of a lost faith, a church for the unorthodox poet, is a legacy of romantic and symbolist tradition. Like David Jones, Hill sees the poet's symbolic making artifice and communication as the secular counterpart for Christ's sacrifice and communion. But while Hill's poems draw many of their symbols from the Bible and literature inspired by the Bible, they rarely promise the traditional rewards of religious experience. The boon of grace is glimpsed but usually as it vanishes into darkness. Hill has stated that "the grasp of true religious experience is a privilege reserved for very few." The poet's task, therefore, is "to make lyrical poetry out of a much more common situation—the sense of *not* being able to grasp true religious experience" (*VP,* p. 89). Of the religious experiences that inform Hill's poems, the most common are creation, crucifixion, purgatory, and apocalypse, which, Hill stipulates, are in many ways equivalent. Although he may not believe in the Christ Word and its ability to alleviate modern anxiety, Hill remains committed to a belief in the poetic word. In a godless age, he is tempted to say, with Stevens, that poetry must act "as life's redemption" (*LL,* p. 16).

Poetry may "make nothing happen," but it at least provides poet and culture with a *via negativa,* a purgative way towards new knowledge and sanctity:

So there is a sense in which the modern artist is called upon to atone for his own illiberal pride and a sense in which he is engaged in a vicarious expiation for the pride of the culture which itself rejects him. He can't win; but, you might say, he can't lose either; for in the words of Grotowski, in his book *Towards a Poor Theatre,* the actor "does not sell his body but sacrifices it. He repeats the atonement; he is close to [secular] holiness" (*LL,* p. 4).

The word imitates the Christ Word, as the poet imitates Christ. Hill's heavens and hells, like Yeats's, are essentially symbolic representations of the elation or despair in imaginative creation. The imagination is in hell when it is torn from its desired image, and it is in heaven when it has grasped it. If there is one ideal or god to which Hill faithfully adheres, it is to the ideal of "creative intellect." Sometimes he calls it the "secondary imagination," at other times the "pillar of fire," the pentecostal flame, the rational mind that is "simple, sensuous, and passionate." For Hill "every fine and moving poem bears witness to . . . [a] lost kingdom of innocence and original justice" (*VP,* p. 88). The seriousness with which Hill pursues his poetry of redemption indicates the measure of his understanding of and sympathy for orthodox religion, rather than any cynical or nihilistic rejection.

"Picture of a Nativity," composed in 1956, provides a good example of Hill's method of transforming biblical doctrines into fables of the imagination. The poem is at once autobiographical, mythic, and sociological, the portrait of Hill's early arrival at poetic maturity (and perhaps, as a teacher at Leeds, on the literary "world's outer shores"), the experience of giving birth to any difficult creation, and the not altogether laudatory response of an audience to an exemplary poem. Although Christ's nativity is at the center of his tale, Hill creates a poem with multiple implications, that is partly about writing. The "arrival" of the "dumb child-king" is Christ, poet, and poem. It is also the arrival of a teacher among students who seem hopelessly bestial and snakelike (but unwilling to be tempted by the fruit of knowledge). They are unfallen; their prehensile torsos and claws, having grown flaccid and buttery, can grasp nothing. They regard words (and the Christ Word) with incomprehension. In the long line of poems about the poetic imagination, "Picture of a Nativity" distinguishes itself by offering in Christian terms an intriguing and humorous portrait of messianic poet and his refractory audience.

Burdened with the wreckage implicit in re-creation, the martyr-poet, somewhat like Christ at the Second Coming (as well as the Nativity), rises above his hardships to create an image that bears witness to them:

> Sea-preserved, heaped with sea-spoils,
> Ribs, keels, coral sores,
> Detached faces, ephemeral oils,
> Discharged on the world's outer shores,

> A dumb child-king
> Arrives at his right place; rests,
> Undisturbed, among slack serpents; beasts
> With claws flesh-buttered. In the gathering
>
> Of bestial and common hardship
> Artistic men appear to worship
> And fall down; to recognise
> Familiar tokens; believe their own eyes.
>
> Above the marvel, each rigid head,
> Angels, their unnatural wings displayed,
> Freeze into an attitude
> Recalling the dead.

"In the act of 'making,'" Hill has written, "we are necessarily delivered up to judgment" (*LL*, p. 14). Hill's new-born poet, who is grandly regal, innocent, and oracularly dumb, delivers up both himself and his published poem for judgment. At odds with the adjudicating culture around him, Hill ridicules the judges. The serpents are "slack" and too thick to be instructed and delighted by poems. The other beasts are timid, domesticated but untutored. The angels, no better, have transcended the natural labors of art altogether by puritanically renouncing them. They are serpents in a different guise. The artists, however, approach the new poem as if they were magi approaching a new incarnation. But they only "appear to worship." They "fall down" in obeisance before something that is ultimately mysterious. Like Yeats in "The Magi," a poem "Picture of a Nativity" resembles, Hill dramatizes equally strong desires for total incarnation and total transcendence and in the icon or "token" depicting the "uncontrollable mystery on the bestial floor" finds a poetic example of "unity of being."

As with the biblical tale of Nativity, Hill uses the orthodox account of Christ's Passion as a metaphor for an exemplary secular passion. He writes as a sceptic, however, who refuses to believe that most communicants feel the full suffering of

Christ's sacrifice, and he confesses his own failure to do so. In his "Canticle for Good Friday," he documents the sharp curiosity and bafflement before Christ that a common man might experience, rather than the "assent from the roots" of the mystic. By placing his doubting Thomas before the cross where he can smell the actual blood and vinegar in Christ's wounds (a privilege not granted Thomas in the Gospels), Hill displays a visceral response and passionate ambivalence. His passion *is* his ambivalence. His modern-day Thomas does not reject belief entirely as superstition; he is drawn toward both the historical and mythical Christ. But, however much he tries, he cannot give up his empirical beliefs and doubts. He cannot make a leap of faith, or even a reasoned assent, as much as he wants to.

If Larkin expresses his generation's desire to abandon the pagan and Christian "myth kitty," Hill dramatizes some of the psychological consequences of its loss. Lacking an understanding of Christ's ordeal on the cross, harrowing of hell, and resurrection, Hill's Thomas remains isolated from orthodox religious experience but also estranged from simple linguistic and artistic experience. Both religious and literary fictions stagger him but fail to transfigure him:

> The cross staggered him. At the cliff-top
> Thomas, beneath its burden, stood
> While the dulled wood
> Spat on the stones each drop
> Of deliberate blood.
>
> A clamping, cold-figured day
> Thomas (not transfigured) stamped, crouched,
> Watched
> Smelt vinegar and blood. He,
> As yet unsearched, unscratched,
>
> And suffered to remain
> At such near distance

> (A slight miracle might cleanse
> His brain
> Of all attachments, claw-roots of sense)
>
> In unaccountable darkness moved away,
> The strange flesh untouched, carrion-sustenance
> Of staunchest love, choicest defiance,
> Creation's issue congealing (and one woman's).

The conversion of Thomas from disbelief to belief in the Bible never happens in Hill's fable. He moves close to Christ but does not touch Christ's wound or commune with Christ's "strange flesh." There is no "carrion-comfort," in Hopkins's phrase, no "at-one-ment." Estranged from "creation's issue," which may be Christ's body (Mary's issue), the blood issuing from His wound, Magdalen's issuing tears (later celebrated in "Lachrimae"), and God's issued Word (which for Thomas is a dead metaphor), Thomas redeems nothing. If Christ once symbolized that staunch love and defiant faith of the martyr, to the modern Thomas, he is simply a carcass on a cross. Thomas walks off, "bored, uninformed," like Larkin's cyclist in "Church Going."

To identify the beliefs and disbeliefs of Hill's Thomas and other personae with the poet himself would be a mistake, as this poem shows. Hill's mode is characteristically satirical, like Jonathan Swift's "poetry of reaction," which, as Hill has observed, possesses "the capacity to be at once resistant and reciprocal" (*LL*, p. 67). In his "Canticle," Hill resembles the woman who creates the Word and weeps over it, as much as Thomas who judges it, or Christ who embodies it. He dramatizes typical attitudes in contemporary society, without giving way to them. His first book originally was to be entitled *Of Commerce and Society,* after a phrase in Allen Tate's "More Sonnets at Christmas." He abandoned this title but never strayed from his intention of expressing society as it is.

Perhaps the most seductive of all Christian themes for Hill, as his history poems demonstrate, is apocalypse. Apocalypse is

For the Unfallen

the revelation (*apokalupsis* means revelation in Greek), of an ideal world by which the past and present can be evaluated and reconstructed. Its method of change is revolutionary, abrupt, uncompromising, rather than gradual and diplomatic. St. John's Apocalypse envisages the final judgment of mankind as a violent and painful experience. In "Little Apocalypse," Hill takes up the theme of apocalypse and examines it once again, but now in the context of a particular poet's (Hölderlin's) private experience. As one of the great German romantics, Hölderlin acts as Hill's mask. Through him he analyzes and evaluates his own apocalyptic temperament, which is an

> Abrupt tempter; close enough to survive
> The sun's primitive renewing fury;
> Scorched vistas where crawl the injured and brave:
> This man stands sealed against their injury:
>
> Hermetic radiance of great suns kept in:
> Man's common nature suddenly too rare:
> See, for the brilliant coldness of his skin,
> The god cast, perfected, among fire.

The tempter is both Hölderlin and apocalypse itself. To stress the abrupt moods and reversals of the apocalyptic mind, Hill scores them into the very abruptness of his syntax.

Hölderlin, like many of Hill's personae, from the Plantagenets to Offa and Péguy, is a paradoxical combination of villain and imaginative hero, mystic and martyr. He is a tough common man, in touch with the fundamental energies of body and nature. He is close to the sun, although it threatens to destroy him. He is also the man of extraordinary brilliance, hermetically sealed from common nature. He is cold and fiery, inhuman and superhuman, a Janus-like figure who faces the sunlit world of history and society ("where crawl the injured and brave") and, at the same moment, looks the other way into the internal world of the imagination. The poem conjoins many opposites and is partly about their conjunction. Hölderlin, like Hill, seeks an "apocalyptic marriage" between the old heaven and old earth and the new heaven and new earth. His goal is to "perfect," to make complete and whole, a god, which is his ideal image and "cast" poem ("cast" like an artifact in bronze or "cast" like a body in fire).

Hill's memorial is as much a diagnosis of apocalypse as a dramatization of it. Lawrence once declared that "the Apocalypse shows us what we are resisting, unnaturally . . . our connection with the cosmos, with the world, with mankind, with the nation, with the family."[21] And Hill concurs that the unnaturalness of apocalypse can be suicidal, a private holocaust, a whole burning, or a plunge into madness.

Subtitled "Hölderlin: 1770–1843," the poem draws attention to events a century later, in 1943, during World War II. Michael Hamburger in *Reason and Energy* (published in 1957, the same year as Hill's poem), recounts that, in Germany in 1943, a special "field selection" of Hölderlin's poems was issued for German soldiers to carry in their packs. It could be argued that the solipsism, hubris, and madness which Hölderlin experienced and wrote of found avid followers in Hitler's Third Reich. The difference, of course, is that Hölderlin attempted to purge destructive energies by making poems, while Hitler purged a society by slaughtering millions. Hölderlin once claimed of his tragic, purgatorial art: "The representation of the tragic is mainly based on this: that what is monstrous and terrible in the coupling of god and man, in the total fusion of the power of Nature with the inmost depth of the man, so that they are one at the moment of wrath, should be made intelligible by showing how this total fusion into one is purged by their total separation."[22] To purge the hubristic imagination of its violence ("the sun's primitive renewing fury" and "radiance of great suns kept in"), the poem must show that the apotheosis (god and man "perfected among fire") is something ultimately separate. In his poems which bear witness to the monstrous and terrible, Hill achieves Hölderlin's sort of catharsis.

For the Unfallen

If there is an apocalypse Hill approves of, it is the sort described in the poem "In Piam Memoriam," in which an empirical bystander unifies, in an act of perception, both the transcendental world of saints and the common world of water and rock. His churchgoer, without the frivolity of Larkin's cyclist or gazer at "high windows," stands before a stained glass window (full of "stained archetypes"), muses on Christianity's orthodox images, and looks beyond them to a new earth rather than a new heaven. At one moment he affirms that his glass saint (like Stevens's "glass man" in "Asides on the Oboe") is a pure fiction, lacking external reference, whose original meaning, stained by time, has decayed:

> Created purely from glass the saint stands,
> Exposing his gifted quite empty hands
> Like a conjurer about to begin,
> A righteous man begging of righteous men.

The saint is the poet's creation (a pure poem), but also an image of the poet himself, a poor man paradoxically rich in imaginative desires and fictions. He begs to be recognized by his audience as he purifies the world's crude substances into luminous poems:

> In the sun lily-and-gold-coloured,
> Filtering the cruder light, he has endured,
> A feature for our regard; and will keep;
> Of worldly purity the stained archetype.

But what lies beneath this masterful image?

> The scummed pond twitches. The great holly-tree,
> Emptied and shut, blows clear of wasting snow,
> The common, puddled substance: beneath,
> Like a revealed mineral, a new earth.

Christian and secular images of "worldly purity" germinate from seasonal earth, scum, snow, tree, and rock. The poem is a revelation of saints and their ways, but also of the earth in its simple, geological grandeur, which remains when all the artificial images have been swept away.

Hill's fundamental attitude towards religious tradition mixes pious remembrance and impious iconoclasm and does not alter significantly throughout his career. Drawn to Christian events of nativity, crucifixion, and apocalypse, he tends to inspect them as a twentieth-century sceptic, aware of their tremendous power as symbols expressing the most fundamental experiences of humanity, but also wary of the exploitation of that power. Whether he calls them tokens, figures, gods, devices, clichés, or archetypes, he is primarily concerned with their capacity as rhetoric. Religion, for Hill, is not so much an agglomeration of atrophied dogmas as it is a language of fiction, complete with impressive ceremonies and symbols, which has controlled the destinies of many people, for better or worse, throughout history.

Modernist Sequences

The two longest sequences in *For the Unfallen*, "Metamorphoses" and "Of Commerce and Society," are ambitious attempts to amalgamate former preoccupations and techniques and to give them a new design. In the poems he wrote at Oxford, Hill experimented with extended sequences, but there he preserved vestiges of plots borrowed from the Bible, novels, or mythology. Now he arranges his sections like pictures in a gallery, with more emphasis on spatial than temporal relationships. Instead of constructing a well-balanced beginning, middle, and end, Hill breaks up his narratives, in the way that innovative modern writers did, into short, self-contained vignettes that focus intense energy. But if Hill's sequences look to the modernists for precedents, they also add something of their own. His compressed syntax, weighted and often tortuously woven with ambiguity and paradox, metaphor and myth, makes for a more militantly ruminative and sceptical utterance than either Pound or Eliot chose to use. The dramatic lyrics of Yeats, Allen Tate, William Empson, Robert Lowell, and Hart Crane are closer in style. But in the space of five or six pages, Hill gives to his sequences almost epic proportions.

Like Ovid, Hill in his "Metamorphoses" charts transformations, this time of emotions, particularly those visited upon the lover in mad pursuit of his beloved image. In five episodes, he traces an erratic path between fear and love, ecstasy and sorrow. The plot resembles an Aristotelian tragedy, which Hill, however, shatters by recording the failure of catharsis rather than its happy fulfillment. It begins in desperation, struggles toward purgatory, comes to a climax with a violent crime, and ends with a failed reconciliation between lovers. Unlike Dante on his purgatorial mountain, Hill's questor returns to the brutal world of society and politics, not as a benevolent mystic or lover but as a shark buffeted by hurricanes. The poem ends with only a glimpse of love. The lovers remain isolated, ill-tempered, devouring each other or gratifying themselves onanistically. They never escape the winding, treacherous path of purgatory, even though they descend from the mountain.

At the beginning, any sense of civilized community is painfully absent. The two lovers lack a common language of "civil intercourse." They remain estranged. Hill tries to express the fear which separates them but finds he can only gesture towards it with a series of negative statements.

> No manner of address will do;
> Eloquence is not in that look,
> But fear of a furred kind. You
> Display the stiff face of shock.
>
> Hate is not in it, nor that
> Which has presence, a character
> In civil intercourse—deceit
> Of a tough weathering-nature.

> This fear strikes hard and is gone
> And is recognised when found
> Not only between dark and dawn,
> The summit and the ground.

Through his negatives Hill delimits boundaries (rather than a particular point) beyond which and between which "the fear" exists. There is no objective correlative, but that is Hill's message. The emotion is subliminal. It transcends civilized, intelligible limits ("dark and dawn, / The summit and the ground"). He has gone some way in articulating its vague, amorphous omnipresence by articulating what it is not.

Hill starts off, then, with a theme common to twentieth-century poetry and philosophy: language's incompatibility with the objects it intends to signify. If Williams said that there are "no ideas but in things," Hill says that things, including words, can only intimate ideas through a glass darkly. In the first section, he entertains the solipsistic position that experience is private and language is too. But in the next section, he criticizes this position for its hubris, as if his hopes for language were too high to begin with. He declares, "through scant pride to be so put out," and, having abandoned his fears, he now tries to return to civilized life and intelligible intercourse. To do this he battles with a symbolist heritage which has led him towards artistic isolation. Mallarmé contended that art "is a mystery accessible only to very few," and that the artist is "a worshipper of beauty which is inaccessible to the mob."[23] Hill wants to demystify the mysteries and make the mob do the same. He fights to break away from his frightful alienation and to reestablish roots in community. He goes to Parnassus, where poetic ghosts issue from the Delphic oracle, to rectify the tradition that has enchanted and stultified him. If there is a purge of hubris, Hill playfully suggests, it is like the catharsis of Greek tragedy, once called a *tragōidia* or goat-satyr play. In Hill's rendition, however, the poet is the goat and, specifically, the scapegoat forced into the wilderness with the community's sins. The poet mocks his vanity by declaring:

> feed, feed, unlyrical scapegoat;
> Plague shrines where each fissure blows
> Odour of laurel clouding yours!
>
> Exercise loftily, your visions
> Where the montainous distance
> Echoes its unfaltering speech
> To mere outcry and harrowing search.
>
> Possessed of agility and passion,
> Energy (out-of-town-fashion)
> Attack every obstacle
> And height; make the sun your pedestal.
>
> Settle all that bad blood;
> Be visited, touched, understood;
> Be graced, groomed, returned to favour
> With admirable restraint and fervour!

The poet recognizes nature's indifference to and society's repugnance for his "harrowing search." His calls for community and love are echoed, like those of Frost's walker in "The Most of It," rather than answered. He may wish to be accepted as a democratic poet with social graces but his symbolist heritage and his commitment to articulating subliminal complexities relegate him to the mountain tops.

When he does descend from his summit, he approaches the civilized world not like Noah's dove flying to Ararat or Moses hiking judiciously down Horeb but as a lawless, ravenous shark. Like Sylvia Plath's "Lady Lazarus," Hill's prophet returns to society to "eat men like air." The estuary to which this predator journeys is Hill's symbolic arena of conflict. The "stayers" and "searchers" who inhabit it are those over whom this new Venus exerts a terrible power:

> And now the sea-scoured temptress, having failed
> To scoop out of horizons what birds herald:
> Tufts of fresh soil: shakes off an entire sea,
> Though not as the dove, harried. Rather, she,
>
> A shark hurricaned to estuary-water,
> (The lesser hunter almost by a greater
> Devoured) but unflurried, lies, approaches all
> Stayers, and searchers of the fanged pool.

The lover, who is androgynous (and much like Yeats's "terrible beauty"), has given up the struggle with articulation that perplexed the first section, as well as the second section's sublime vision of civility, in which love was the guiding principle. She rises like an atomic explosion (that "shakes off an entire sea") rather than like Botticelli's delicate Venus born from sea-foam and whisked toward land on a shell.

Although it is partly about emotional metamorphoses, the poem also metamorphoses old poems and myths into a new one. The first sections of the poem, for instance, transform sections of Wordsworth's "Prospectus" and redefine his quest for sublime moments. Wordsworth invoked the god of sublime poetry, Urania, to help articulate his deepest fears and ecstasies and accomplished this (like Hill) through negative statements.

> Not Chaos, not
> The darkest pit of lowest Erebus,
> Nor aught of blinder vacancy, scooped out
> By help of dreams—can breed such fear and awe
> As fall upon us often when we look
> Into our Minds, into the Mind of Man—
> My haunt, and the main region of my song.

For Hill, however, visionary paradise is a "fiction of what never was." His dove, like Wordsworth's dream, attempts to "scoop out" a portion of the paradisal Ararat above the Atlantic's flood but comes back unrequited.

For the Unfallen

While borrowing diction from Wordsworth, Hill rejects the notion of happily wedded antinomies, whether of man and woman or mind and world. His marriages are battles as much as concords, bonds of hate as much as love. The gods of romantic love are dead, he affirms, and for an elegiac model, he goes to Allen Tate's "Seasons of the Soul":

> All the sea-gods are dead.
> You, Venus, come home
> To your salt maidenhead,
> The tossed anonymous sea
> Under shuddering foam-
> Shade for lovers, where
> A shark swift as your dove
> Shall pace our company
> All night to nudge and tear
> The livid wound of love.

But what is the result of abandoning romantic notions of Elysian fields and majestic sea gods? An obsession with war? In Section IV, Hill transforms Henry Newbolt's "Drake's Drum," a poem about Sir Francis Drake which once inspired young men to fight in World War I, into a terse elegy that also imitates "News for the Delphic Oracle." Both Newbolt and Yeats presuppose afterworlds for the dead, but Hill renounces these as fictions in order to stress the horror of war. For Newbolt, heroes such as Drake, hammocked in his sea grave, may be resurrected at will:

> Call him on the deep sea, call him up the Sound,
>   Call him when ye sail to meet the foe;
> Where the old trade's plyin' an' the old flag flyin'
>   They shall find him ware an' wakin', as they found
>   him long ago!

For Yeats, the dead proceed to the "Isles of the Blest" on the backs of dolphins. For Hill, they simply dissolve in the sea:

> Those varied dead! The undiscerning sea
> Shelves and dissolves their flesh as it burns spray
>
> Who do not shriek like gulls nor dolphins ride
> Crouched under spume to England's erect side
>
> Though there a soaked sleeve lolls or shoe patrols
> Tide-padded thick shallows, squats in choked pools
>
> Neither our designed wreaths nor used words
> Sink to their melted ears and melted hearts.

Once again Hill affirms the separateness of language and reality (his words fail to redeem the dead) and does so in a terse lament.

Like many forms of meditational exercise, "Metamorphoses" is a search for an object commensurate with the poet's desire for both ascetic love and sexual requital. Its immediate goal is reunion with an estranged beloved, but when Hill's lovers meet they do so only to plot strategies of evasion. The woman chooses to confront all storms, because bad weather promises chastening and toughening. The other contemplates castration as a possible antidote to love's trials. Following Venus, who originated from Uranus's castrated phallus, Hill's lover enters the sea, with phallus "hammocked" in salty underclothes, rather ludicrously preparing himself for amorous transformation.

But Hill's poem forecasts torments of sexual abstinence and desire (bleaching and burning), rather than their alleviation. Like Yeats's sacrificial man in "Vacillation," Hill's persona continues to run a course between extremities, but without consolation. Rather than justify renunciation, the poem embraces the purgatorial quest for love, imitating in its tortuous syntax the agony of sacred and secular passion:

> Doubtless he saw some path clear, having found
> His love now fenced him off from the one ground
> Where, as he owned, no temperate squalls could move
> Either from the profession of their love.

> Storm-bound, now she'd outweather him, though he,
> Between sun-clouded marshworld and strewn sea
> Pitched to extremities, in the rock's vein
> Gripped for the winds to roughen and tide stain.
>
> But when he tore his flesh-root and was gone,
> Leaving no track, no blood gritting the stone,
> Drawn freely to the darkness he had fought
> Driven by sulphurous blood and a clenched heart,
>
> Grant the detached, pierced spirit could plunge, soar,
> Seeking that love flesh dared not answer for,
> Nor suffers now, hammocked in salt tagged cloth
> That to be bleached or burned the sea casts out.

The path of "Metamorphoses," spiraling through love and hate, is anything but "doubtless." But by articulating his sulphurous hell, this errant lover seems able to contain his "intemperate squalls" of emotions, if only behind a fence of words. The diction recalls Hart Crane, another poet "drawn" and "driven" by fractious moods. In the end, the poem is oddly affirmative, although its ending is ambiguous. The narrator's otherworldly love, the cause of his troubles, has abated. Through a sea change (which amounts to a baptism in the gutter), the lover will either return enriched by experience or purified of experience altogether.

Begun in 1956, the year "Metamorphoses" was completed, "Of Commerce and Society," resembles the earlier poem in its technique of arranging seemingly disparate fragments, but now, instead of depicting metamorphoses in individuals, Hill widens his scope to incorporate the flux of history and western culture. "The historian's business," Henry Adams wrote in his *Education*, a book Hill read before writing his poem, is "to follow the track of the energy; to find where it came from and where it went to; its complex source and shifting channels; its values, equivalents, conversions."[24] Although Hill's view of history is not as rigid and deterministic as Adams's, he traces its complex track as well. Events from religion, politics, economics, science, agriculture, literature, and mythology intersect. The eclectic modernist poem is Hill's model, and, to a certain extent, he reflects on the literature and politics of the modernists. Like the authors of *The Waste Land*, *The Cantos*, and *Ulysses*, Hill attempts to X-ray a culture broken by the First World War.

As before, Hill owes much to Allen Tate's "More Sonnets at Christmas" and also to his "Ode to our Young Pro-Consuls of the Air," which sketches the history of World War I and modernism as well, asserting that the rise of totalitarianism which precipitated the Second World War was caused by the failure to reach a just conclusion of the earlier war. In his opening fable "The Apostles: Versailles, 1919," Hill uses the story of the Annunciation to highlight the collapse of civilized virtues at the end of the Great War. Without referring to the actual treaty debated by Lloyd George, Orlando, Clemenceau, and Wilson, he suggests that it was the mistake that opened the gates for Hitler. At Hill's Versailles, the politicians are apostles of the wrong word. They betray Christ's word like Judas. As in many other poems, Hill exposes the invidious connection between the abuse of language and political destruction. Once he said to a reporter of *The Illustrated London News*: "Language *contains* everything you want—history, sociology, economics: it is a kind of drama of human destiny. One thinks how it has been used and exploited in the past, politically and theologically. Its forthrightness and treachery are a drama of the honesty of man himself. Language reveals life."[25] The annunciation at Versailles formulated the destiny of twentieth-century Europe. It revealed greed, arrogance, and vengeance rather than Christian humility and forgiveness. Hill likes to begin poetic sequences with annunciations which mime and parody the original Annunciation, and here he wittily imagines its modern equivalent as the hot, smoky linguistic breath (the *aer* or *spiritus*) of the "Big Four" thickening in the halls of Versailles to the consistency of flesh, mud, or sour milk. In deflated, almost simplistic sentences, he imitates the deflation of values and the concomitant deflation of Germany that set the country, and the rest of Europe, on the track towards holocaust.

> They sat. They stood about.
> They were estranged. The air,
> As water curdles from clear,
> Fleshed the silence. They sat.
>
> They were appalled. The bells
> In hollowed Europe spilt
> To the gods of coin and salt.
> The sea creaked with worked vessels.

Because of this debased annunciation, in which words and emotions curdled into a stagnant mass, Europe was turned from a potentially hallowed land to a wasteland of hollow men. The church, having broken up like a pitcher of milk, "spilt religion" into a shallow romanticism. T. E. Hulme denounced this "spilt religion" for its devotion to utilitarian and capitalistic ideals ("the gods of coin and salt"—the gods of taxes) and its ignorance of traditional values. In using language, Hulme stated, "the great aim is accurate, precise and definite description."[26] Hill points out that such clarity has been muddled by the politicians. Like Eliot, Hill composes an elegy for "the mind of Europe," whose established culture after the Great War is a heap of broken images.

Civilization, Hill has stated, is a struggle to control anarchical energies, and in the second section, "The Lowlands of Holland," he makes the Netherlands' struggle to keep the sea controlled behind dikes a synecdoche for Europe's effort to remain civilized. He sets the period *entre deux guerres* beside the interminable scourings and scarrings of European history. As in Robert Lowell's "Children of Light," where Holland serves as a mythical Eden from which historical crimes exfoliate, Hill's poem turns the Eden myth into a fable of historical falls and redemptions. A latter-day Gerontion, Hill's narrator regards Europe as a labyrinth and imitates some of its puzzling directions and indirections in a syntactical maze:

> Europe, the much-scarred, much-scoured terrain,
> Its attested liberties, home-produce,
> Labelled and looking up, invites use,
> Stuffed with artistry and substantial gain:
>
> Shrunken, magnified—(nest, holocaust)—
> Not half innocent and not half undone;
> Profiting from custom: its replete strewn
> Cities such ample monuments to lost
>
> Nations and generations: its cultural
> Or trade skeletons such hand-picked bone:
> Flaws in the best, revised science marks down:
> Witness many devices; the few natural
>
> Corruptions, graftings; witness classic falls;
> (The dead subtracted; the greatest resigned;)
> Witness earth fertilised, decently drained,
> The sea decent again behind walls.

If spirit and word dominated the first section, the body and its wounds dominate the second. The perverse annunciation creates a harrowing incarnation, which leads to a crucifixion and holocaust in which Christ's physical body represents the scoured terrain of Europe, and His Gospels and communion wafers represent the "artistry" which invites the historical sensibility to remember it. Joyce once imagined history's cycle of creations and cataclysms as the nightmarish dream ("produce") of a gigantic body (Earwicker's). Hill similarly thinks of Europe as a mythical body that burns up (like the Phoenix) only to renew itself from its nest of ashes.

Although Holland remained neutral or "innocent" during the world wars, Hill's poem implies the opposite. Passive bystanding and spiritless drifting (as with the apostles at Versailles or "the lost generation" a decade later) Hill condemns. Not to oppose the politicians when they shrink nations or blow them up ("shrunken, magnified") is to partly endorse them. This is Hill's history lesson, communicated to the survivors for their "substantial gain." Civilization's body, after the wars, is a skeleton. Its trade routes, which supported and transported culture for centuries, are bones "hand-picked" by vultures and archaeologists. Twentieth-century scientists have "marked-down" the value of supportive myths (such as Adam and Eve eating the flawed, "hand-picked" apple) and devalued the humanities, which study myths, although myths are all the more necessary in periods of chaos.

Europe's fall, Hill hopes, will include a fall into a greater understanding of ways to repair, graft, or reclaim its ruins. For Hill, making is the art of remaking, a damming up of potential power ("The sea decent again behind walls"), and a sequestering of criminal passions behind prison walls. The Netherlands farmer, who reclaims his land from the sea and cultivates it, is Hill's figure for the modern artist and culture hero, who brings civilization (as well as agriculture) to the wasteland. After the Holocaust reduces Europe to a "nether-land" or hell, he "grafts" new limbs on old stalks and once again makes culture flourish.

Donald Davie argues that "to dislocate syntax," as Hill does in "The Lowlands of Holland," "is to threaten the rule of law in the civilized community,"[27] but Hill's syntax does not subvert communal laws so much as mime their subversion. As a historian of modernism and the breakup of Europe, Hill elegizes the romantics in his third section, since they, Davie also contends, honored civilized laws by retaining "urbane" syntax. In "The Death of Shelley," Hill does not bury Shelley, as Pound and Eliot tried to do, so much as bear witness to the idealism which Shelley, with varying degrees of success, attempted to uphold. As in Yeats's later poetry, Hill dramatizes the romantic hero descending into slime, barbarism, and desolation for renewal.

Remembering the shattered relics of past refinements (the utopian ideals of the ninteenth century), Hill correlates Shelley's drowning off Italy with civilization's death at the beginning of the twentieth century. He begins with an abrupt portrait of culture reduced to its primordial elements:

> Slime; the residues of refined tears;
> And, salt-bristled, blown on a drying sea,
> The sunned and risen faces.

Reincarnated into the modern era, Shelley appears as a new Perseus, not as in the heroic myth, where he quests after his ideal lover, Andromeda, but as a wasteland figure, impotent, purposeless, jaded, who mirrors a shore of ruins:

>   There's Andromeda
> Depicted in relief, after the fashion.
>
> 'His guarded eyes under his shielded brow'
> Through poisonous baked sea-things Perseus
> Goes—clogged sword, clear, aimless mirror—
> With nothing to strike at or blind
>   in the frothed shallows.

Perseus's Medusas are romantic images (like the angels in Allen Tate's "Ode") whose poisonous enchantments threaten to turn him to stone. Ideals of love and culture ebb and flow through Hill's poem, as they do through history, giving way to bestiality and refinement by turn.

> Rivers bring down. The sea
> Brings away;
> Voids, sucks back, its pearls and auguries.
> Eagles or vultures churn the fresh-made skies.
>
> Over the statues, unchanging features
> Of commerce and quaint love, soot lies.
> Earth steams. The bull and the great mute swan
> Strain into life with their notorious cries.

For the Unfallen

Established forms or "unchanging features" of commerce, love, and communication bring people together. When the old forms break up, an influx of bestial anarchy, for which the twentieth century is notorious, shakes the dust off the statues. Whether this heralds renaissance or decadence Hill, for the moment, leaves unanswered. Following Yeats, he imagines the avatars of Zeus (bull and swan) as both creative and destructive. But if the sexual crimes committed against Leda and Europa propel the world towards war, it is not an ancient, legendary war but the Holocaust of World War II. In his fourth section, which is about the Holocaust, Hill speaks of communal guilt and how the mind deals with it, how it projects guilt into symbolic figures, represses, and sublimates it. He begins with an elegiac recognition of the dead which entertains, with Shelley, the notion that poets should be the world's unacknowledged legislators, the memories and consciences of the statesmen. Visionary poet and apocalyptic politician mingle as Hill declares:

> Statesmen have known visions. And, not alone,
> Artistic men prod dead men from their stone:
> Some of us have heard the dead speak:
> The dead are my obsession this week
>
> But may be lifted away. In summer
> Thunder may strike, or, as a tremor
> Of remote adjustment, pass on the far side
> From us: however deified and defied
>
> By those it does strike. Many have died. Auschwitz,
> Its furnace chambers and lime pits
> Half-erased, is half-dead; a fable
> Unbelievable in fatted marble.

If symbols which recollect historical atrocities have accumulated fat, Hill encourages the artist to scrape the fat off as well as to open the graves and let the dead speak with the pentecostal vigor of Christ. His job is to make history, no matter how horrible, live.

The crux of the poem, and of so many of Hill's poems that acknowledge atrocities, arises from the issue of sacrifice. Is burning a symbolic body on an altar the same as purifying a poem or purging fatty, desensitized nerves? Is the martyr-poet's painful act of witnessing the same as a holocaust? Hill juxtaposes the "whole burning" of holocaust with the therapeutic cleansing of art, the sacrificial purification of language with the barbaric purification of the tribe, and points to the differences of their means and ends.

Commentators on the Holocaust, among them Adorno and George Steiner, have suggested that its unbelievable horrors transcend linguistic description. "No poetry after Auschwitz"[28] was Adorno's famous cry. Steiner wondered if silent witnessing was best. Hill's poetry, in contrast, stands for an articulate "demonstration" (whose Latin root means both a showing and a warning) so that the brutal facts and the myths which engendered them are engraved deep in public memory. The question of propriety, of how many acts of witnessing the Holocaust needs, and when and where they should be made, appears again in this poem:

> There is, at times, some need to demonstrate
> Jehovah's touchy methods, that create
> The connoisseur of blood, the smitten man.
> At times it seems not common to explain.

That statesmen and artists often serve similar gods of destruction makes Hill's attitude of cautious restraint, indicated by the poem's use of verbs like "may" and "seems," adverbial qualifiers such as "at times" and "some," and ambiguous diction, seem admirable and correct.

"Common explanation," as Davie quotes Hulme as saying, means "ex-planing" the mind's contents according to traditional rules of syntax. In the section on Auschwitz, Hill keeps his syntax relatively straightforward. In the fifth section, "Ode on the Loss of the 'Titanic'," however, he turns back to the expressive syntax used in "The Lowlands of Holland," where syntactical dislocations mirrored cultural dislocations in history. The sinking of the *Titanic* in 1912 fits into the poet's scheme not simply because it involves a misuse of language, but because it provides an adequate symbol for the relations between Europe and America during the modernist era. The *Titanic* is Hill's symbolic boat that ferries the political and poetic spirit across the Atlantic. He reveals some of its significance in his essay on Allen Tate when he discusses a century in which

reality becomes the incestuous possession of a dedicated few; while millions are deployed for war or profit by the crassest of political jargonings. Was not the "Titanic" disaster partly the result of rhetoric? A sinkable ship was called "Unsinkable"; and the realists and practical men, who are always the blindest dreamers of this world, were swamped by a slogan. And the innocent, as always, died too. No poet would dream of booking a passage on an unsinkable ship![29]

Hill's poem records not the arduous redemption of "fatted marble" by poets but the holocaust of both language and bodies by political demagogues. Babel is toppled and the politicians' babbling tongues are let loose over the world. Hill takes arms against a sea of rhetoric in a magnificent rhetorical display of his own:

> Thriving against façades the ignorant sea
> Souses our public baths, statues, waste ground:
> Archaic earth-shaker, fresh enemy:
> ('The tables of exchange being overturned');
>
> Drowns Babel in upheaval and display;
> Unswerving, as were the admired multitudes
> Silenced from time to time under its sway.
> By all means let us appease the terse gods.

Poseidon, the earth shaker, Christ, the cleanser of temples, and Jehovah, the destroyer of linguistic towers, coalesce in Hill's portrait of those who, rather than recultivating the modernist's "waste ground" and restoring to it community and commerce, make it even more uninhabitable by undermining what is most essential—its language.

In "Of Commerce and Society," the sea of turbid words and drowned bodies is Conrad's "destructive element," into which Hill's poet, like Marlow, must dive. Hill also associates the sea with Hardy's "Immanent Will," as depicted in "Lines on the Loss of the Titanic." Hardy's sea "stirs and urges everything" towards crisis, just as Hill's "inertia of language . . . is also the coercive force of language" (*LL*, p. 2). Hill ends his sequence, however, with a glance at another artist—Henry James. In "The Martyrdom of Saint Sebastian, Homage to Henry James," he describes, fancifully and sarcastically, the aquatic poet-martyr prepared for a plunge into linguistic chaos.

More emphatically than in any other section, Hill now associates writing with crime but distinguishes between "cold-blooded" crimes and linguistic mistakes which art sacrificially redeems. Both James and Hill, as the poem's epigraph from Corinthians indicates, desire to confront the dilemma of social responsibility and artistic commitment "face to face," rather than to peer at it through a glass darkly. But James, as E. M. Forster pointed out ("so enormous is the sacrifice that many readers cannot get interested in James. . . . They cannot grant his premise, which is that most of human life has to disappear before he can do his novel")[30] is more like Sebastian, punctured with arrows on his cross above the linguistic sea rather than crucified (as Hill seems to be) in the sea itself. The Jamesian artist, in Hill's playful portrait, is vulnerable to great sufferings, but he is so sensitive that he cannot fend off even the simplest colds:

> Naked, as if for swimming, the martyr
> Catches his death in a little flutter
> Of plain arrows. A grotesque situation,
> But priceless, and harmless to the nation.

For the Unfallen

Bearing witness to life's complexity through fastidiously crafted artifice, as James did, requires great pains. The artist pays a price which receives inadequate remuneration in commercial society. Ostracized by society, he is harmless to it. Hill imagines him sweating and weeping salt tears, which he then shapes (as in "Lachrimae") into pure crystals. Hill asks us to consider what must seem a futile, destructive exercise:

> Consider such pains 'crystalline': then fine art
> Persists where most crystals accumulate.
> History can be scraped clean of its old price.
> Engrossed in the cold blood of sacrifice,
>
> The provident and self-healing gods
> Destroy only to save.

These are the artist-gods, whose artifacts redress the wounds of society and history. They are "terse gods" compared to the bombastic and verbose politicians. They destroy to save.

Hill finishes his sequence with a humorous contribution to the "international theme," so central to the poem and to the fiction of James. America and Europe, as Hill portrays them, are two mythical giants, who, after all their mistakes, still blunder towards ill-defined goals. America, fat on material goods, marches toward a dubious star of prosperity (Lucifer) while Europe, materially depleted after two world wars, dreams of culture like a muddled, overly-refined somnambulist:

>   Well-stocked with foods,
> Enlarged and deep-oiled, America
> Detects music, apprehends the day-star
>
> Where, sensitive and half-under a cloud,
> Europe muddles her dreaming, is loud
> And critical beneath the varied domes
> Resonant with tribute and with commerce.

If America is a ponderous refrigerator or deep oil field, Europe is a sensitive, impractical intellectual trying to carry on business as best he can.

Both "Metamorphoses" and "Of Commerce and Society" envision well-governed forms of culture and lament their continual collapse. They arrange sequences of intense, fragmentary glimpses of civilization's battle to contain immense passion and barbarism's opposing battle to shatter those containments. Like Pound and the modernists, Hill exploits the "ideogrammic method" to string together luminous details and epiphanies. But while his poems may resemble short encyclopedias with many brief chapters, his intense fears and desires give them a lyrical complexion. In a century noted for unprecedented violence and politically maladroit poets, Hill's artistic self-consciousness, political wariness, and uncompromising demand for perfection are welcome antidotes.

3 / POWER AND AUTHORITY

King Log

Continuities

That Hill should be ignored in a decade when many poets tried their hand at metaphysical poetry is strange. A. Alvarez, one of the few critics to take notice of *For the Unfallen*, called it "an extraordinarily fine achievement" and "one of the three or four important first books of poetry . . . in the fifties," but he also voiced a complaint that would dog Hill with every new book: "Where Mr. Hill's poems falter it is because they are overconcentrated; he works by a logic so compressed as to be at times squashed out of all recognition."[1] While John Wain and the Movement praised Empson for his "miraculous blend of the colloquial immediacy of Donne and the immense weight of Hopkins,"[2] they could not discover similar qualities in Hill. For his part, Hill did not capitulate; instead, like Swift, a writer he was studying at the time, he attacked his attackers. The strained relationship between Hill and his audience persisted through *King Log*, informing his poems with high tension and explosive wit.

Early on, in poems like "Picture of a Nativity" and "Canticle for Good Friday," Hill ridiculed his audience for its indolence and incompetence. He taunted the serpents and Thomases to become better readers. In the last poem in *For the Unfallen*, "To the (Supposed) Patron," his arrows are as sharply barbed as ever. Here he draws a portrait of the reader of unexceptional talents, who is likely to pay for (and therefore patronize) his work but to reject it for its convolutions. Unlike Baudelaire, who forced his reader into an ambiguous identification with him ("*Hypocrite lecteur,—mon semblable,—mon frère!*"), Hill notes the separation between poet and reader. He mocks the reader in a symbolic language destined to baffle even the most adept interpreters. To seal his contempt, he dedicates his book to "the unfallen," who have not yet fallen into knowledge and may never do so. "To the (Supposed) Patron" identifies unfallenness with ignorance and culpable innocence.

The reader, in Hill's fable "To the (Supposed) Patron," is a connoisseur of barbecues; art and poetics are merely pastimes he dabbles in. He prefers the soft, inner meat of poems (the barbecued sacrifices) rather than the exterior char and gristle:

> For his delight and his capacity
> To absorb, freshly, the inside-succulence
> Of untoughened sacrifice, his bronze agents
> Speculate among covertible stones
> And drink desert sand.

An intelligence bureau of athletic, well-tanned agents (literary critics) decodes the cryptic inner meanings for the patron. As Robert Lowell said, "Two poetries are now competing, a cooked and a raw. The cooked, marvelously expert, often seems laboriously concocted to be tasted and digested by a graduate seminar. The raw, huge blood-dripping gobbets of unseasoned experience are dished up for midnight listeners. There is a poetry that can only be studied, and a poetry that can only be declaimed, a poetry of pedantry, and a poetry of scandal."[3] Hill's poetry is both cooked and raw, and it requires "bronze agents," trained to speculate among Christian rocks and waste lands, to discover its inside succulence. Hill imagines his critics sweating over fiery charcoal (the convertible stones) and preparing poems so that patronizing readers, protected from the heats of imaginative creation, can relax and digest them in water-cooled rooms:

> That no mirage
> Irritate his mild gaze, the lewd noonday
> Is housed in cool places, and fountains
> Salt the sparse haze.

Incorrigibly insular, blissfully unillusioned and incapable of disillusionment, Hill's English reader is an upholder of "the gentility principle." His mild gaze and air-conditioned rooms protect him from the "lewd" holocausts, religious crises, literary revolts, and political upheavals which the poet is embroiled in.

Unlike Crashaw, who imagines an ideal lover in his poem "To his (Supposed) Mistresse," Hill depicts neither ideal lover nor ideal reader. His patron is a perpetual vacationer (a figure scorned by Hill). He is a prodigal son, a man who quests for amorous affairs like a botanist after ever rarer species; he is the negligent, unworried man of Matthew's parable of the lilies:

> Prodigal of loves and barbecues,
> Expert in the strangest faunas, at home
> He considers the lilies, the rewards.
> There is no substitute for a rich man.
> At his first entering a new province
> With new coin, music, the barest glancing
> Of steel or gold suffices. There are many
> Tremulous dreams secured under that head.

As if to mock Eliot's spiritual voyager in the *Four Quartets*, Hill portrays him in his everyday clothes: exchanging money for his holiday, listening to music on the radio as he enters new provinces, dazzled by materialistic splendors. "The realists and practical men . . . are always the blindest dreamers of this world,"[4] Hill stated the same year he wrote the poem. To this man he dedicates his book:

> For the unfallen—the firstborn, or wise
> Councillor—prepared vistas extend
> As far as harvest; and idyllic death
> Where fish at dawn ignite the powdery lake.

Under "prepared vistas," sentimental visions of happy ends ("idyllic harvests") and fresh beginnings, an inferno of sulphurous gunpowder, detonated by Leviathans (the fish), goes unnoticed. With less genteel manners than his patron, Hill rebukes everything he stands for.

Embedded in *For the Unfallen* is Lawrence Binyon's poem "For the Fallen, " an elegy for the dead of the Great War. Binyon writes:

> England mourns for her dead across the sea.
> Flesh of her flesh they were, spirit of her spirit . . .
>
> They shall grow not old, as we that are left grow old:
> Age shall not weary them, nor the years condemn.
> At the going down of the sun and in the morning
> We will remember them.

Hill's book is "for the unfallen" in the sense that it is a history lesson in fallenness for the innocent and ignorant. *King Log*, Hill's second book, is also for the unfallen. Here he alludes to the fable by Aesop in which frogs, tired of having no ruler to govern them, send a deputation to Zeus to request a king. Expecting to fool the frogs with a decoy, Zeus drops a log into their midst, but the frogs, frightened at first, soon grow contemptuous. They approach Zeus again and ask him for a more vigorous king. Zeus, now impatient and irritated by their presumption, sends a water snake to devour them. Aesop appends the moral: "This fable teaches us that we are better off with an indolent and harmless ruler than with a mischief-making tyrant."[5] By entitling his book *King Log* and his postscript "King Stork" (a figure in medieval versions of Aesop's fable who gobbles up frogs), Hill manages to pillory both parties—authoritarian authors as well as lethargic readers. If the poet is Zeus, then his audience is comprised of frogs. His artifice is the log, the historical record and fictitious being sent to them. Hill's postscript gives ample evidence of the treachery and indolence of kings. It condemns those, like Henry VI (his weakness allowed the Wars of the Roses to continue), who possess power but fail to use it effectively.

Besides the poet's buffoonery and Zeus-like attitude to his reader, there are graver connections between *For the Unfallen* and *King Log*. In the second book, the dominant themes are violence and suffering, whether political (war and persecution), religious (as in the martyr or zealot), artistic (as with the poet), or amorous (between lovers). The epigraph from Francis Bacon, "From moral virtue let us pass on to the matter of power and commandment," locates the book in historical problems of power, in which, as Yeats claimed, "the best lack all conviction, while the worst / Are full of passionate intensity." "How does one govern with force?" rather than "what is the most virtuous form of government?" is the book's central question.

In *King Log*, several poems aim for the syntactical and metaphorical density of poems like "The Lowlands of Holland" or "Elegiac Stanzas," but there is a new simplicity which draws on the energies of colloquial speech and vivid prose. "The Songbook of Sebastian Arrurruz," for example, mixes prose poems and verse and maintains a "simple, sensuous, and passionate" diction throughout. One of the "Three Baroque Meditations" traces Hill's development in miniature, from a style vulnerable to emotional convolution and rhetorical bloating to a purified austerity:

> Anguish bloated by the replete scream.
> Flesh of abnegation: the poem
> Moves grudgingly to its extreme form,
>
> Vulnerable, to the lamp's fierce head
> Of well-trimmed light.

Although *King Log* retains the knotted ambiguities, abrupt ellipses, and truculent sarcasm of the earlier volume, its poems in general have a new repose and clarity. Even "Funeral Music," with its disjointed narrative and compressed logic, is more finely contrived than earlier sequences such as "Metamorphoses" and "Of Commerce and Society." Hill, perhaps the harshest judge of his work, once said he found *King Log* his most satisfactory book. Its vehemence is matched at every point by its control.

The Poetry of *Poesis*

Hill's awareness of himself as a poet writing for an intransigent audience is related to his more general obsession with the poetic process itself. Hill began his career by writing, in "Genesis," a poem about becoming a poet. In his first book, the poet was the "dumb child-king" or virile combatant, strangling the monuments of tradition or casting them into fire to make them new. In *King Log*, however, there is a shift of emphasis from the rebellious neophyte to the toughened and often embittered elder. Rather than "Genesis" and "Picture of a Nativity," we now have "Old Poet with Distant Admirers" and "Four Poems Regarding the Endurance of Poets." In the first book, Hill's personae generally appeared in vehement postures of rebellion. In *King Log*, they are more sedentary. They dream of the imaginative life as a nightmare ordeal, sit at the poetry banquet and gaze at the exotic meats with ironic detachment, or lie in self-imposed or politically imposed exile. Although their attitudes may seem uncommonly bleak, they never submit entirely to despair. They remain wry, caustic, articulate.

Almost all the poems in *King Log* are, to some degree, concerned with poets and poetry, but with poetry in its most general application. Hill views the poet as a representative maker whose vocation gives him special authority to comment on "the nature and condition of those arts which are composed of words" (*LL*, p. 2). Hill writes a poetry that displays "the theory of poetry / As the life of poetry," and that affirms, as Stevens also remarked, that "the theory / Of poetry is the theory of life" ("An Ordinary Evening in New Haven"). In an essay, Hill extolled Stevens and partly agreed with his "magnificent agnostic faith whose summation is in the 'Adagia'. . . . 'After one has abandoned a belief in god [sic], poetry is that essence which takes its place as life's redemption' " (*LL*, p. 16). With the symbolists in Arthur Symons's portrayal, Hill considers "the making of poetry as a sacred task" (*LL*, p. 17) in a secular world of imperfection.

Hill is too aware of language's duplicity, slipperiness, and opacity to assent to the symbolist creed of poetic perfection. With Eliot he would agree that

> Words strain,
> Crack and sometimes break, under the burden,
> Under the tension, slip, slide, perish,
> Decay with imprecision, will not stay in place,
> Will not stay still.
> ("Burnt Norton")

Hill explains in an essay that "the arts which use language are the most impure of arts, though I do not deny that those who speak of 'pure poetry' are attempting, however inadequately, to record the impact of a real effect. The poet will occasionally, in the act of writing a poem, experience a sense of pure fulfilment which might too easily and too subjectively be misconstrued as the attainment of objective perfection." These rare moments culminate in what Hill calls an "act of at-one-ment, a setting at one, a bringing into concord, a reconciling, a uniting in harmony" (*LL*, p. 2) in which the poet experiences a transient feeling of exhaustion and beatitude. But what does the poem actually "at-one" with? Hill suggests that whatever menaces the poet's search for perfection, whether political harassment or the recalcitrance of language itself, is his most compelling subject.

In the poem "The Imaginative Life," Hill puts his poetic theories into dramatic form. The title is reminiscent of Stevens, but the rhetoric has more in common with Yeats's "Magi" and "The Second Coming." As in the earlier poem "Picture of a Nativity," Hill associates the magi with the "artistic men" and with all who make or worship images. His imaginative magi are night-dreamers and magicians who transform everyday fears and desires into spectacular images. The magi are neither the wise men of the Bible, however, nor the "pale, unsatisfied ones" of Yeats's poem but "part-barbarians" who quest for sublime visions with murderous ferocity. They renounce the "wisdom" of the everyday intelligence and live dangerously at extremities. Like Rimbaud, who wanted to be part saint and part criminal, Hill's magi sacrifice health and sanity in order to write great poems. Rimbaud averred:

> A Poet makes himself a visionary through a long, boundless, and systematized *disorganization of all the senses*. All forms of love, of suffering, of madness; he searches himself, he exhausts within himself all poisons, and preserves their quintessences. Unspeakable torment, where he will need the greatest faith, a superhuman strength, where he becomes among all men the great invalid, the great criminal, the great accursed—and the Supreme Scientist![6]

Of these lawless, quixotic visionaries Hill says:

> Evasive souls, of whom the wise lose track,
> Die in each night, who, with their day-tongues, sift
> The waking-taste of manna or of blood . . .

Like the souls of the dead in classical mythology, Hill's artists come to life by drinking blood. They are strangely living and dead, and they make poems as a normal person might make new cells from digested food. Their diet is sensual and spiritual (blood and manna). The poetic magi taste, select ("sift"), break down, and transform common day materials into nocturnal visions. Their night journeys, however, are ascetic, grueling, revelatory. Hill calls these poets

> The raw magi, part-barbarians,
> Entranced by demons and desert frost,
> By the irregular visions of a god,
>
> Suffragans of the true seraphs.

King Log

Suffragans are technically bishops who serve their archbishops by attending synods and delivering prayers for the souls of the dead. For Hill, the poet dreaming of seraphs and gods in his death-in-life exile is also a suffragan speaking to and for history's dead.

But Hill does not embrace these self-styled suffragans or the seraphs they serve with unequivocal assent. The dying-away from the world, the demonic repression of sexuality, the subliminal visions, all depend on a renunciation of nature which may be criminal. Hill does not share Rimbaud's unabashed reverence for criminals, no matter how visionary they may be. The entire poem may be read as a sardonic confession—and a splendidly formulated one—of the poet's hatred for natural limitations and desires which get in the way of supernatural desires but which he must abide by to remain sane.

> Lust
> Writhes, is dumb savage and in their way
> As a virulence natural to the earth.

Natural desires, to these militantly ascetic imaginations, are satanic serpents, insurrectionary savages, poisonous diseases. When lust is purged, Hill says derisively:

> Renewed glories batten on the poor bones:
> Gargantuan mercies whetted by a scent
> Of mortal sweat: as though the sleeping flesh
>
> Adored by Furies, stirred, yawned, were driven
> In mid-terror to purging and delight.
> As though the dead had *Finis* on their brows.

Hill exaggerates the blessings of the purgatorial journey in order to express disaffection with its means and ends. The "gargantuan" dispensations of glories depend on a brutal denial of self and society. The dead are never "finished" in Hill's war, as the demons are never completely purged. Furies pursue the high-strung poet day and night.

Compressed with allusions to religious myths and other poems, an earlier poem, "Annunciations," may serve as Hill's poetic testament. It has been regarded by some critics, with good reason, as the best summation of how and why Hill writes poems and, by Harold Bloom, as one of the best poems written in the last few decades. Bloom maintains that "in 'Annunciations,' Hill wrote what later tradition may judge to have been the central shorter poem of his own generation, a poem that is itself a despairing poetics, and a total vision both of natural existence, and of the necessary limitations of what we have learned to call imagination."[7] Although the poem describes the relationship between imagination and nature, as Bloom contends, it does so in terms of the word, the body, and the poet's quest for love. The word *is* the body in Hill's poem, an incarnation of odors, sounds, tastes, sights, and textures. It feeds on other bodies and feeds the readers. But Hill sees the word, half-jokingly, as a botanist with nets, scalpels, and specimen jars on a trip to the bog to gather samples that will be preserved in the poem. The bog could be society, language, or common nature. In this comical myth of *poesis*, the word is an agent, who walks through the world like Christ (the Word) to recreate it. It is no static counter for reality. Hill declares:

> The Word has been abroad, is back, with a tanned look
> From its subsistence in the stiffening- mire.
> Cleansing has become killing, the reward
> Touchable, overt, clean to the touch.
> Now at a distance from the steam of beasts,
> The loathly neckings and fat shook spawn
> (Each specimen-jar fed with delicate spawn)
> The searchers with the curers sit at meat
> And are satisfied.

The Word, Hill satirically implies, is a tourist tanned from his holiday abroad. But the Word may also be tanned from the acids and stains of the mire. Is the journey a flight from or a descent into the world of ordinary passions? In 1959, the year Hill commenced writing this poem, he traveled to America to teach at the University of Michigan, but the mire is not so much an American university as all history, into which living things fall, die, and get preserved. Words, for Hill, are fossils which need to be periodically exhumed and cleansed, and he goes to the bog, although it nearly kills him, to do his digging.

If "the reward" or finished poem is the Christ Word, miraculously resurrected, then the poet is doubting Thomas judging the sacrifice, which contains, like the "specimen-jar," the poet's preserved passions and wounds. Hill has said of Yeats that "it is as though the very recalcitrance of language—and we know that Yeats found the process of composition arduous—stood for the primary objective world in one of its forms of cruelty and indifference."[8] "Annunciations" specifically dredges from the recalcitrant world the two words *sacrifice* and *love*. To the anthologist Kenneth Allot, Hill explained:

> I suppose the impulse behind the work is an attempt to realize the jarring double-takes in words of common usage: as "sacrifice" (I) or "Love" (II)—words which, like the word "State," are assumed to have an autonomous meaning or value irrespective of context, and to which we are expected to nod assent. If we do assent, we are "received"; if we question the justice of the blanket-term, we have made the equivalent of a rude noise in polite company.[9]

Running through "Annunciations" like a spine is the story of Christ's incarnation, wordly mission, sacrificial death, descent into hell, and dispensation of grace upon resurrection. Hill alludes to Gabriel's Annunciation, in which the angel announces that the spiritual Word will be made flesh. The Church's feast on March 25, commemorating the Annunciation, is matched, in Hill's poem, by a poetry feast and raucous festival, at which the poet disseminates his spirited words among the attendants. At the festival are scholars, critics, readers, writers, and all those, for better or worse, involved with "the nature and condition of those arts which are composed of words." In a mock communion, they consume the poet's word rather than the angel's Word:

> Such precious things put down
> And the flesh eased through turbulence the soul
> Purples itself; each eye squats full and mild
> While all who attend to fiddle or to harp
> For betterment, flavour their decent mouths
> With gobbets of the sweetest sacrifice.

Once passed through digestive turbulence, the poet's sacrifice ennobles ("purples") the soul of the communicant.

The ludicrous picture of the poet feeding jars of linguistic spawn to avid admirers at a literary festival is partly "an attack upon everyone who has to do with poetry,"[10] as Harold Bloom claimed, but partly also a lampoon to deflate romantic and symbolist mystiques which surround poetry. Behind the far-fetched metaphors and sardonic mask, Hill is both fascinated and haunted by the spawn and beasts contained by the poem. In the prose gloss published in Allot's *Penguin Book of Contemporary Verse*, he goes to great length to explain his poem and the poetics expressed in it:

I should take lines 6 and 7 as the key antithesis around which the section moves: "fat shook spawn" v. "delicate spawn." Line 6 stands for pain, lust, in the blubbery world; line 7 for pain, lust, by the time it is distilled by the connoisseurs. The connoisseur is as likely to be the poet as the critic. The "setting" of this section is a banquet where the men who have been hunting the beasts (the searchers) are in a mood of mutual adulation with the chemists and distillers and picklers and putters-right (the curers). And they listen to violin and harp, because the function of art is to instruct by delight ("for betterment" = "for moral improvement"). At the same time, they fiddle and harp, in the vulgar sense of the term, they pull strings to get on (they try to "better themselves"). Still a long way from here the beasts go on copulating, steamily, breeding more art-fodder; but this can be put behind us (as it is in the imagery) because Art is "decent": it "reconciles the irreconcilable"; it serves to pay lip-service to heritage (hence the persistent sense of being at a banquet). It will not soil the decent mouth.

The Word (line 1) is the impulse that makes and comprehends. Poetry *before* the poetry-banquet. The Word is an Explorer (cf. *Four Quartets, passim*). By using an emotive cliché like "The Word" I try to believe in an idea that I want to believe in: that poetry makes its world from the known world; that it has a transcendence; that it is something other than the conspicuous consumption (the banquet) that it seems to be.

What I say *in* the section is, I think, that I don't believe in the Word. The fact that I make the poem at all means that I still believe in words.[11]

Although Hill's poetics are complex, they are governed by simple laws. The poet devours his materials and transforms them into art; the audience devours the artifacts and creates more art-fodder by turning them into clichés; the poet returns to the mire or dump (like Stevens in "The Man on the Dump") to gather new materials for his poems. "The words of a dead man," Auden said in his elegy for Yeats (and the words of a living man, Hill might add) "are modified in the guts of the living."

Hill has written with dissembling candor that "however much and however rightly we protest against the vanity of supposing it [the poem] to be merely the 'spontaneous overflow of powerful feelings', poetic utterance is nonetheless an utterance of the self, the self demanding to be loved, demanding love in the form of recognition and 'absolution' " (*LL*, p. 17). With this in mind, it is not surprising that Hill completes his pair of sonnets in "Annunciations" with a love poem. The poem attempts to restore to the cliché, "love," its Christian significance as *caritas*, which for Hill implies self-sacrifice, commitment to community, and consolation of the damned. The poem begins with an abrupt salutation and command, and then proceeds to document love's trials:

> O Love, subject of the mere diurnal grind,
> Forever being pledged to be redeemed,
> Expose yourself for charity . . .

To find love above "the mere diurnal grind," Hill, like Dante, undertakes a purgatorial ascent as demanding as Christ's. He dies away from the flesh and admonishes his disciples in a facetious outburst.

> be assured
> The body is put husk and excrement.[12]
> Enter these deaths according to the law,
> O visited women, possessed sons!

Hill entertains complete spirituality, however, only to expose it for what it is, the psychological equivalent of a military battlefield or butcher shop where the body is not so much chastened as murdered:

> Foreign lusts
> Infringe our restraints; the changeable
> Soldiery have their goings-out and comings-in
> Dying in abundance. Choicest beasts
> Suffuse the gutters with their colourful blood.

In this spiritual warfare, the spirit dies when the body dies. If the god and goal of both the "in-coming" meditational exercise and the "out-going" military exercise is *caritas*, both fail to achieve their desired end. Hill surveys the wreckage in the wake of spiritual and amorous pursuits:

> Our God scatters corruption. Priests, martyrs,
> Parade to this imperious theme: 'O Love,
> You know what pains succeed; be vigilant; strive
> To recognize the damned among your friends.'

Like Lowell, who imagines God as a "snow-monster" that "wipes the coke-fumes from his eyes / And scatters his corruption" in his early poem "Winter in Dunbarton," Hill views God and His attendants as "scattering" damnation by defeating it, but also as "scattering" or littering the world with the dead, wounded, and damned. What pains "succeed" or win in the struggle for love?

What pains "succeed" or come after the battle and never end? Is salvation, in the form of requited love, ever permanently attained? Hill says in his gloss:

The "germ," I think, is the key phrase in line 11. "Our God scatters corruption" = "Our God puts corruption to flight" or "Our God disseminates corruption." I may have been thinking of Mr. Dulles's idea of God as Head of Strategic Air Command.
  Lines 1 and 12. Two appearances of Love in the World: Line 1— as habit (the vulgarism "grind" is intentional); line 12, Love as militant conformity (the whole army of martyrs is suggested). Any idea of Love, simply as Love, fails to appear. It struggles to be heard in the last two lines but is twisted by a pun.
  O Love, *acknowledge* (admit, confess, recognize as valid) the claims of those in need (your friends) difficult though this may be (strive) and unsavoury as they may be (damned). This is a prayer for contact. OR: Love, look to yourself, you know the drill, among your friends some are non-elect; keep a sharp look-out for these (and, I hope to imply, when you do find them, look quickly the other way). But I want the poem to have this dubious end; because I feel dubious; and the whole business is dubious.[13]

"Annunciations" berates religious symbols and rituals, which both sanctify life and hideously stifle it. Rather than a felicitous revelation and incarnation, Hill's "annunciation" forecasts a series of debilitating crucifixions and ambiguous purgatories. Hill may pursue beatific *caritas*, the way Dante pursued Beatrice, but, unlike Dante, he finds nothing but a reflection of his "perplexed persistence" at the end of his quest. Damnation is below and redemption agonizingly above. His poem strives towards love, *in imitatione Christi*, and succeeds brilliantly in articulating the struggle but does not culminate in amorous requital.
  For Hill, there is little relaxing on middle ground, only a perpetual vacillation between extremities. If the modern poet, as Wallace Stevens contended in "Of Modern Poetry," writes "the poem of the mind in the act of finding / What will suffice" and aims at "finding a satisfaction," Hill would argue that writing

about the act of searching is his only satisfaction. In "An Order of Service" (1966), written several years after "The Imaginative Life" and "Annunciations," Hill again reflects on the poet's vocation, his sacrifice and "service" and wonders whether it has any compensatory value. If poets form an "order," like a religious community of monks who have "orders" to serve, what do they serve? Their own destruction? Their private visions? Nothing at all? Hill wittily transmogrifies the poetic servants into visionary surveyors and then mocks them. The poetic surveyors, unlike their practical counterparts, who with theodolites, range poles, measuring tapes, and stadia rods measure the boundaries of property, are vacant snowmen who flaunt a mystical indifference to all but god and self. "An Order of Service" is a ruthlessly self-conscious portrait of the artist with a "mind of winter" whose inner weather fluctuates, like the "sacred river" in Coleridge's "Kubla Khan," between mania and despair. Hill says:

> He was the surveyor of his own ice-world,
> Meticulous at the chosen extreme,
> Though what he surveyed may have been nothing.

Like Steven's "Snow Man" and Frost's "Old Man" in his winter night, Hill's inward gazer has withdrawn so far from normal human community that his mind is virtually dead. Unlike Stevens and Frost, who do not overtly judge "the mind of winter" and, indeed, seem partially enchanted by it, Hill appraises and judges, just as an English "surveyor" would appraise the value of a house. In the second stanza Hill's tone turns hortatory and sarcastic:

> Let a man sacrifice himself, concede
> His mortality and have done with it;
> There is no end to that sublime appeal.

Perhaps with this poem in mind, Harold Bloom said of Hill: "He is indeed a poet of the Sublime, a mode wholly archaic yet always available to us again, provided a survivor of the old line comes to us."[14] But Hill employs the word "sublime" only to ridicule it. His "sublime" is not the sublimation which allows for civilized contact but the sublime of the egoistical hermit and false mystic. He says:

> In such a light dismiss the unappealing
> Blank of his gaze, hopelessly vigilant,
> Dazzled by renunciation's glare.

The poet-mystic's sensual deprivation prepares him for dazzling visions and provides what Stevens calls "the stale grandeur of annihilation" ("Lebensweisheitspielerei"), for its bliss depends on mental blankness and self-obsession. To this sublimity, Hill does not show the normal romantic response. Its influx sends the manic depressive reeling.

If the poet's sacrifice is so pernicious to himself and his society, why does he continue to write? Hill has pondered over this and come to the following conclusion: "let us suggest that a man may continue to write and to publish in a vain and self-defeating effort to appease his own sense of empirical guilt. It is ludicrous, of course" (*LL*, p. 7). Hill's perplexity has drawn him to T. H. Green, the nineteenth-century Hegelian, whose dilemmas are similar to his own:

In the sacrificial nature of his perplexed persistence and in his vulnerability to the accusation which his servitude draws upon itself, Green achieves his own substantial freedom and power. . . . There are triumphs that entrap and defeats that liberate. Green is creative in his distress. To speak of his exemplary failure is to see him in the light of a noble phrase borrowed from Forsyth; it is to say that he "passed through negative stages to his positive rest" (*LL*, p. 120).

Often in Hill's poetry there is this same entropy—an enervation or winding down of the psyche through stages of failure to a point where the poet, after writing his poem, attains momentary peace.

Few poets criticize poetry as fiercely as Hill. One of the clearest examples of Hill's self-excoriation is "Three Baroque Meditations." The poem is baroque as many of Donne's poems are baroque, in its mingling of splendor and morbid gloom and in its hermetic concentration on form and the anarchic forces which dissipate form. The argument of the poem fastens on the familiar incompatibility of life and art. In pursuing perfection, the poet alienates himself from natural existence; in pursuing the natural life, he alienates himself from perfection. Seeking love, justice, and a reconciliation of opposites in his verse, he stirs up despair, antagonism, and indifference in other people. Hill begins by questioning poetry's power to put things right:

> Do words make up the majesty
> Of man, and his justice
> Between the stones and the void?

Is art the only place where utopias and panaceas exist? Inexorable demons menace Hill however much he tries to quell them:

> How they watch us, the demons
> Plugging their dumb wounds! When
> Exorcized they shrivel yet thrive.

A predatory world of sexuality and violence, governed by brutal laws of survival, surrounds both poet and poem:

> An owl plunges to its tryst
> With a field- mouse in the sharp night.
> My fire squeals and lies still.

The poetic imagination (the fire), however diminutive and vulnerable (it squeals like the mouse), resembles the predatory owl as much as its victim. Hill finds these antinomies embodied in Minerva, the goddess of both martial and poetic arts, whose bird is the "wise bird" or owl. Although Hill praises her, his praise is laced with hyperbole and irony:

> Minerva, receive this hard
> Praise: I speak well of Death;
> I confess to the priest in me;
>
> I am shadowed by the wise bird
> Of necessity, the lithe
> Paradigm Sleep-and-Kill.

The fact that living depends on killing shadows Hill like the owl itself. To accept the instincts, he avers, is a necessity. It is the only "wise" thing to do in a world of killers.

Ted Hughes, in *Hawk in the Rain* (pubished five years before Hill began his "Baroque Meditations"), uncaged a bestiary of ferocious animals and poetic monsters. Hill opens a similar cage but also locks it up. His poetry, as the second "Baroque Meditation" demonstrates, battles to restrain the grotesque and pathetic. While Hughes gravitates towards baroque rhetoric, which can dull and bloat its message, Hill yearns for sinewy articulation. When Hill approaches nature's rapacious animals and gothic landscapes, he dons the mask of a foreign evangelist entering a heathen country. Rather than merge with the lusty inhabitants (the foxes) or the indifferent masses (stones and the dead), he tries to inculcate a humanizing knowledge of sin and death. "Death is the mother of beauty," Stevens said in "Sunday Morning." Hill affirms that the consciousness of death is the "suave power" behind civilized minds:

> In darkness outside,
> Foxes and rain-sleeked stones and the dead—
>
> Aliens of such a theme—endure
> Until I could cry 'Death!' 'Death!' as though
> To exacerbate that suave power;
>
> But refrain.

The bestial world remains recalcitrant and the poet restrains his manic effort to rectify it. Underneath Hill's mask of tactful restraint, however, there is a landscape of barbarous Furies that will not be quelled. Hill ends his poem with an observance of his embittered perfectionism:

> I am circumspect,
> Lifting the spicy lid of my tact
> To sniff at the myrrh. It is perfect
>
> In its impalpable bitterness,
> Scent of a further country where worse
> Furies promenade and bask their claws.

Tactfully circumspect, Hill is still a Pandora's box of exotic spices and unsavory goblins. His Furies may carry themselves with ceremonial dignity, but beneath their disguises are sharp claws.

The last section of the poem, unlike the first two, is not so much about writing poems as about the suffering which overheated imaginations cause to loved ones. "The Dead Bride" is a soliloquy and reminiscence delivered by the poet's wife, which condemns him for manipulating her like a poem. Hill implies, with Oscar Wilde, that the poet can make his life into a work of art, but when he tries to make the lives of others into art he is doomed. He kills those he loves, as Wilde also said, because in love he tries to make them conform to his ideal image. As wife and mother, Hill's protagonist bears many burdens; she is midwife to her husband's poems, nurse to his anxieties, martyr to his patriarchal values, muse, and sexual partner. Her complaint is understandably vindictive:

> I writhed to conceive of him.
> I clawed to becalm him.
> Some nights, I witnessed his face in sleep
>
> And dreamed of my father's
> House. (By day he professed languages—
>   Disciplines of languages)—
>
> By day I cleansed my pink tongue
> From its nightly prowl, its vixen-skill,
>   His sacramental mouth

> That justified my flesh
> And moved well among women
> In nuances and imperatives.
>
> This was the poet of a people's
>   Love. I hated him. He weeps,
> Solemnizing his loss.

Like other poems in the baroque tradition, this one ends with passions evoked and tears ceremoniously shed.

The conflict between the lovers, to the poet's ironic view, is predominantly oral. The poet has a sacramental mouth which transfigures everyday speech into poetry. His wife has a "vixen's" tongue, whose language (*lingua* or tongue is language) is vehemently down-to-earth. He "justifies" or perfects her everyday words into poems. Without her, he might withdraw into a private language. He is like Paul Valéry's Monsieur Teste, a consciousness separated from others as well as himself, devoted to intellectual and linguistic exercises that are all his own. Madame Emilie Teste, his wife, declares that "his head is a sealed treasure, and I don't know whether he has a heart."[15] And he answers: "I was suspicious of literature, even of the fairly precise demands of work in poetry. The act of writing always requires a certain 'sacrifice of the intellect'. It is quite clear, for instance, that the conditions of literary reading do not allow for an excessive precision of language. The intellect would readily exact of ordinary language certain perfections and purities that are not in its power."[16] Hill shares the same reverence for linguistic exactitude as Teste, which makes him suspicious of all writing and sets him at odds with his wife.

Hill's "Baroque" marriage is founded more on linguistic relations than on sexual or amorous ones. It breaks down when oral exchanges collapse. With a frankness characteristic of the confessional poets, Hill proclaims the woe that is in marriage, but with a notable difference. Rather than divert personal guilt towards a ghoulish father figure, which was the way of Sylvia Plath and Robert Lowell, Hill admits and atones for personal guilt. He *is* the father figure, the linguistic master. The poem is an act of self-judgment; it allows the poet's wife to step into the witness box and voice her indictment. It is a confession of failure in which both parties play different roles rather than a self-righteous harangue by the poet.

"The sphere of Art and the sphere of Ethics are absolutely distinct and separate,"[17] Oscar Wilde claimed, but Hill constantly conjoins the two. He is no aesthete, although he obsessively reflects on art and its separation from life. Torn between a priestly devotion to his craft and a common man's love for fellows and mistresses, he makes his poetry speak for both. He is a humanist whose symbolist garb is a hair shirt but whose rituals are intended to bind people together rather than split them apart. Although he fails, he does not fail completely. As quoted earlier, Hill said of T. H. Green: "There are triumphs that entrap and defeats that liberate. Green is creative in his distress" (*LL*, p. 120). Hill's defeats, like Green's, are negative successes. Disenchanted and disillusioned, he is less deceived by utopian ideals. He falls into a "new knowledge of reality" which is both despairing and inspiring. He never capitulates to melancholy but embodies it wittily in poems. Although his life may descend into chaos, his art continues to exert a masterful control. His poems about poetry are winning testaments to the imagination's ability to survive life's reproaches.

The Nightmare of History

Hill has been accused of evasiveness in his history poems, but the only thing he evades is pat judgment. He considers private events in a public context and public events in a private one, evaluating both with uncommon candor. "Jousts, slush and uproar of battles, the frozen deathspew of the slain"[18] constitute history's nightmare, from which Hill, like Joyce's Dedalus, attempts to awake. "All history moves towards one great goal, the manifestation of God,[19] says the doddering headmaster in *Ulysses*. For Hill and Dedalus, however, history is cyclical, secular, and bloody.

A poem which broods on God and history and which has proven baffling to critics is "Ovid in the Third Reich," the first poem in *King Log*. Its simple syntax, colloquial sentences, and loosely rhymed quatrains recall the "The Apostles: Versailles, 1919." In the earlier poem, Hill dramatized the conflict between Christian *caritas* and worldly vengeance. "Ovid in the Third Reich" examines a similar split between political innocence and experience. For Hill, Ovid exemplifies the fallen idealist who has, in Robert Frost's words, "a lover's quarrel with the world" ("The Lesson for Today"). The crux of Ovid's *Amores*, from which Hill takes his epigraph, is the difficulty of loving that which is no longer lovable. Ovid speaks of a man's illusioned and disillusioned love for a woman. Hill, working on a larger scale, speaks of a man's perplexed love for humanity, which includes indifference and repugnance:

> I love my work and my children. God
> Is distant, difficult. Things happen.
> Too near the ancient troughs of blood
> Innocence is no earthly weapon.
>
> I have learned one thing: not to look down
> So much upon the damned. They, in their sphere,
> Harmonize strangely with the divine
> Love. I, in mine, celebrate the love-choir.

If God represents innocent, transcendent charity, what good is He to the man confronted with the Holocaust? After such knowledge, how can he (and why should he) forget and forgive? Innocence may be the mystic's "unearthly weapon" against history's nightmare, but for the soldier facing it, it is no "earthly" good.

Hill's Ovid could be an Allied soldier or a civilian witnessing the concentration camps for the first time. His reaction is divided as he tries "not to look down" with smug detachment on their suffering. The ambiguity implies solicitude, humility, and restraint. At the beginning, he speaks like Jehovah gazing over his creation, or like any father talking affectionately about his job and family; at the end, he speaks fully aware of the sins of Jehovah-like fathers. As an innocent bystander, he observes that the damned in their extreme privation are close to divine grace. Justly or unjustly punished, they harmonize "with the divine / Love." He celebrates the "love choir," the cherubic singers, who express unqualified love for life's victims. But *he* never actually expresses love for the victims. He applauds the concord between the god of love and the damned, as if it were the harmony of the spheres, but he remains in his own earthly sphere of family and job at a safe remove from the "troughs of blood."

For Jon Silkin, Hill's Ovid resembles Eichmann, as depicted by Hannah Arendt in her study of "the banality of evil."[20] Ovid is no mechanical butcher, however, but a well-intentioned, vacillating lover. He resembles one of Yeats's innocents in "News for the Delphic Oracle," who, having died from the world, relives his wounds among "the choir of love" and realizes that innocence is foolhardy. Hill's love-poet, however, never pitches off his burden of doubt, anxiety, and vacillation. He merely acknowledges them in the ambiguities of his poem.

When Hill examines early American history, as in "Locust Songs," his nightmarish vision takes on apocalyptic proportions. The poem begins with a self-styled "Emblem," like one in a seventeenth-century emblem book (chronologically apt in a poem about America's beginnings), in which Pilgrim Fathers quest through wilderness and desert for a paradisal "new heaven and new earth." Searching for religious, industrial, and agricultural opportunity, they conform to an old paradigm of romantic voyage. They have therefore to suffer the disillusionments and to commit the same errors of all romantic questers:

King Log

> So with sweet oaths converting the salt earth
> To yield, our fathers verged on Paradise:
> Each to his own portion of Paradise,
> Stung by the innocent venoms of the earth.

Ambitious and self-righteous, the American founders confront the native soil like the locusts of Revelation. But they are also Christian farmers, who vow to convert what they take to be a venomous desert (inhabited by Indians) into a cultivated Eden. Like Lowell, Hill satirizes the Calvinists' contempt for the indigenous wilderness and the Indians. Their "sweet oaths" are actually blasphemies; "the salt earth" is poisonous only because they think and make it so. Blinded by Christianity's myth of Eden, they believe that America can be plucked and chopped up like an apple, made into a pie, and devoured in portions. The Protestant ethic assures them that each man, if he works hard, can have "his own portion of Paradise." The Pilgrims, however, are the real snakes, venomous and satanic, full of evil machinations, while the natives who suffer them are comparatively innocent.

The ravage of the American wilderness precipitates a fall and eviction. Robert Lowell imagines a similar event in his elegy "At the Indian Killer's Grave" and wonders if "the great mutation" of the Last Judgment will punish and rectify the sins of the American Fathers. If the fruits of his sins are rotten apples, Hill's American Adam tries to rectify them by digging them back into the ground, by growing new crops from the compost. The second section, "Good Husbandry," may allude to Thomas Tusser's *Five Hundred Good Points of Husbandry* (1571), a calendar instructing farmers in everything from peason-sowing to sheep-shearing, but Hill describes his good husbandry in terms of mythical apple picking:

> Out of the foliage of sensual pride
> Those teeming apples! Summer burned well
> The dramatic flesh; made work for pride
> Forking into the tender mouths of Hell

> Heaped windfalls, pulp for the Gadarene
> Squealers. This must be our reward:
> To smell God writhing over the rich scene.
> Gluttons for wrath, we stomach our reward.

Rather than magnify the splendors of a well-husbanded, agrarian America, which was Allen Tate's way, Hill obliquely refers to America's scapegoats and victims. His poem, like the windfall apples, is for the Gadarene pigs, who, as Matthew recounts, "ran violently down a steep place into the sea, and perished in the waters" (8.32) after Christ exorcised the demons in two men and transferred them to the pigs. The "Gadarene squealers" in Hill's humorous fable are those who confess their own and their culture's sins (they "squeal" on them, as in American slang) in order to purge them. This oblique section owes something to Hart Crane and is partly an argument with him. Hill's "Summer burned well" recalls the line "Dangerously the summer burned" in Crane's "Passage" and echoes Crane's themes of vision, memory, and guilt. But Hill repudiates Crane's impulsive, suicidal romanticism, which culminated in his death-leap into the sea, like the Gadarene pigs. Yvor Winters argued that Crane's ideas and actions found precedents in the heralds of American culture, Whitman and Emerson, and Hill partly agrees:

The doctrine of Emerson and Whitman, if really put into practice, should naturally lead to suicide: in the first place, if the impulses are indulged systematically and passionately, they can lead only to madness; in the second place, death, according to the doctrine, is not only a release from suffering but is also and inevitably the way to beatitude. There is no question, according to the doctrine, of moral preparation for salvation.[21]

Salvation, however, may depend on the suicidal penchant of a savior who dies so that the community can be reborn. As in Blake's fable of the repressed man who devours the apple of wrath, Hill points to the price the savior pays as he "stomachs" the sins of his culture.

If "Good Husbandry" portrays Jefferson's America of small, independent farms, the last section gives evidence of bad husbandry, of Lincoln's America torn by westward expansion and civil war. The battle of Shiloh, where in 1862 Johnston and Grant left twenty-three thousand dead, is Hill's synecdoche for the strife into which early agrarian America tumbled. At Shiloh, the Union forces barely defeated the Confederates, but it was an ultimate loss for Grant, whose army was afterwards placed under the command of General Halleck. Hill does not describe the battle in any detail, but its horror permeates the poem like a dark cloud. His principal interests are metaphysical and teleological. As he reflects on America's destiny, he avers that the pattern of conquest does not change through history; only its means change. Hill's poem is a tortured and ironic soliloquy by an early American:

> O stamping-ground of the shod Word! So hard
> On the heels of the damned red-man we came,
> Geneva's tribe, outlandish and abhorred—
> Bland vistas milky with Jehovah's calm—
>
> Who fell to feasting Nature, the glare
> Of buzzards circling; cried to the grim sun
> 'Jehovah punish us!'; who went too far;
> In deserts dropped the odd white turds of bone;
>
> Whose passion was to find out God in this
> His natural filth, voyeur of sacrifice, a slow
> Bloody unearthing of the God-in-us.
> But with what blood, and to what end, Shiloh?

Entertaining notions subscribed to by the Mormons, Hill imagines Christ ("the shod Word") traveling to America and going west to settle among the Indians, but he blasts all Protestant denominations ("Geneva's tribe") who revel in apocalyptic fanaticism. As if to parody de Tocqueville, who declared that "this gradual and continuous progress of the European race toward the Rocky Mountains has the solemnity of a providential event; it is like a deluge of men rising unabatedly and daily driven onward by the hand of God,"[22] Hill sees the "deluge" as locusts "feasting Nature," apocalyptic horsemen following a maniacal cavalry officer, and the "shod" horse itself stampeding westward.

For Hill, the Civil War represents a crisis of conscience in American history. The shock, he conjectures, began an inward quest, where as before an outward one had predominated. He alludes to the spiritual warfare inherent in the Protestant's pursuit of the "inner light" ("the God-in-us") and places it in suggestive proximity with the Civil War. Is the struggle to realize the spirit of freedom in nature (as in Hegel's conception of history) simply America's competitive battle for private gain at the expense of public good? "With what blood, and to what end" is this battle fought? Hill remembers Shiloh in Tate's "Ode to the Confederate Dead," in Lowell's "Quaker Graveyard in Nantucket," and in the Old Testament and suggests that "there is one story and one story only," which is the history of paradise lost. Hill directs his question to Shiloh because Shiloh (the name of an ancient city in Palestine) was once associated with Christ and meant "bringer of peace," but it was also, paradoxically, a place of numerous battles. With Milton, who said at the beginning of *Paradise Lost* that his story came from the "Oracle of God" beside Shiloh's waters, Hill believes that Shiloh possesses similar clues to man's destiny.

"Our Fathers wrung their bread from stocks and stones," Robert Lowell wrote in "Children of Light,"

> And fenced their gardens with the Redman's bones;
> Embarking from the Nether Land of Holland,
> Pilgrims unhouseled by Geneva's night,
> They planted here the Serpent's seeds of light . . .

For Hill and Lowell, the American *voyant* is also the perverse "voyeur of sacrifice" who perpetrates a "bloody unearthing." The presence of Jehovah as an actual agent in history haunts both poets, as if he were the image of their own shadows. But Hill is more capable of standing back and wondering painfully over his dark side, while Lowell, at least in his early work, does not question the evil around him so much as glare with indignation at it and then, with Jehovah-like vehemence, record it detail by detail.

Frequently, Hill entertains the possibility of returning from history's nightmare to a prelapsarian innocence; then, like Milton's Adam in *Paradise Lost*, he recognizes that it would be a regression to infantile ignorance. Forlornly contemplating the world's future wars, Milton's Adam proclaims:

> O Visions ill foreseen! better had I
> Liv'd ignorant of future, so had borne
> My part of evil onely . . .
>   I had hope
> When violence was ceas't, and Warr on Earth,
> All would have then gon well, peace would have crown'd
> With length of happy dayes the race of man;
> But I was far deceav'd; for now I see
> Peace to corrupt no less than Warr to waste.
>   (*Paradise Lost*, XI, 763–784)

History verifies Michael's prophecy and justifies Adam's despair. A poem entitled "I had hope when violence was ceas't," with its obvious reference to *Paradise Lost*, describes a concentration camp where the last vestiges of hope have vanished:

> Dawnlight freezes against the east-wire.
> The guards cough 'raus! 'raus! We flinch and grin,
> Our flesh oozing towards its last outrage.
> That which is taken from me is not mine.

Naked, dispossessed, like Muir's personae in "The Absent," these camp victims have won the martyr's indifference to all worldly possessions, including their bodies. They have lost everything, even the awareness of loss itself.

In his discussion of martyrs with Haffenden, Hill described the "ability to overcome the animal self, which . . . has been marvellously caught in Eliot's line about the 'reluctance of the body to become a *thing*' . . . [as] an achievement which may be inspiring in some ways but is profoundly chilling in others" (*VP,* 91). "September Song," another poem depicting the terrors of the Third Reich, uses the elegy form to remember those victims who were reduced with factorylike efficiency into things. Hill begins in a mood of satirical effrontery. Hitler's rigidly hierarchical society paradoxically accepts even the "untouchables" (the lower caste) into its great death machine. Herod's systematic killing of the innocents, the Egyptian plagues that "passed over" the houses of the Jews but killed everyone else, and Hitler's slaughter of the Jews are all of a piece in Hill's poem. The epitaph "born 19.6.32—deported 24.9.42" recalls events in the life of a child in Nazi Germany but also Hill's birthday (18.6.32), one day before. Hill identifies with the child's fate but also indicates the distance between them:

> Undesirable you may have been, untouchable
> you were not. Not forgotten
> or passed over at the proper time.
>
> As estimated, you died. Things marched,
> sufficient, to that end.
> Just so much Zyklon and leather, patented
> terror, so many routine cries.

The instruments of death, the Zyklon crystals of toxic gas, the patented machines and authorized routines through which victims "passed," are "things" like the humans they destroy. Hill tabulates the vicious ironies of the camps. The undesirables are desirable, but only as meat for the fire. The untouchables are touched—as Hill says in another poem about the Holocaust, by "Jehovah's touchy methods"—but to be damned rather than saved. Those who are normally forgotten, forsaken, or banished by the elite are remembered in order to be dismembered. The Jews, over whom the plagues once passed, are now the victims of the worst plague of all—the Nazis.

Hill ends his poem with a self-conscious, bracketed reflection on making elegies for those whose experiences transcend "human" experience. Can the poet speak knowingly of history's nightmares or is he bracketed by his own experience? Hill scores his worries into the very punctuation of his lines:

(I have made
an elegy for myself it
is true)

September fattens on the vines. Roses
flake from the wall. The smoke
of harmless fires drifts to my eyes.

The poet, at a safe distance from the actual fires of crematoriums, broods on emblems of fallen innocents (the roses). Even the season reminds him of victims "fattened" for the fire, as if all nature were ripening toward some great unholy harvest. Hill remains sombre, stoical, sardonic, taciturn. He refrains from saying too much, since a garrulous fattening of language would indicate complicity with the decadent world he documents.

To let the dead speak of their historical crises may be a futile exercise, but Hill persists with masterly dexterity. In his "Four Poems Regarding the Endurance of Poets," he speaks for the victims of other totalitarian regimes. The act of ventriloquizing for the dead raises many dramatic problems, some of which are solved by Tommasso Campanella, the poet Hill honors in his first elegy. Campanella was a poet and priest born in Stilo, Spain, in 1568. Arrested during the Inquisition, tortured, and then thrown into prison, he spent more than a quarter of a century fortifying his friends and cultivating messianic dreams of man's renovation in a "city of the sun." Edmund Burke once described his character and his insight into other characters in the following way:

When he had in mind to penetrate into the inclinations of those he
had to deal with, he composed his face, his gesture, and his whole
body, as nearly as he could into the exact similitude of the person he
intended to examine; and then carefully observed what turn of mind
he seemed to acquire by this change. So that . . . he was able to enter
into the dispositions and thoughts of people, as effectually as if he
had been changed into the very men. . . . [He] could so abstract his
attention from any sufferings of his body, that he was able to endure
the rack itself without much pain . . . by inducing in the body a
disposition contrary to that which it receives from these passions.[23]

Actor, dramatist, and martyr intersect in this description. In the
first poem of the sequence, Hill puts on the mask of Campanella
himself and calls to mind his techniques of surviving great pain.
The slug they meditate on suggests ways to "scale" or transcend
imprisonments:

> Some days a shadow through
> The high window shares my
> Prison. I watch a slug
> Scale the glinting pit-side
> Of its own slime. The cries
> As they come are mine; then
> God's: my justice, wounds, love,
> Derisive light, bread, filth.
>
> To lie here in my strange
> Flesh while glutted Torment
> Sleeps, stained with its prompt food,
> Is a joy past all care
> Of this world, for a time.
> But we are commanded
> To rise, when, in silence,
> I would compose my voice.

A shadow his only companion, Campanella broods on "the track
left by human beings like the slime left by a snail," which, Hill
explains, "is full of false directions and self-pity and nostalgia

as well as lust, wrath, greed and pride" (*VP,* p. 89). It is the substance of history and poetry but Campanella, enjoying a dubious freedom from bodily torments, has no time to transubstantiate it into artifice.

Campanella's dream of a utopian 'city of the sun' may have inspired Hill's next section, "A Prayer to the Sun," for it imagines the sun's ascent over the prisoner's shadowy confinement, as if it were the radiant mind itself. It is dedicated, however, to Miguel Hernandez, the twentieth-century Spanish poet (1910–1942), who wrote not of utopias but of their ruins. A Catholic and Communist, Hernandez fought in the Spanish Civil War against Franco and died in prison while awaiting execution. His sunlit city is an embattled one, over which vultures and a predatory sun (rather than a benign deity) circle. His poems, as Hill conceives them, are brief prayers, shaped as crucifixes, which attest to an insidious dialectic between light and dark, predator and prey:

> i
> Darkness
> above all things
> the Sun
> makes
> rise

> ii
> Vultures
> salute their meat
> at noon
> (Hell is
> silent)

> iii
> Blind Sun
> our ravager
> bless us
> so that
> we sleep.

The force of destiny, as Hill and Hernandez imagine it, is like Hardy's "immanent will." It is indifferent, brutal. It pitches the everyday world into nightmare as unconscionably as the sun turns day into night.

Hill's poems form a guidebook on how to endure suffering. In his homage to Robert Desnos, the French poet who died in Terezin Camp during World War II, Hill offers scholastic methods of contemplation and self-mortification as possible antidotes. The Church Fathers, Hill declares, "cultivate the corrupting flesh" by contemplating the most gruesome images of death and bodily decay, but, by doing so, they toughen themselves to actual corruption and decrepitude when it comes. As trainers to spiritual athletes, they break down the body to build it up. As mentors to poets, they inculcate an ascetic skill with language through suppression of "hysterica passio." Their regimens help pare down rhetoric into lithe, sinewy poems.

Hill's sequence on poets under political duress finishes with "A Valediction to Osip Mandelshtam," the Russian poet who spoke out against Stalin and suffered exile in a number of detention camps, where he eventually died. Mandelshtam's "Tristia," which speaks of a "science of good-byes," informs Hill's "Tristia" and his scholastic or "scientific" methods of dealing with suffering. But Hill's poem is concerned more with the vanity of remembering past crimes and victims than with actually memorializing them in accomplished valedictions. He laments:

> The dead keep their sealed lives
> And again I am too late. Too late
> The salutes, dust-clouds and brazen cries.
>
> Images rear from desolation
> Look . . . ruins upon a plain . . .
> A few men glare at their hands; others
> Grovel for food in the roadside field.

King Log

> Tragedy has all under regard.
> It will not touch us but it is there—
> Flawless, insatiate—hard summer sky
> Feasting on this, reaching its own end.

The communication of the living, Hill might say to Eliot's ghost, is tongued with fire beyond the language of the dead. Salutations and brazen elegiac cries to the dead all seem belated efforts to stir up the dust over impenetrable graves. What comes back to haunt the living are images of history's tragic waste. The "blind Sun / Our ravager" hovers over the scene like the secret police, who will not touch the visiting poet (Hill traveled to the USSR in 1966, a year after the poem was written) but who keeps continual watch. The final irony is that tragedy is the only unflawed thing (a perfect killer with a boundless appetite) in a cosmos of imperfection and ruin. Tragedy may simply be Hill's emblem for Nature, like Ted Hughes's hawk, who surveys all creation and periodically descends to devour it. Nature destroys, consumes, and then creates anew. Hill stares at the tragic scene with little "tragic joy."

Whether the imagination can know and accurately represent anonymous victims of concentration camps, little-known martyrs of the Inquisition, afflicted American Indians, politicians and soldiers butchered during the Wars of the Roses, and artists who die under dictatorial regimes is a question for epistemology, linguistics, historiography, and poetics. A poem which Hill worked on throughout the composition of *King Log* and which touches on many of these disciplines is "History as Poetry." Begun in 1961 and collected in the pamphlet *Preghiere* (1964) but then substantially revised between 1967 and 1968, the poem avers that the history of language and the history of society follow similar patterns. As Hill said in an interview, "In handling the English language the poet makes an act of recognition that etymology is history. The history of the creation and the debasement of words is a paradigm of the loss of the kingdom of innocence and original justice" (*VP,* p. 88). History is a record of creations, falls, and redemptions. Poetry is the same. But Hill witnesses the collusion between poetry and history, in which "poetic" rhetoric incites atrocities and atrocious dictators silence poets.

The poem begins with a salutation across history to old words, dead writers, and buried deeds. The greeting is a communion, but one that leaves a bitter taste in the poet's mouth. Tradition can be a dead feast for the communicant who wants to recollect past passions. The poet feels the ash on his tongue:

> Poetry as salutation; taste
> Of Pentecost's ashen feast.

Eliot imagined the dead speaking to the living in unintelligible, pentecostal tongues; Hill imagines the living consuming the pentecostal ash of what the dead have said. As Christopher Ricks pointed out in an early review, Hill "persistently tackle[s] the problem of what to do about dead language, clichés, the phrases which have gone sour, flat, or heartless on us."[24] The dead language, however, is not completely dead. Pentecost's ashen words, like communion wafers, recall the wounded Christ and those who have suffered similarly. They reveal the "blue wounds" and "the tongue's atrocities" which have caused the wounds. Poetry's purpose is an "at-one-ment" with "empirical guilt," which for Hill is synonymous with the "anxiety about *faux pas,* the perpetration of 'howlers', grammatical solecisms, misstatements of fact, misquotations, improper attributions" (*LL,* p. 7). These are "the tongue's atrocities," too, the poet's worrisome (but less cataclysmic) version of the demagogue's linguistic improprieties and atrocities.

For Hill, poetic history is a tale told by a common man whose buried innocence (objectified by Lazarus and the gouged lily) is exhumed to give significance to the idiocies of fortune:

> Poetry
> Unearths from among the speechless dead

> Lazarus mystified, common man
> Of death. The lily rears its gouged face
> From the provided loam.

Lazarus comes back from the compost of tradition (as Eliot's Lazarus does in "Prufrock") to tell us all. With him comes a mixture of artifacts, cries of ecstasy and pain, and didactic auguries. In his retinue are also priests and instruments (presumably gramophones preserving historical records), all of which Hill satirizes as the dubious boons of the archaeological dig. Hill lists them:

> Accomplished
> Auguries: bleatings: tarred golden dung;
>
> Glittering instruments; sober priests
> Who now beyond danger memorize
> The names in error and justice drawn
> From oblivion, blood-embroiled souls . . .
>
> 'An achievement' as they say.

This is very much like the excavation in "Solomon's Mines," where Hill excoriated the "priests, soldiers and kings." This time he belittles their safe, hermetic, often inaccurate rituals of remembrance. Compared to the "blood-embroiled souls" of those who fought and died in the world, they are bloodless, otherworldly, and too innocent to bear accurate witness.

In the final version of the poem, which Hill published in *King Log*, the third quatrain is missing. It reads:

> Fortunate
> Auguries; whirrings; tarred golden dung:
>
> 'A resurgence' as they say. The old
> Laurels wagging with the new: Selah!
> Thus laudable the trodden bone, thus
> Unanswerable the knack of tongues.

"Accomplished auguries" is changed to "fortunate auguries" and "an achievement" to "a resurgence." Accomplishments and achievements, in a poem about resurrecting the dead, may imply too unambiguous a success. "Fortunate" introduces the idea of fortune and the notion, which is Hill's firm belief, that history should provide a scholarly index for fortunetellers. Like Dylan Thomas, Hill jokingly envisions the accomplished artist (wreathed in laurels) as a dog (rather than a god) who wags his tail with anticipation as he excavates the "trodden bones" of the dead. Is the bone his reward? Must his bones be trodden down before he can understand history's dark lessons? To learn the pentecostal "knack of tongues," Hill's Lazarus-poet must accept death-in-life. His art of ventriloquy derives from harrowing initiations and, because it transports him beyond known boundaries, is ultimately "unanswerable." "You can refute Hegel," Yeats said, "but not the Saint or the Song of Sixpence."[25] You can refute the logic of the living, Hill would add, but not the logic of the dead.

The dramatic impact and credibility that the poet accords history depends upon a "suspension of disbelief" which, in turn, depends upon the poet's "knack of tongues," his ability to make ghosts of the past vividly real. Mnemosyne is Hill's muse but also his demon. She impels him to resuscitate the dead language of the tribe (the "ashen feast"), as well as the dead tribe itself. She instigates his journey into the underworld as well as his journey above it to the "lost kingdom of innocence and original justice" which is his true heritage.

Doctor Faustus and the Poetry Banquet

Convinced that writing is akin to damnation, Hill seized upon the legend of Doctor Faustus. Hill's Faustus, although related to lengendary forbears, is unique. To begin with, he is a poet who finds damnation thrust upon him; he does not choose it like Marlowe's Faustus. He shuns the devil's alchemical magic and promises of supremacy, while Marlowe's Faustus craves them. Unlike Thomas Mann's Dr. Faustus (another artist), he rebels against diseased genius, inhumanity, and "aristocratic nihilism."[26] Hill's Faustus is a poet who begins his career blissfully unaware that "one . . . writes under judgment"[27] and who, through writing, falls into an inferno of moral perplexity, guilt, and tentative cures.

Marlowe, Mann, and Hill follow the Genesis example of depicting the fall into damnation as a symbolic eating. First Adam eats the fruit of the tree of knowledge; then he is told that "cursed *is* the ground for thy sake; in sorrow shalt thou eat *of* it all the days of thy life; Thorns also and thistles shall it bring forth to thee; and thou shalt eat the herb of the field; In the sweat of thy face shalt thou eat bread, till thou return unto the ground; for out of it wast thou taken" (Gen. 3. 17–19). Marlowe's Faustus eats the apple of knowledge and similarly stumbles:

> falling to a devilish exercise
> And glutted more with learning's golden gifts,
> He surfeits upon cursèd necromancy.
> ("Prologue")

The cultured musician of Mann's Dr. Faustus, Adrian Leverkühn, consumes past musical forms as if they were so many poisonous apples. His demonic muse, an avatar of Lucifer, contends that culture is passed on through a series of morbid, necromantic eatings: "A whole host and generation of youth, receptive, sound of core, flings itself on the work of the morbid genius, made genius by disease; admires it . . . carries it away, assimilates it unto itself and makes it over to culture, which lives not on home-made bread alone, but as well on provender and poison from the apothecary's shop."[28] For Hill, too, tradition is proliferated by one generation feeding on the artifacts of another.

Although Hill's poem "Doctor Faustus," appeared in *For the Unfallen*, it was one of the last poems to be collected (1958) and focused on a preoccupation that would receive greater attention in *King Log*. Composed of three sections, two quatrains each, its compressed but resonant lyricism made it Hill's favorite poem of the volume. It is a *Bildungsroman* in brief, like "Genesis." It traces the short, downward arc of the poet's fall from an original, undistracted, innocently self-involved writing, through painful self-consciousness and guilt, to a final ambivalent affirmation of poetic vision. In the first section, Faustus conjures up a "god" from a steaming pool of blood. It is the sacrificial blood squeezed from his own body and the body of his poem. He seems to create himself as he creates his poem. Hill has said that through the craft of poetry "we rise to a discovery of true personality" (*LL*, p. 17). Birth and death, killing and creating, mingle disturbingly in Hill's fable. The birth of poems (the "gods"), according to Faustus, is comparable to Christ's birth from the immaculate womb and His miraculous resurrection from the tomb. Although a magician of sorts, Faustus does not deem poetic creation magical. It is a common, workmanlike task. Hill's poem enters the world as a common swan, swaddled in clean, ordinary feathers. Writing poetry, Hill affirms, is only one of many ways that the common imagination (the god-man) expresses itself:

> A way of many ways: a god
> Spirals in the pure steam of blood.
> And gods—as men—rise from shut tombs
> To a disturbance of small drums;
>
> Immaculate plumage of the swan
> The common wear.

Entitled "The Emperor's Clothes," this is a portrait of the artist as a young swan. His flight from the world will soon crash. He is Icarus, the king in Hans Christian Andersen's story, and Adam and Eve before the fall, sublimely oblivious to his vulnerability. Although his birth "to a disturbance of small drums" is ominous, he fails to hear (Hill was partially deaf as a child) the distant rumbling of critical voices that expose the naked animal beneath the imperial feathers.

> There is no-one
> Afraid or overheard, no loud
> Voice (though innocently loud).

A child's voice roused the fairy-tale king from his vain enchantments. Here an unspecified person rends the substanceless garments off the soaring poet.

Caught in mid-flight, he now spirals into a hell of self-consciousness. The sin of Mann's Dr. Faustus, Hill has claimed, is his Christian supernaturalism, his "refusal . . . to submit or be ruled by any of the exigencies of the created natural order" (*LL*, p. 4). Hill's Faustus rises from the earth in the first section; in the second, he falls back to it. He falls from linguistic innocence into an inquisitorial attitude toward all words. His fall from heaven mimics Lucifer's, but his task in hell is not to build Pandemonium so much as to redeem those words whose sacred meanings have fallen into decrepitude.

Poetry's banquet table is now a refuse dump of spoiled meats. It is the litter left after a beach party attended by Hill's notorious antagonists, the English holiday makers. The second section, "the Harpies," dramatizes the corruption of language by recalling the Greek myth of monstrous birds that descend on the prophet Phineus to defile his meat before he can eat it. The Harpies, for Hill, represent all those who make language meaningless and unpalatable, but also the critics (like himself) who harp on the definitions and implications of words so much that they make polite, fluent conversation impossible. Although Marlowe's Faustus, clothed in Mephistophilis's invisible girdle, indulges in the Pope's "politic banquet," Hill's Faustus, after losing his transparent clothes, practices ascetic discernment, which amounts to linguistic mortification. He walks among the graceful "gods" of fashionable English society (who expose their gristled bodies on the beach) and suffers their meaningless chat:

> Having stood hungrily apart
> From the gods' politic banquet,

> Of all possible false gods
> I fall to these gristled shades
>
> That show everything, without lust;
> And stumble upon their dead feast
> By the torn *Warning to Bathers*
> By the torn waters.

Faustus, no demigod and certainly no politic god of the bourgeoisie, still stumbles in their wake. How else will he transform the language of the tribe into something rich and strange? Into the linguistic sea, polluted and roiled by dangerous currents, he dives (like Sebastian in the poem dedicated to Henry James).

Despite his linguistic agonies, Hill's Faustus avoids the irrevocable perdition of Marlowe's Faustus and the premature sterility of Mann's. As "Another Part of the Fable" tells, he no longer pretends to innocence in a world governed by wolves and no longer practices a hermetic art without a shrewd knowledge of history and society. He has grown up, although he still guards his early innocent plumage. The innocents are not ferried to Elysian isles of the blessed, as in Yeats's "News for the Delphic Oracle;" they stay behind to confront worldly gods and laugh in their teeth.

> The Innocents have not flown;
> Too legendary, they laugh;
> The lewd uproarious wolf
> Brings their house down.
>
> A beast is slain, a beast thrives.
> Fat blood squeaks on the sand.
> A blinded god believes
> That he is not blind.

The swanlike innocents, Hill implies with revisionary panache, are the defenceless pigs whose house the wolf blows down in the fairy tale. At the end, beast and poet, body and spirit, are unified, but not without painful sacrifice (the pigs are burnt and squeaking on the sand). Rather than inflict blindness on himself like Oedipus or the romantic poets who "transform . . . their blindness towards their precursors into the revisionary insights of their own work,"[29] as Harold Bloom claims, Hill's Faustus accepts blindness as part of his nature and redeems it by envisioning it in a poem.

Faustus transfigures his "dissipation by a metaphor that perfectly comprehends it" (*LL*, p. 13). The unmoral nature becomes moral through damnation, so Eliot argued in an examination of Beatrice in Middleton's *The Changeling*, which Hill quotes and qualifies: "The reason why the poet's 'discovery' is finally not to be confused with Beatrice's 'discovery' is perhaps implied by my reference to that '*vision* of "the unmoral nature . . ."' by which I attempt to set at one the piercing insight and the carnal blundering" (*LL*, p. 16). The task of "Doctor Faustus," accomplished most overtly in the final lines, is to "set at one" the antinomies of blindness and insight.

Faustus's poetry of spectacular flights and falls resurfaces in Hill's "Bibliographers." In the twentieth century, Hill wittily remarks, in "the finest-possible light" (Lucifer is the "light-bearer") of psychoanalysis and mythology, the devils of Lucifer's army abound. Hill's bibliographers map the fallen angels reincarnated in books:

> Lucifer blazing in superb effigies
> Among the world's ambitious tragedies,
> Heaven-sent gift to the dark ages,
>
> Now, in the finest-possible light,
> We approach you; can estimate
> Your not unnatural height.

The effigies of Lucifer are emblems of the tragic mythos. Lucifer's "discrete progeny" (the "politic" beach partiers and summer vacationers), who avoid history's undertow in order to lounge on sunny sand, draw from Hill another scornful rebuke. They have fallen with Lucifer into hell, into the underworld of the dead, but refuse to recognize the fact. The Faustian bibliographers, on the other hand, know Lucifer intimately.

> Though the discrete progeny,
> Out of their swim, go deflated and dry,
> We know the feel of you, archaic beauty,
>
> Between the tombs, where the tombs still extrude,
> Overshadowing the sun-struck world:
> (The shadow-god envisaged in no cloud).

The heroic insubordination of "the shadow-god," Lucifer, makes him a seductive beauty, who may be averted only if envisaged in unclouded language. He is Jung's shadow as much as Freud's id, through which the ego must pass, naming the demons, and in which the naive find themselves "out of their swim."

Hill's Faustus, despite his demonic and angelic attributes, is fundamentally a humanist who confronts hell and heaven to better comprehend what lies in between—civilized virtues. "The Bibliographers" are writers and students who sit at the poetry banquet, like Faustus, in various postures of judicious or injudicious eating. Table manners, it would seem, are all-important. Before the selection of meats, the banqueters exercise moral discernment or gobble the food with wild abandon. Faustus is one of the connoisseurs, abstemious, highly discriminating, which is why he complains so bitterly when he finds nothing but gristle and fat. Like Lowell, Hill divides poetry between the well-cooked and the raw, the spoiled and the fresh. In "The Humanist," his Faustian persona stands before a portrait of a Renaissance man who has just finished writing a poem and now searches through tradition's memorabilia for a suitable epigraph. In the picture, Hill finds his own stance mirrored. The Renaissance man sits at the poetry banquet of linguistic meats:

> The *Venice* portrait: he
> Broods, the achieved guest
> Tired and word-perfect
> At the Muses' table.
>
> Virtue is virtù. These
> Lips debate and praise—
> Some rich aphorism;
> A delicate white meat.
>
> The commonplace hands once
> Thick with Plato's blood
> (Tasteless! tasteless!) are laid
> Dryly against the robes.

Moral perfection (virtue) is achieved through artistic virtuosity (virtù). Having perfected his poem, the Faustus-poet experiences one "of those rare moments in which the inertia of language . . . seems to have been overcome" (*LL*, p. 2). His sense of ecstatic fulfillment, Hill says, is "commonplace," although his original inspiration was the divine frenzy of Plato's *Ion*. He could be a painter who has just finished a portrait, a carpenter who has finished building a perfectly shaped box (Hill likes the adage—"a poem comes right with a click like a closing box" *LL*, p. 2), or a diner who has just finished his main course. The bardic excitement, the passion in the blood, has drained away. The craftsman's hands, once "tasteless" because completely subliminal and wholly engaged in rectifying "tasteless" mistakes, return to their natural repose.

Many writers have written about becoming artists and writing poems, but few have put so much emphasis on the actual moment of finishing a poem. For Hill, the attainment of poetic perfection, when the poet can finally relax, is a form of beatitude to which he directs his life and art. He quotes Eliot approvingly in his discussion of the moment of atonement: ". . . when the words are finally arranged in the right way—or in what he comes to accept as the best arrangement he can find—[the poet] may experience a moment of exhaustion, of appeasement, of absolution, and of something very near annihilation, which is in itself indescribable" (*LL*, p. 2). For Dr. Faustus, this ecstatic moment of completion is as close as he ever gets to "the lost kingdom of innocence and original justice" from which he has fallen and to which he continually aspires.

"Funeral Music"

In "Funeral Music," a sequence of eight unrhymed sonnets which form the centerpiece of *King Log*, Hill examines one of England's principal upheavals, the prolonged, petty, and bloody civil wars during the second half of the fifteenth century, known as the Wars of the Roses. In these wars, like Eliot in the *Four Quartets*, Hill finds a correlative for the present. The poem resembles a series of photographs laid out in a row, spliced with commentary in which the poet identifies the action and points to motives and consequences. Hill digresses from historical events to speculate on religious and philosophical issues. He also recounts experiences from personal life and from the society around him which parallel similar ones in the wars. He remains, all the while, continually aware of himself writing a poem in which all events collide and correspond. To the end, "Funeral Music" is a twentieth-century meditation rather than a dramatic narrative of political and military events.

Seeking instruction from periods of decadence and renaissance, so as to cultivate the latter, Hill finds in the wars exemplary material. Just as two world wars in the twentieth century broke the British Empire, so the Wars of the Roses buried the aristocratic society of medieval England. "The old feudal nobility had destroyed itself in the Wars of the Roses; the medieval structure of society, based on guild and manor, had broken down; the Medieval Church had been pillaged and shaken to the ground."[30] The wars occured shortly before Catholic Europe divided into a Catholic and Protestant Europe and shortly before the Renaissance flowered from the cleft. In the wars, aristocratic lords allied to the families of Lancaster and York made private squabbles public ones. The wars, according to the historian R. L. Storey, were "no more than a sordid scramble by various great lords for control of the king's government."[31] The strife resulted from a degenerate, war-minded aristocracy in its death throes. Although thousands were killed, Storey argues, "the country as a whole . . . was barely affected by this blue-blooded bickering."[32] For Hill, however, the private melees were public catastrophes. An old order died and so did many soldiers:

> It is now customary to play down the violence of the Wars of the Roses and to present them as dynastic skirmishes fatal, perhaps, to the old aristocracy but generally of small concern to the common people and without much effect on the economic routines of the kingdom. Statistically, this may be arguable; imaginatively, the Battle of Towton itself commands one's belated witness. In the accounts of the contemporary chroniclers it was a holocaust. (KL, p. 68)

Beside this, the plucking of white and red roses by Shakespeare's Richard Plantagenet and Somerset is idiotic glamorizing. The title "The Wars of the Roses," originally coined by Sir Walter Scott in *Anne of Geierstein*, impels Hill to interrogate and reject all rosy, poeticized accounts.

"Funeral Music" is not all solemn dirge and muffled rumination, however, but also "a commination and an alleluia" (KL, p. 67). It formally denounces the barbarisms of the wars and formally praises those who successfully or unsuccessfully resisted them. The cries of victims and groans of victors can be heard throughout. Hill's "ornate and heartless music punctuated by mutterings, blasphemies and cries for help" (KL, pp. 67–68), unsurprisingly, echoes Shakespeare's rhetoric in *Henry VI:* "Your hearts I'll stamp out with my horse's heels / And make a quagmire of your mingled brains" (Part 1, I, iv, 108–9). Discussing the genesis of "Funeral Music," Hill admitted the allegiance by saying that "it was a happy accident that in order to give a lecture course on Shakespeare I found myself re-reading the *Henry VI* plays at exactly the right time; discovering the power of a certain kind of rhetoric which I'd been educated to think of as inferior to Shakespeare's later work. This came at a time when my thoughts were beginning to stir towards the writing of the sequence 'Funeral Music' " (*VP,* p. 80–81). Hill's rhetoric, although halted by meditative silences, is not quiet or smoothly-flowing. While Eliot discourses on "timeless moments" and historical patterns with dampened, twilit humility, Hill marches with a staccato tread. When he confronts history's battlefield of corpses and mud, his tone varies between sarcasm, disbelief, repugnance, and despair.

Old themes converge in Hill's sequence, and many derive from Shakespeare. The poet intentionally places the ceremonies of aristocratic society and the rituals of the Catholic church against the brutal beheadings, military slaughters, isolated tortures, and unseemly couplings that rage beside them. Since the wars were primarily the fault of an ineffectual king, questions of authority and power predominate. The poem begins with a funeral march inside a church, just as *Henry VI* commences with the king's funeral inside Westminster Abbey. But Hill's symbolic procession represents not just one funeral but all ceremonies of remembrance:

> Processionals in the exemplary cave,
> Benediction of shadows. Pomfret. London.
> The voice fragrant with mannered humility,
> With an equable contempt for this World,
> 'In honorem Trinitatis'.

In this dark cathedral, which is as much Plato's cave as Westminster Abbey, shadows of the dead gather to trade benedictions with the living. But Hill is neither Platonic idealist nor hermetic priest, although he might like to be. Outside are murders and wars, and he recalls them by naming the cities where they occurred. Pomfret is where Richard II, who for many symbolized high decorum and art, was murdered in prison and where Richard Neville, Earl of Salisbury, a renowned combatant in the Wars of the Roses, was killed. London, no seat of benevolent justice during the wars, was the capital of internecine squabbles and executions.

Among history's ruins the poet pieces together gruesome facts. Eliot, who contemplated similar events (wasted cities, murders in cathedrals, worldly renunciations), advocated the purgative way of the saint. But otherworldly quietism, Hill points out, is suicidal where predatory slaughters are common occurrences. Unresisted, the butchers chop heads with ever-increasing alacrity. Otherworldliness, by definition, is inhuman. Both axe and angel, in Hill's poem, are emblems of "an equable contempt for this world." He provides the sound effects of their assault:

> Crash. The head
> Struck down into a meaty conduit of blood.
> So these dispose themselves to receive each
> Pentecostal blow from axe or seraph. . . .

To "dispose" oneself humbly and sacrificially to a greater power (as in "Two Formal Elegies") is literally to "dispose" of one's humanity like trash. One gets beheaded for the obeisance. In his epigraph, Hill lists specific beheadings from the Wars of the Roses (William de la Pole, John Tiptoft, and Anthony Woodville) but includes within the purview of his poem all brutalities and their strange symbiosis with religious and literary formalities. De la Pole was a poet and perhaps, Hill recounts, a racketeer; Tiptoft, "patron of humanist scholars, was known as the Butcher of England because of his pleasure in varying the accepted postures of judicial death" (KL, p. 67); Woodville was a poet and religious mystic. In the sacred places, the axe falls with horrible repetition.

For Eliot in the *Four Quartets*, pentecostal communion ("Benediction of shadows") also possessed both creative and destructive aspects. The pentecostal "dark dove with the flickering tongue" was the dove of grace transformed into a German bomber descending on London during the Second World War. Hill's vision, like Eliot's, subsumes these paradoxes. Murders create the need for psalms; out of the world of butchers grows the empyrean for angels; from heaven the imperial, axe-wielding angels descend in fiery bombers. The crimes of history encourage writers to record them. Memory's shadows burgeon out of history's dump.

If Plato's cave is a church (psalms mingle there with fiery ghosts), it is not a crowded one. In fact it is a no man's land, a barren haven, a demilitarized zone in a violently militarized world:

> Psalteries whine through the empyrean. Fire
> Flares in the pit, ghosting upon stone
> Creatures of such rampant state, vacuous
> Ceremony of possession, restless
> Habitation, no man's dwelling-place.

Only ghosts, and not necessarily holy ones, inhabit God's dwelling place. The church, like a history book, can bring the past beneficially to bear on the present, but for most, Hill observes, communion with the dead, and even with the living, has become a lost art.

Like Shakespeare's plays, which so often address questions of power and virtue, Hill's "Funeral Music" repeatedly addresses itself to Christian ideas of goodness (humility, *caritas*, sacrifice), but as they appear in an unchristian world. Do Christian virtues, as Nietzsche argued, condone weakness and promulgate a herd morality? Do they make the conscientious man weak in the presence of real terrors? Does the reconciliation of salvation simply lead to ineffectual governance and the ideal of sacrificial service to mindless obedience? Hill directs many of these questions at Henry VI. During the Wars of the Roses, the majority of citizens served Henry VI, the "ritual king," but for that reason, England faltered through forty years of anarchy. In Hill's poem,

Henry VI is Christ-like, an exemplar of *caritas* (historically, he was fair-minded and kind). But he is also a mysterious, Yeatsean sphinx vexing civilization to years of stony sleep and nightmare. A reflective soldier sarcastically wonders why he is fighting for such a figurehead. His sacrifice, he realizes, is utterly fruitless:

> For whom do we scrape our tribute of pain—
> For none but the ritual king? We meditate
> A rueful mystery; we are dying
> To satisfy fat Caritas, those
> Wiped jaws of stone.

Spiritual and political warfare collide in this interrogation of high-minded idealism. The King's lands, which are waste, remain so because he cannot command the power to rejuvenate them.

Hill, who does not subscribe to timeless moments or sempiternal reconciliations, hypothesizes in an ironical parenthesis:

> (Suppose all reconciled
> By silent music; imagine the future
> Flashed back at us, like steel against sun,
> Ultimate recompense.)

The flashback travels two ways, from future time to present time, and from past time to the historical present. If silent music exists, Hill contends, it exists only in the imagination. More sceptical and more worldly than Eliot, Hill envisions silence as what comes before and after history's cacophonous, muck-drenched, blood-stained battles. His music, like Wilfred Owen's, redeems the noises and colors of war, its desolate fields of sleet and wind and clashing bodies, rather than the quiet of the godlike mind musing on patterned moments.

> Recall the cold
> Of Towton on Palm Sunday before dawn,
> Wakefield, Tewkesbury: fastidious trumpets

> Shrilling into the ruck; some trampled
> Acres, parched, sodden or blanched by sleet,
> Stuck with strange-postured dead. Recall the wind's
> Flurrying, darkness over the human mire.

On this Palm Sunday, no godlike mind resurrects dead soldiers into a timeless empyrean. The Battle of Towton, on March 29, 1461, was the worst in the Wars of the Roses. According to Hill, "one finds the chronicler of Croyland Abbey writing that the blood of the slain lay caked with the snow which covered the ground and that, when the snow melted, the blood flowed along the furrows and ditches for a distance of two or three miles" (*KL*, p. 68). Thirty thousand were killed in the battle. The Battle of Wakefield, on December 30, 1460, was fought by Queen Margaret (York died in it). In the later Battle of Tewkesbury, in 1471, Margaret's army was crushed.

England's decaying aristocracy, during the Wars of the Roses and during Hill's lifetime, shares the destiny of all apocalyptic builders. At the midpoint of the second millennium, Hill says in a playful reference to Yeats's cosmic gyres, the medieval world spirals towards the Renaissance; the opposed factions of York and Lancaster collide; and at the climactic point of intersection there is apocalyptic destruction and revelation, an "appearance," as Hill humbly calls it. St. John's apocalyptic marriage makes way for an earthly, sexual one. According to Shakespeare, apocalyptic expectations were endemic to the period surrounding the wars. He begins *Henry VI* with Bedford's exclamation:

> Hung be the heavens with black, yield day to night!
> Comets, importing change of times and states,
> Brandish your crystal tresses in the sky
> And with them scourge the bad revolting stars
> 						(I, i, 1–4)

In equally grand rhetoric, Hill depicts the magilike armies tearing up the "bestial floor" to prepare for a renaissance.

> They bespoke doomsday and they meant it by
> God, their curved metal rimming the low ridge.
> But few appearances are like this. Once
> Every five hundred years a comet's
> Over-riding stillness might reveal men
> In such array, livid and featureless,
> With England crouched beastwise beneath it all.

Mythically, barbarians always congregate in the north and renew delapidated civilizations in the south (Hill's "old northern business" also refers to England's industrial north). Out of blood and carnage comes a new birth, crying and struggling:

> A field
> After battle utters its own sound
> Which is like nothing on earth, but is earth.
> Blindly the questing snail, vulnerable
> Mole emerge, blindly we lie down, blindly
> Among carnage the most delicate souls
> Tup in their marriage-blood, gasping 'Jesus'.

To pitch life "into the frog-spawn of a blind man's ditch" so that it can recreate itself is one form of purgatory, a form both Yeats and Hill deem gruesome but inevitable.

Yeats's baptism in "A Dialogue of Self and Soul" inspires Hill to conduct a similar metaphysical debate in his fourth section. The baptism has taught him to beware of excessive cerebration. Fearful that intellect, having crawled from the didactic carnage, will now forget its past and reign with terror, Hill summons it for questioning. For Hill, "intellect" is the mind of uncompromising principles, "soul" the mind of instinctive passions. In a poem centered around a king whose intellect snared him in conflicting allegiances, whose vacillations made practical political decisions impossible and atrocities inevitable, a debate between the mind's contrary faculties is apt. Hill begins with an echo of Donne's "Riding Westward," another dialogue between mind and soul:

> Let man's soul be a sphere, and then, in this,
> The intelligence that moves, devotion is . . .

Intelligence, the angel, guides the soul's sphere. But Hill reverses Donne, and offers some unsettling observations:

> Let mind be more precious than soul; it will not
> Endure. Soul grasps its price, begs its own peace,
> Settles with tears and sweat, is possibly
> Indestructible. That I can believe.
> Though I would scorn the mere instinct of faith,
> Expediency of assent, if I dared,
> What I dare not is a waste history
> Or void rule.

When the withdrawn mind shows little involvement with expediency, contemplating the world rather than acting in it, it will not endure. Soul, the grasping, passionate self, full of imaginative desire, will build up endurance by fighting battles in the world but, for all its labors, gain little but tears and sweat. The void rule of the Wars of the Roses occurred because Henry VI lacked the necessary instinct and faith to make quick, expedient decisions. Unschooled in history's gutter, he did not endure. Wondering whether faith or reason should reign, Hill unexpectedly addresses Averroes, the medieval Spanish philosopher (1126–1198), who affirmed the power of worldly reason over divine revelation (Aquinas later rebutted him) and the eternity of the world over man's spiritual immortality. Hill, like Averroes, sees a place for instinctual faith and sudden revelation when they lead to right action. What he deplores is the intellectual muddle-headedness which fails to avert war's waste. He says, with gentle mockery:

> Averroes, old heathen,
> If only you had been right, if Intellect
> Itself were absolute law, sufficient grace,

> Our lives could be a myth of captivity
> Which we might enter: an unpeopled region
> Of ever new-fallen snow, a palace blazing
> With perpetual silence as with torches.

The political intellect must tap the common ground of unreasoned intuitions, although, as Hill realizes, this way is dangerous. The instinctual politician is often the demagogic tyrant.

Hill's poems, and especially his long ones, strive to dramatize the informed mind arguing with itself, presenting for contemplation the raw data of experience (battles, beheadings, funerals), then fabricating hypotheses (suppose there *is* ultimate recompense; suppose Averroes *is* right), and then posing tentative conclusions. Through Averroes, Hill traces his own enchantments, doubts, and resolutions. In an interview he revealed:

When I was writing "Funeral Music", I was much interested in Averroism, which is, or was, a heresy. . . . Averroism was the doctrine of monopsychism, that is, that there's only one single Intellect, or "intellective" soul for the whole of humanity, and it seemed to me at first sight a most comforting doctrine—the idea that all kinds of personal guilt, a burden of culpability for all eternity, might be absorbed and absolved in that one "Intellect"—but afterwards I felt it was not a doctrine to be embraced at all; it seemed to be the archetype of the totalitarian state. And so I reacted very violently against it. . . . What at first seemed comforting ended up being desolate, rather like one of those beautiful but terrifying fairy stories where one enters a palace which is either totally empty or full of sleeping people, a dead sleep which is lit by blazing torches, never replenished and yet never extinguished. (*VP,* pp. 98–99)

In Hill's fifth sonnet, the instinctive man invades the torchlit, wintry palace to indulge in sanctified murder:

> As with torches we go, at wild Christmas,
> When we revel in our atonement
> Through thirty feasts of unction and slaughter,
> What is that but the soul's winter sleep?

Religious desire is here turned from revelation to revelry, from "unity of being" to mindless fanaticism.

Having convinced himself that too much intellect is as bad as too much soul, Hill's meditator moves on to contemplate judicious compromises. Can there be a just state, he wonders, or have the apocalyptic trumpets of doom already sounded and the consummate state (full of injustices) appeared in its final, irrevocable form?

> So many things rest under consummate
> Justice as though trumpets purified law,
> Spikenard were the real essence of remorse.

Here emotions are merely things (like spikenard) and disposed of remorselessly. The victims "dispose" themselves once again to the axe:

> these dispose themselves to receive each
> Pentecostal blow from axe or seraph . . .

Here the dispensers of justice terrorize humans for sport. As in the Third Reich, to mention one example, language is manipulated to dispose real emotions and to motivate atrocities. The distance between the articulate propagandist's loom, on which he weaves captivating arguments, and the torturer's rack is short. "Funeral Music" is composed of many voices, and one of them is the messianic terrorist's, who (like Hitler or Goebbels) employs oratorical devices to seduce the innocent and ignorant into hell. He renders his victims pitiful but shows no pity:

> When we chant
> 'Ora, ora pro nobis' it is not
> Seraphs who descend to pity but ourselves.
> Those righteously-accused those vengeful
> Racked on articulate looms indulge us
> With lingering shows of pain, a flagrant
> Tenderness of the damned for their own flesh . . .

The damned value their flesh; the transcendental seraphs do not. Those who believe they serve God ("I believe," Hitler said, "it was the will of God to send a boy from here into the Reich"[33]), when hailed as supreme powers ("ora, ora pro nobis"), consign multitudes to infernos of their own making.

The relationship between the highest and the lowest, the ruler and the ruled, typifies a more familiar relationship in "Funeral Music," namely that between father and son. Father-and-son relations run through *Henry VI* like leitmotifs, and Shakespeare intimates that the wars result from family bonds upset or broken. To dramatize the Battle of Towton, for example, he presents a parricide from one stage door and a father who has killed his son from the opposite door (Part 3, II, v). In "Funeral Music," father and child also fall asunder. The poet regards childhood, as Wordsworth and Blake did, as a period of Adamic namings and visionary gleams, but he does not sentimentalize the mercilessness that also exists in childhood:

> My little son, when you could command marvels
> Without mercy, outstare the wearisome
> Dragon of sleep, I rejoiced above all—
> A stranger well-received in your kingdom.
> On those pristine fields I saw humankind
> As it was named by the Father; fabulous
> Beasts rearing in stillness to be blessed.

The child's kingdom, unlike the snowy, torchlit palace of the intellect and soul, is sleepless, bestial, and pristine. Recollections of Eden, however, bring with them recollections of falls. The Wordsworthian child falls from his visionary paradise; the Blakean child plucks the fruit of the mystery tree and falls into an awareness of paralyzing contraries.

> The world's real cries reached there, turbulence
> From remote storms, rumour of solitudes,
> A composed mystery. And so it ends.
> Some parch for what they were; others are made

> Blind to all but one vision, their necessity
> To be reconciled. I believe in my
> Abandonment, since it is what I have.

Wordsworth "parched" for what he was and his poetic powers dried up. Blake, with imperious single-mindedness, "blind to all but one vision," strove for the reconciliation of Albion's divided self. More modest and more difficult, perhaps, Hill aims to heal psychic losses by expressing them as they are.

Divided against himself in contemplation, Hill wonders why he tortures himself with questions of power and war. Was such tergiversation the undoing of Henry VI?

> 'Prowess, vanity, mutual regard,
> It seemed I stared at them, they at me.
> That was the gorgon's true and mortal gaze:
> Averted conscience turned against itself.'
> A hawk and a hawk-shadow.

Too much self-examination can turn the acting mind to stone. To avert paralysis, the Perseus hero mirrors his own penchant for self-mirroring and then, hawk that he is, goes to battle. Hill conjoins spiritual and martial combat again to underscore their complicity:

> 'At noon,
> As the armies met, each mirrored the other;
> Neither was outshone. So they flashed and vanished
> And all that survived them was the stark ground
> Of this pain.

After the ecstatic cry in the sexual ditch and the painful cry in Eden, a redemptive cry intimates relief from pain. But it is an illusion; only pain and carnage remain:

> I made no sound, but once
> I stiffened as though a remote cry
> Had heralded my name. It was nothing . . .
> Reddish ice tinged the reeds; dislodged, a few
> Feathers drifted across; carrion birds
> Strutted upon the armour of the dead.

The ludicrously strutting birds, the new militia, are a flock of merciless vultures. Less self-conscious (and less self-destructive) than their human victims, they survive them.

The poem begins with ghosts exchanging benedictions in memory's cave. It ends with communication between ghosts in the same cave, but now the ghost talk is aimed at the world outside:

> Not as we are but as we must appear,
> Contractual ghosts of pity; not as we
> Desire life but as they would have us live,
> Set apart in timeless colloquy:
> So it is required; so we bear witness,
> Despite ourselves, to what is beyond us,
> Each distant sphere of harmony forever
> Poised, unanswerable.

Like Eliot's coda at the end of the *Four Quartets*, which draws poetic and historic fragments into "the crowned knot of fire," Hill's end envisions a "sphere of harmony," but one which promises little consolation. If "the existing order is complete before the new work arrives,"[34] like a poised sphere, a dialogue with the dead is comparable to shouting at planets on a windy night. Hill yearns to commune with both living and dead; as it is, he finds himself in "no man's dwelling-place," the ghostly cave between the two.

Solemnly, bitterly, he finishes his meditation with a spate of conundrums. Are the artists really ghosts, or do they just appear so to the public? If they inhabit timeless zones, brood on phantasmal creations, and talk only to themselves, is it simply because ordinary folk have evicted them from the common-day world? Are their failures compensated for in language? Hill answers:

> If it is without
> Consequence when we vaunt and suffer, or
> If it is not, all echoes are the same
> In such eternity.

If eternity is indifferent

> Then tell me, love,
> How that should comfort us—or anyone
> Dragged half-unnerved out of this worldly place,
> Crying to the end 'I have not finished'.

In his "Preface" to *Poems* (1920), Wilfred Owen declared that his subject was war "and the pity of war" but that his elegies were "in no sense consolatory."[35] Hill's elegies, also, are not consolatory. Opposed to Platonic and Christian notions of redemptive ends, Hill finishes his poem with a cry for finality that never comes. His denial of transcendental resolutions and perfect completions, paradoxically, is not an affirmation of the imperfect, unfinished world either. His last cry is a call for human contact, for renewed love between estranged parties, and for an end to history's wars, which, he knows, will never end. The poet never finishes his poem, Auden remarked; he simply abandons it. In poetry as in history (the Wars of the Roses ended one era but began another), endings are at best tentative resolutions. Hill's poem articulates a continuous music, a dialectic of stresses and calms, of atrocious crimes and penitential redemptions, and it painfully affirms an anguished persistence.

"The Songbook of Sebastian Arrurruz"

For the poet eager to be "simple, sensuous, and passionate," the lyric tradition of the Renaissance and twentieth-century Spain offers many stirring and supportive models. Hill turned to Spain to garner material for his "Songbook," the group of eleven poems in prose and verse which end *King Log*. Although the Spanish sources remain intentionally obscure, the collection resembles the *cancioneros* or songbooks of sacred and profane love lyrics popular in Spain's Golden Age. These songbooks developed from earlier Castilian love poems, whose notable virtues were a simple vocabulary and a narrow range of rhetorical devices, chief among them oxymoron, antithesis, and polyptoton (repetition of a word or phrase). Applied to crisis, as R. O. Jones says, they were "expressive of the tormented obsession of the lover, helpless in the grip of contradictions, willing his own martyrdom but yearning for release, thrown from extreme to extreme of joy and pain, hope and despair."[36]

Like his Spanish ancestors who wrote of their excruciating romances in sincere, untrammeled language, Arrurruz (Hill's Spanish spokesman) is both lyricist and martyr of love. His sacrifices so exhaust him that his life as a poet, as well as his life as a person, is near collapse. Having lost his wife and mistress, he finds other human contact impossible or repugnant and gradually gives way to despair. He produces nearly a dozen jeweled lyrics, but their anachronistic passion is entirely for a sensuality now dead. His present life is a memory of "circumstantial disasters," whose fragments he determines to put into some sort of coherent shape.

But who is Sebastian Arrurruz? Are his poems originals, translations, or Hill's own? Hill guards his secrets by saying that *"The Songbook of Sebastian Arrurruz* represents the work of an apocryphal Spanish poet. Various *Cancioneros (Songbooks)* are referred to in bibliographies of Spanish poetry. The Arrurruz poems contain no allusion to any actual person, living or dead" (KL, p. 70). In his interview with Haffenden, Hill was more expansive:

> My main inspiration for the idea was in the work of Antonio Machado, who had created an "apocryphal professor" called Juan de Mareina and an imaginary poet-philosopher called Abel Martín. I gave Arrurruz the chronology 1868–1922, which enabled him to celebrate the centenary of his birth on the date of publication of my second book, which was advantageous to both of us (we shared a celebration party), and also enabled him to die on the very threshold of modernity, without having had the advantage of reading *The Waste Land* or *Ulysses*. Arrurruz is a shy sensualist with a humour that could be said to balance the sensuality . . . (VP, p. 95)

Like Eliot's Prufrock, Pound's Mauberley, Joyce's Dedalus, or Berryman's Henry, Hill's Arrurruz is a persona that never exactly mirrors its author. Unlike Lowell's *Imitations*, which Hill lauded as one of his "most resolute and fruitful methods"[37] two years before beginning "The Songbook," Hill's poems are fabrications without originals. Themes and tones from Spanish Renaissance lyrics, as well as from Petrarchan sonnets that influenced them, may be detected in Hill's "Songbook," but they are merely echoes.

According to Hill, Arrurruz belongs to the old line; he is a poet who straddles, with noticeable pain, the idealism of the nineteenth century and the disillusionment and despair of the twentieth. We are led to assume that he has remained innocent of the upheavals of modernism, but his method of composition (resembling a collage) bears many resemblances to work done in the period surrounding the First World War. Arrurruz's ribald humor and linguistic playfulness are reminiscent of Joyce's. His personality, as with many of Joyce's characters, may be conjured etymologically from his name. As Sebastian, he is a martyr, related to the third-century Sebastian shot full of arrows for converting Roman soldiers to Christianity. Hill begins the poem with Sebastian at the age of Christ when he died, thirty-three, and makes Arrurruz's deaths and resurrections imitate His. Arrurruz's desire to sink his roots into tradition and earth is revealed in his surname, which derives from the Spanish for rice, *arroz*. Also embedded in his name is the word *arrows*, just as Roman arrows were once embedded in Sebastian and Cupid's arrows in Arrurruz. Suffering the wounds of love and their obsessive memories on sleepless nights, Arrurruz searches for a cure through writing. He is like the Spanish mystics St. John of the Cross and St. Teresa, who composed poems to relieve their "wounds of love," but he is also like the American Indians, who once cured arrow wounds with a salve made from the plant arrowroot. A civilized, scholarly man, Arrurruz traces his lineage to Ararat (with playful euphony), and he travels there to survey the origins and failures of civilization. Like Pound and Eliot, Arrurruz dreams of culture revitalizing itself but finds the ruins—caused by Turkish massacres and World War I—depressingly intractable.

Arrurruz's "Songbook" begins with an imitation of Petrarch's sonnets to Laura as well as modern poems about European desolation. Like Petrarch, Hill announces the number of years elapsed since his beloved's departure and plunges into inveterate gloom:

> Ten years without you. For so it happens.
> Days make their steady progress, a routine
> That is merciful and attracts nobody.
>
> Already, like a disciplined scholar,
> I piece fragments together, past conjecture
> Establishing true sequences of pain;
>
> For so it is proper to find value
> In a bleak skill, as in the thing restored:
> The long-lost words of choice and valediction.

Ten years before "Arrurruz," Hill wrote "Asmodeus," a poem which ended with a broken relationship and a valedictory farewell to a lover. Now, with "the rending pain of re-enactment," he shores up memories of lost love. His "bleak skill" (his writing) restores to consciousness words which will ultimately extricate him from amorous confusion. "The long-lost words of choice and valediction," when resurrected, remind him that he is still free to choose and act.

Dipping into the quick of past wounds, Arrurruz, like Hill in many other poems, debates proper and improper ways of expressing them. Shall he retain discipline and disdain, so as to keep down as well as heighten his explosive memories? In his "Coplas," traditional forms in which lovers serenade each other, the poet writes with sardonic stoicism not of felicitous trysts and serenades in the night but of lovers abrasively grieving over separation. Baldly possessive, he juggles the idea of possession in such a way that it finally appears as if he wants to lose what he has never possessed (his lover). He mocks his nostalgia for sensual romance but then mocks his mockery.

Struggling to remain well-mannered in extreme anguish and anger, however, he fails to exercise a Sebastian-like composure on his cross. As the poem progresses, the inner battle is fought between what the poet envisions as the masculine and feminine principles entrenched in his own personality and culture. The conflict is between speech, which he associates with femininity, and writing, which he believes is masculine. Arrurruz writes while his wife speaks, and even when he speaks, he preserves the scholarly exactitude and abrupt discourse of his writing. While his writing and speech are fractured monologues, weighted with lengthy, contemplative pauses, her speech is natural, unreflective, smoothly-flowing, like the water that bubbles from her fountain later in the poem. While he dreams and withdraws from the daily social world of trivia and chat, she burrows more deeply into it. While he is the snow on Ararat, cold and forbidding, glittering high above the world, she is the ripe flower and warm cypress that blossoms in the valley below. He abstains from abundant sexuality; she indulges in it. He stays at home, making metaphors that appease his desire for beauty; she roams outside, shamelessly lusting and loving. Arrurruz is as barren as a desert. She is as fertile as the earth after rain. He is Monsieur Teste to her Madame Emilie. He has made of his mind a house of mirrors, as Valéry says of Teste, and now lives in it by himself. Teste's wife finds her husband barricaded behind walls that love can no longer penetrate. Arrurruz is possessed with Teste's passion to acknowledge himself simply as he is, "without omissions, pretences, or indulgence,"[38] and does so in the same haphazard form of letters, recorded conversations, and poetic prose.

When Arrurruz observes the portrait of a saint in the middle of the poem, he enviously imagines himself metamorphosed into ascetic artifice. His wife, however, wants to escape the rigors of artifice and vacation in wind and sun. For Arrurruz, writing alienates a person from everything in the world; for his wife speaking is a form of sociability. Writing for him demands repression of powerful instincts; speech for her requires spontaneity and a degree of recklessness. Throughout the poem, the dialectic of writing and speech, the imaginative life and the social life, defines and exacerbates their relationship. Although Arrurruz would like to unify oppositions, in the end he fails to. He imagines writing and speech as poetic figures and wonders if they will come together in a happy marriage, in himself, in his poem, and in the world outside:

> It is to him I write, it is to her
> I speak in contained silence. Will they be touched
> By the unfamiliar passion between them?

In the end, they do not touch.

Like Petrarch, Arrurruz indulges in a belated and finally posthumous dream correspondence with his departed lover. Yet he is neither wholly dead nor wholly somnolent. He is bitterly cognizant of the sexual affairs of others and of his own subliminal affairs:

> What other men do with other women
> Is for me neither orgy nor sacrament
> Nor a language of foreign candour
>
> But is mere occasion or chance distance
> Out of which you might move and speak my name
> As I speak yours, bargaining with sleep's
>
> Miscellaneous gods for as much
> As I can have: an alien landscape,
> The dream where you are always to be found.

Arrurruz begins like a level-headed man of the world but soon becomes a desolate insomniac. In the first stanza, he dismisses "sacred" and "profane" love (love as "sacrament" or "orgy") as old-fashioned taxonomies. Love and sex are for him mundane, fortuitous, a matter of chance affairs rather than premeditated commitments. *Candor* in Latin means whiteness and purity, and

Arrurruz declares he is not innocent. In fact, he is well schooled in the language of love, especially in its impurities—its innuendos, hyperboles, clichés, and obvious lies. That Arrurruz regards sexual intercourse as linguistic discourse, however, is a measure of his abstract, writerly imagination, and of his predisposition to see all activities (like many modern philosophers) as functions of language. He is professorial and ascetic. Although he wants to regain contact with his estranged wife, he succeeds only in the silence of a dream.

In Ovid's *Metamorphoses*, the landscape of dream and the gods of sleep are charmingly described in the tale of Ceyx and Alcyone, the two lovers who separate when Ceyx, the husband, embarks on a sea journey and drowns. Announcing the death of the husband to Alcyone, Morpheus, god of sleep, whom Arrurruz supplicates, assumes the husband's shape and appears before her in a dream. Waking, she travels to the sea, finds her husband's corpse and attempts suicide but suddenly finds herself alongside her husband, metamorphosed into a bird. Myths of separation, return, and metamorphosis are on Arrurruz's mind when he wakes. But it is not into a halcyon day of benign transformations that he wakes. Remembered sorrows return to him, not metamorphosed into conjugal birds but into hard, didactic facts. Arrurruz bitterly derides the myth of return and reconciliation as "A workable fancy" which never works:

>   Old petulant
> Sorrow comes back to us, metamorphosed
> And semi-precious. Fortuitous amber.
> As though this recompensed our deprivation.
> See how each fragment kindles as we turn it,
>   At the end, into the light of appraisal.

In a moment of petulant reflection, Arrurruz appraises the detritus of his life preserved (like old insects) in amber and, like amber, cut into semi-precious gems (the "abrasive gems" of the second section). In his art, which captures and shapes his fortuitous disasters, he finds little to praise.

Having lost his original happiness, Arrurruz broods on the ludicrous economy of his life. Has he gained anything from his losses? Has he forfeited everything to be poet and scholar? At times, he regards the loss of sexual life as a gain for his poetry but shows little joy over this apparent compensation. In a passage that resembles Eliot's "What the Thunder Said" in *The Waste Land*, where rain finally inseminates the sterile earth without resuscitating the poet, Arrurruz acknowledges and satirizes his stormy, unfulfilled desires:

> Love, oh my love, it will come
> Sure enough! A storm
> Broods over the dry earth all day.
> At night the shutters throb in its downpour.
>
> The metaphor holds; is a snug house.
> You are outside, lost somewhere. I find myself
> Devouring verses of stranger passion
> And exile. The exact words
>
> Are fed into my blank hunger for you.

The vegetal realm of rain and earth is the provenance of Arrurruz's wife, the *Gea Mater*, and having contained her chaotic energies in his metaphor, he keeps her at a safe distance. He has lost her but has found himself, and he has briefly found the words for "the unfamiliar passion between them." He has failed to consummate his sexual desires, but his failure has opened a way for fresh poems.

A shy, sensitive man, whose liaisons with women threaten him, Arrurruz contemplates abandoning sexual love altogether. He imagines refining himself out of existence, like young Stephen Dedalus, of becoming a rarefied aesthete or saint. He yearns for reconciliation between warring desires, even if that means becoming androgynous. He wants to pull love's arrows from his corpse and convert his turbulent marriage into a ceremony as elaborately stylized and passionless as an illuminated manuscript.

> I imagine, as I imagine us
> Each time more stylized more lovingly
> Detailed, that I am not myself
> But someone I might have been: sexless,
> Indulgent about art, relishing
> Let us say the well-schooled
> Postures of *St. Anthony* or *St. Jerome,*
> Those peaceful hermaphrodite dreams
> Through which the excess of memory
> Pursues its own abstinence.

Although Arrurruz would like to transmogrify his life into art and, once out of nature, never take the form of any natural thing, he finally rejects (as Yeats partly does) total transcendence. He may pursue abstinence in art, but the weight of memory always brings him, like gravity, back to earthly imbroglios.

Nostalgically, dreamily, Arrurruz considers a rapprochement with his wife and a new, shared life of sexualized speech, linguistic sex, and quiet but passionate communication. This, however, is the world of the "would have been," which points to one end, his present anguish:

> There would have been things to say, quietness
> That could feed on our lust, refreshed
> Trivia, the occurrences of the day;
> And at night my tongue in your furrow.

Silence in which to write (to "refresh" the "tongue" of the tribe) is Arrurruz's paradise. Again he imagines relationships in linguistic terms. Poetic verse, its name derived from the plow "reversing" at the end of the field and carving a new furrow, is Arrurruz's only satisfaction after abandoning related pleasures with his wife. Other women, Arrurruz complains, are linguistically unappealing:

> Without you I am mocked by courtesies
> And chat, where satisfied women push
> Dutifully towards some unneeded guest
> Desirable features of conversation.
> [1922]

Postscripted 1922, the year *The Waste Land* appeared and the year Arrurruz died, this may be taken as the poet's nemesis and last testament, his final descent into a linguistically barren society where poetic delicacies and fastidious exactitudes have vanished.

Although Arrurruz dies from this life, he is granted (it would seem from the chronological arrangement of his letters) a posthumous, ambulatory existence. He walks among the dead to examine their ruins. He journeys back to the origins of his life and culture, and, like the medieval Christians who made pilgrimage to Armenia (as in *Piers Plowman*), he ends at Mt. Ararat. From there, he gazes at the Tigris and Euphrates river basin, the Fertile Crescent, and, as a postdiluvian and postlapsarian man, recollects the original sins of history. Temporally and geographically remote, he sends his wife a "Letter" which glimpses the genocide and deportation inflicted by the Turks on the Armenians.

> So, remotely, in your part of the world:
> the ripe glandular blooms, and cypresses
> shivering with heat (which we have borne
> also, in our proper ways) I turn my mind
> towards delicate pillage, the provenance
> of shards glazed and unglazed, the three
> kinds of surviving grain. I hesitate amid
> circumstantial disasters. I gaze at the
>   authentic dead.

Civilization's provenance (origin) is both agricultural and artistic, but for Arrurruz it is now a dump. Pottery shards and winnowed grains lay about, synecdoches of old cultures. As in "An

Ark on the Flood," Hill's undergraduate elegy, Ararat is not a permanent haven of vision but a summit where civilizations rise and collapse.

Only ghosts frequent Ararat now. With the Great War behind him, Arrurruz utters a Blakean song of experience, a "Song from Armenia." Beyond Ararat's leaves, snow, and shadows, he sees nothing transcendent or even living. If Blake imagined angels singing hosannas behind the leaves, Hill sees only a desiccated woman sucking at a fountain. The daughters of inspiration have dried up into the daughters of memory. The fountain bubbles only a hand's breadth above the rim. Images of life frozen, darkened, and shriveled, and memories of a gone world of sensual delight are the arrows in Arrurruz's corpse. Leaves and snow emblematize his death. He says with melancholy terseness:

> Roughly-silvered leaves that are the snow
> On Ararat seen through those leaves.
> The sun lays down a foliage of shade.
>
> A drinking-fountain pulses its head
> Two or three inches from the troughed stone.
> An old woman sucks there, gripping the rim.
>
> Why do I have to relive, even now,
> Your mouth, and your hand running over me
> Deft as a lizard, like a sinew of water?

About the same time (1919–20), Ezra Pound was making similar observations about ruined romance, comparing civilization, in "Hugh Selwyn Mauberley," to "an old bitch gone in the teeth." Several years later, in 1928, Osip Mandelshtam would be exiled to Armenia and witness similar collapses.

Arrurruz's penultimate letter, dated 1921 (the year before his death), is more deeply rooted in the living world but pertains to a former house of fiction, a life-in-death of writing and silence. Addressed "To His Wife," the letter again recounts Arrurruz's failure to achieve conjugal intimacy. His wife, he states with ironic insight, would rather have real sex in a real house than witness the linguistic conjugations and poetic climaxes arrived at in the imagination. She finds herself a foreign guest in Arrurruz's house of language. The poet explains:

> You ventured occasionally—
> As though this were another's house—
> Not intimate but an acquaintance
> Flaunting her modest claim; like one
> Idly commiserated by new-mated
> Lovers rampant in proper delight
> When all their guests have gone.

Although the written evidence proves that rampant desire still exists in Arrurruz, it remains sequestered in his head. His wife, not well-acquainted with his interiors, somehow probes them but is only "idly commiserated" by what she finds.

A brief coda ends Arrurruz's "Songbook" with a witty, despairing summary of his losses and Pyrrhic gains. It brings together many of the disparate elements which have assailed him throughout: speech and writing, community and solitude, waking and dreaming, nature and artifice, sexuality and abstinence, memory and forgetfulness, public propriety and private abandon. His battles terminate in gloom:

> Scarcely speaking: it becomes as a
> Coolness between neighbours. Often
> There is this orgy of sleep. I wake
> To caress propriety with odd words
> And enjoy abstinence in a vocation
> Of now-almost-meaningless despair.

If love of others and vigorous speech are twin roots of civilized community, Arrurruz's roots, although withered, have not died completely. The heat has gone out of his relations, but by retaining a sense of ironic propriety, he still enjoys his daily rhythm of waking, working, and sleeping, which connects him to the larger rhythm of society and cosmos. His death occurs in the middle of the poem, his death of love ten years before the poem begins, but Arrurruz lives on, a broken man, "feeding / A little life with dried tubers." Not wholly devoid of passion, he looks upon his somatic dilapidation as an "orgy of sleep."

In the review of Lowell's *Imitations* that preceded the "Songbook," Hill indirectly reveals a good deal about Arrurruz's desolation and its relation to his imaginative life. By way of a discussion of Leopardi, whose poems appear in Lowell's book, Hill says:

The terrors of Leopardi's life are made to obtrude, in an exaggerated way, upon the plain statements of the poem, so that where he originally wrote "your mortal life" he now says:
"this life overhung by death"
and his "fascinating studies" in the "bolted room" are suggestive of onanistic excitement.

One would accept this as a positive view of a life so spiritually and physically desolate as Leopardi's; and as a restatement of the romantic hypothesis that poetry is a substitute for the poet's personal deficiencies.[39]

Arrurruz is another Leopardi. Out of his failures and fears he pieces together a faceted poem of romantic hopes and tragic disillusionments. Despair has become so typical of his life that, he jokingly declares, the word *despair* has become a cliché. But his estrangement from present life has advantages; it allows him the freedom to give significant shape to his past. That poetry leaves him cold makes his despair more complete, but it also makes for what Yeats called the "cold snows of a dream" ("Meditations in Time of Civil War"), in which he can at least imagine a vestigial passion. Desolation makes new creations possible. Hill's poems, in their wit and clarity, confer upon Arrurruz's suffering an aura of triumphant gloom.

4 / THE ANGLO-SAXON HERITAGE

Mercian Hymns

Precedents

Mercian Hymns is a more intense onslaught upon historical realities than Hill's previous books. Nowhere else does he dig up and "ex-plane" his personal and cultural roots with such sustained animosity and delight. Committed to scholarly fact, he simultaneously revels in myth, fantasy, and satire. The *Hymns*, like *The Waste Land* and *The Cantos*, make extensive use of old books but are refreshingly original. As Hill glances over his shoulder at the past, his despair serves only to sharpen his sense of irony and comedy. His poem is an indictment, but often a funny one, of a particularly English inheritance.

King Offa, the first Anglo-Saxon king strong enough to unify England and claim the title *Rex Totius Anglorum Patriae*, is the archetypal ruler in *Mercian Hymns*, a Jehovah-figure who overlooks and participates in the offenses and virtues of his world. Hill uses Offa the way Joyce uses Finnegan, as a mythical body which contains all history and all geography but which also encompasses a specific location, namely England's West Midlands (the modern name for the ancient kingdom of Mercia ruled by Offa). The poem is a compendium of autobiographical and historical incidents which unites Hill's childhood during the Second World War and Offa's brutal but accomplished career during the second half of the eighth century. Like William Carlos Williams's *Paterson* and Olson's *Maximus Poems, Mercian Hymns* repudiates ordinary limitations of time and space so that the legendary Offa can embody "the presiding genius of the West Midlands . . . from the middle of the eighth century until the middle of the twentieth" (*MH*), which was when Hill left Bromsgrove in Worcestershire for Oxford.

The metrical and narrative freedom which Olson and Williams favor, however, differs from Hill's compressed, rhythmical prose. While *Paterson* and *The Maximus Poems* are thoroughly American and find their closest ally in Whitman, Hill's *Hymns* go to American expatriates, Eliot and Pound, for models. With them, Hill renounces Whitman's affirmative ebullience and replaces it with a more refined and cautious discrimination. All three stand by the political and moral intelligence that makes distinctions, that proscribes and prescribes. *Mercian Hymns* is a diagnosis of a king and his nation (Offa *is* the English nation), and Hill is the surgeon who appears in many guises—usually with spade, plow, sword, axe, chisel, or pen—to cut open the body, discover the sickness, and administer the cure.

As an emblem of personal and cultural disease, Offa bears many resemblances to Eliot's wounded Fisher King. In section V, he is described as "a king of / some kind, a prodigy, a maimed one." He suffers many wounds (marital turmoil, deracination, mental breakdown, wars), and as a vegetation deity, he suffers the collapse of the natural environment at year's end. He desperately needs an infusion of spring-like vigor before he and his lands can be restored to order. Jessie Weston says of the Fisher King that "the story postulates a close connection between the vitality of a certain king, and the prosperity of his kingdom; the forces of the ruler being weakened or destroyed, by wound, weakness, old age, or death, the land becomes waste, and the task of the hero is that of restoration."[1] Offa may be a mythical king, but he retains a much more political complexion than Eliot's kings in *The Waste Land*. He appears at his office desk, signing charters and laws, on the battlefield, fighting Welsh invaders, in his gardens, examining food supplies, on the shore, greeting Charlemagne and his French armies, in Europe on diplomatic and religious pilgrimage, and under his lamp, inspecting his famous coinage. Eliot and Hill, however, share the conviction that the standards of culture, and specifically European and English culture, are in decline. For Hill, however, that is a permanent condition except during those rare moments when the forces of decadence are overcome.

When asked by Haffenden about the genesis of his *Hymns*, Hill was quick to distinguish his prose poems from others by saying that "they're versets of rhythmical prose. The rhythm and cadence are far more of a pitched and tuned chant than I think one normally associates with the prose poem. I designed the appearance on the page in the form of versets. The reason they take the form they do is because at a very early stage the words and phrases began to group themselves in this way" (*VP*, pp. 93–94). Although Hill's versets may have shaped themselves, they were compelled to do so in part by past models, one of the most important ones being *Sweet's Anglo-Saxon Reader*, which contains six passages from the Roman Psalter and Hymns translated from Latin into the Anglo-Saxon dialect Old Mercian and entitled "Mercian Hymns." When the Psalter, with its interlinear Anglo-Saxon glosses, was compiled during the early ninth century by a scribe at Canterbury (shortly after Offa's reign), Anglo-Saxon prose was just beginning to assert itself. In the seventh and eighth centuries, when *Beowulf*, "The Seafarer," and "The Dream of the Rood" were composed, English literature was mainly oral poetry. The slow transformation from oral poetry to written prose began with the laws of Ethelbert of Kent (around 600), Ine of Wessex (in the late 600s), and Offa in the late 700s. Although Offa's laws are lost, Hill fancifully reconstructs them in several sections of his poem. He also alludes to Offa's charters, written in a kind of prose poetry during the late 700s, and to Alfred the Great and his famous ninth-century translation of Boethius's *The Consolation of Philosophy*, which established English prose as a conscious literary mode.

Hill's *Hymns* reconstitute this transitional moment in English letters through overt allusion and oblique adaptation. Like Anglo-Saxon poems and early poeticized prose, the *Mercian Hymns* abound in clanging, alliterated vowels and consonants, weldings of Latinate Christianity and Germanic paganism, abrupt, ungrammatical howls and suave, legalistic declarations. The original manuscripts of Anglo-Saxon poetry, in fact, were first written in continuous prose and only later broken into parallel columns. Anglo-Saxon poets juxtaposed two half-lines, in which the first letter of the first stressed word in the second half-line alliterated with a word in the original half-line. Hill echoes the sounds of early English poems:

> We have a kitchen-garden riddled with toy-shards,
>   with splinters of habitation. The children shriek
> and scavenge, play havoc. They incinerate boxes,
> rags and old tyres. They haul a sodden log, hung
> with soft shields of fungus, and launch it upon
>   the flames.

This section, "Offa's Laws," refers to Offa's legal prose, just as the earlier description of Offa, "contractor of the desirable new estates," remembers his prose in charters. The image of children launching a diseased log in a ruined garden recalls the funeral and ship burial in *Beowulf* of Scyld Shefing (lines 36–44), a ritual Offa was probably familiar with, since *Beowulf* was possibly composed by another Mercian and may have been dedicated to Offa's court. Hill, as the later Mercian scribe, muses on vestiges of Anglo-Saxon culture—heroic deeds, ornamented ships, treasure hoards, and dolorous ceremonies—but as they reappear in the games of children. He discloses continuities, but with quiet irony rather than indulgent nostalgia. The childish barbarisms of his Anglo-Saxon forbears loom large against the background of their ornate artifacts.

Poetic rhythm and rhythmical prose, Hill affirms in his essay "Redeeming the Time," can act as a seismograph, "registering, mimetically, deep shocks of recognition" (*LL*, p. 87). *Mercian Hymns* celebrates language's capacity to record past upheavals in the abruptness of its rhythms. It also indicts language for causing such upheavals. Hill's first two sections, subtitled "The Naming of Offa," describe both King Offa and his word as earth shakers and earth movers. Offa builds dikes and monasteries and wages wars, but so does language. The word is spade and sword, a digger of etymological and cultural roots and a warrior that severs those roots.

Like David Jones in *The Anathemata* and *In Parenthesis*, Hill proposes in *Mercian Hymns* "to make a shape out of the very things of which one is oneself made."[2] And, like Jones, Hill takes all of European civilization as his provenance. If Jones's fragments are scattered, Hill's versets by comparison are fastidiously ordered and symmetrically arranged, like pictures in a gallery. St.-John Perse's sequence of prose poems, *Anabasis*, may have contributed to the craft of the *Hymns*. What Eliot said of Perse's poem is equally true of Hill's, namely that "the justification of such abbreviated method is that the sequence of images coincides and concentrates into one intense impression of barbaric civilization. The reader has to allow the images to fall into his memory successively without questioning the reasonableness of each at the moment; so that, at the end, a total effect is produced."[3] Through hammering rhythms, Perse tracks the course of a primitive Asiatic conqueror (like Offa) as he builds cities, mixes with his brawny compatriots, and traverses deserts to found new civilizations (as *anabainein*, going up or forward, means in Greek). His lust for travel and identification with elemental processes resembles Offa's. Hill ends his poem, like Perse, not with a grand resolution but a new faring forth, not with Christian redemption but with Adam leaving behind red mud and coins— the tokens of the original sin out of which he was formed and of the sins he commits while forming his nation.

Hill found a less modern precedent for *Mercian Hymns* in the Latin prose hymns or canticles of the early Christian Church. Frederick Brittain's *Penguin Book of Latin Verse*, with Saint Nicetas's famous "Te Deum" (the "canticle in rhythmical prose . . . used in Christian worship from the fourth century to the present day"⁴), is mentioned in Hill's notes. The "Te Deum" and other prose canticles are derived from the Jewish psalter (as Sweet's "Mercian Hymns" are derived from the Roman psalter) and deploy a swaying, incantatory line broken into half-lines for hypnotic effect. Brittain observes that "as the Jewish psalter was the sole hymn-book of the early church, it is not surprising that the "Te Deum" is characterized throughout by the parallelism which is the basis of Hebrew poetry. Another striking feature of the canticle is that most of the lines in its first three sections end in one of the three varieties of the rhythmical *cursus*."⁵ Hill, on the other hand, does not use parallelism or set patterns of rhythmical stress (cursus) with any regularity, but echoes of Hebrew rhythms resonate among Hill's Latin, Anglo-Saxon, and modern phrases.

Hill alters his paradigms for ironic effect. While the "Te Deum" celebrates the virtues of God the Father, *Mercian Hymns* is an "objective correlative for the inevitable feelings of love and hate which any man or woman must feel for the *patria*" (*VP*, p. 94). The beginning of "Hymn VI," "The Childhood of Offa," plays upon Sweet's *Canticum Deuteronomii in Die Sabba [ti]*, the Song of Moses (translated from the "Old Latin" Bible into Old English by a Mercian). In this biblical passage, Moses praises God, the rock, for sustaining Jacob in the desert and wilderness, but then laments man's subsequent disobediences:

> As an eagle stirreth up her nest,
> fluttereth over her young,
> spreadeth abroad her wings, taketh them,
> beareth them on her wings:
> *so* the LORD alone did lead him,
> and *there was* no strange god with him.
> He made him ride on the high places of the earth,
> that he might eat the increase of the fields;
> and he made him to suck honey out of the rock,
> and oil out of the flinty rock.
> (Deut. 32, 11–13)

In Hill's modern English, biblical events appear metamorphosed. Jacob is the bestial child (young Offa and young Hill) and more beast than human. He digs in the wild for roots and is enthralled by strange gods:

> The princes of Mercia were badger and raven. Thrall
> to their freedom, I dug and hoarded. Orchards
> fruited above clefts. I drank from honeycombs of
> chill sandstone.

The eagle (*earn* in the Anglo-Saxon version) is a Machiavellian raven-prince; the burgeoning fields (*cennende londa*) are the frutiful orchards; the honeyed stone (*hunig of stāne*) is watery sandstone.

In his essay "Redeeming the Time," Hill praises George Eliot for her "sense of traditional rhythmic life," and goes on to explain how liturgy and liturgical prose (as in his *Hymns*) can reunite the uprooted soul with the rhythms of body, nature, and culture:

The collects of the Anglican Church are composed of liturgical prose; they could properly be said to possess rhythm, though not metre. Here again, however, "familiar rhythm" is both liturgical and extraliturgical, telling of a rhythm of social duties, rites, ties and obligations from which an individual severs himself or herself at great cost and peril, but implying also the natural sequences of stresses and slacks in the thoughts and acts of a representative human being. (*LL*, p. 89)

For Hill, Offa is the "representative human being" of the Midlands but also an emblem of "social duties, rites, ties and obligations" which Hill seeks to recapture through his rhythmical prose. Hill's *Hymns* recall his early involvement in the church ("I sang in the church choir from about the age of seven until I went up to Oxford," he said in an interview [*VP*, p. 76]) and conjure up a whole world of childhood associations. Like George Eliot, Hill "reads" his Midlands landscape for its historical significance. His attitude towards past and present is radically conservative, if that term is taken to mean conservationist. It is concerned with establishing fertile relations with the soil from which he sprang. It is not to be confused with modern-day interpretations of *'conservatism'.* Hill's sympathies are with the radical Tories of another century when he says that "my admiration for Oastler and the whole radical Tory tradition that he represents is considerable: I find it one of the most attractive political traditions of the nineteenth century and something quite apart from what we now know as Conservatism. Modern Conservatism, which is Whiggery rampant, could be beneficially instructed by radical Toryism, but of course won't let itself be. Conservatives conserve nothing" (*VP*, p. 86). The radical Tories, for Hill, stand for moral perception won from a studious examination of the past and directed towards right action in present and future.

For Hill, the past was always a site to excavate. On leaving Bromsgrove for Oxford in 1950, he confessed that "the boy born and brought up in Worcestershire . . . is still to all intents a local boy. He does not, unless he is very unfortunate, lose touch with his home ground. His roots still ache for their soil."[6] Homesick for familiar ways and wary of new ones, Hill returned to his home ground on actual and poetic journeys. With its Anglo-Saxon kings and constabulary fathers, *Mercian Hymns* is another return to the *patria*. These pseudohymns resemble real ones in that they articulate personal grievances and assert that evils recur. Many are confessional, but Hill's method is fundamentally mythic. If he confesses, he does so in the third person, finding for his personal acts correlatives in history and legends. Myth interweaves with fact. Confession, carried to its limit, changes character. Biography becomes myth.

Hill's plot is only loosely chronological. While the first two sections describe "The Naming of Offa" and bear some resemblance to the Christian nativity (an incarnation through words) and the last four sections describe Offa's death, the middle sections shift back and forth between the adulthood and childhood of both Offa and Hill. The collage emphasizes Hill's point that the poetic child often behaves like the political adult. But

Mercian Hymns

in the flux of the poem, demarcations, however shadowy, assert themselves. Sections III to X, with the exception of VIII, illustrate the poet's Worcestershire boyhood in and around pubs, Roman ruins, churches, schools, and home. In the next eight sections, from "Offa's Coins" (section XI) to "Offa's Journey to Rome" (section XVIII), Hill focuses on the ruler's affairs in the state. Offa appears inspecting the nation's coinage, collating its historical and mythical records, punishing criminals, signing laws, dividing up his realm, welcoming diplomats from France, and traveling to Rome. From sections XIX to XXVI, Offa is the older man musing over his photograph album or watching children from his kitchen window repeat the past. He returns to childhood and to England's long history of wars and labor movements, but now with the perspective of a man near death. In the last four sections, entitled "The Death of Offa," Hill describes the comical funeral of Offa but also uses the occasion to remember his parents and grandparents and to consider the future of the nation's "children and our children's children," which he finds increasingly gloomy. Few other English poets have submitted their culture to such an extended interrogation and portrayed the political animal with such persistent insight.

Offa Revealed

Hill begins his *Hymns* as an Anglo-Saxon poet might, with a rhapsodic catalog of Offa's accomplishments. As history books reveal, Offa was a brutal, dilligent, and effective politician who exerted a tremendous influence over the medieval world. An artist of multiple talents, he engineered the monumental dike and ditch between the Dee estuary and the Bristol Channel (running along the Wye River), which protected the Mercian frontiers from Welsh insurgents. An economist, he minted the silver penny and established the basis of a money economy which lasted in England for six hundred years. A good businessman, he enlarged England's commercial trade with Europe.

He was also a patron of monasteries, a friend of the Pope, who made Mercia the seat of an archbishop, a lawmaker, and a writer of charters. Enthroned at Tamworth, the palace of Mercian kings, he is, for Hill, an archetypal king of the sacred grove, a guardian of the "perennial" golden bough made famous by the mythologist James Frazer. Ancient, he is also modern: the guardian of iron bridges and asphalt motorways. Hill celebrates him in a half-serious and half-humorous eulogy:

> King of the perennial holly-groves, the riven sandstone: overlord of the M5: architect of the historic rampart and ditch, the citadel at Tamworth, the summer hermitage in Holy Cross: guardian of the Welsh Bridge and the Iron Bridge: contractor to the desirable new estates: saltmaster: moneychanger: commissioner for oaths: martyrologist: the friend of Charlemagne.

As father and child, political bully and humiliated citizen, mythic body of all history and individual body of the poet, Offa is perplexed by contradictions but, as later hymns demonstrate, can act with unswerving conviction. A brutal animal, he is also a man of graceful culture.

W. F. Bolton, in his *History of Anglo-Latin Literature*, observes that "Offa is a common name,"[7] and in *Mercian Hymns*, Hill makes Offa embody all 'names'. As heir to the Anglo-Saxon poets, Hill confers upon the act of naming and the name itself the utmost significance. His meditation plays upon "Offa" and catalogs the names he conjures up:

> A pet-name, a common name. Best-selling brand, curt graffito. A laugh; a cough. A syndicate. A specious gift. Scoffed-at horned phonograph.

In this fanciful but meaningful elaboration, Offa appears as a domesticated animal (a pet), bound to the laws of human culture, but also a savage (horned) political animal. He possesses the awesome power usually attributed to words in illiterate societies, but he is also a ludicrous and obscene graffito. Like an advertisement for a brand-name product or a best-selling book, he appeals to primordial impulses rather than refined tastes. He is an antiquated phonograph with an amplifying horn and a "scoffed-at horned" scapegoat who arouses laughs and coughs of derision; but he is also a charismatic leader and a phonographic guardian of his tribe's records. (Notice how the sound "Offa" generates "graffito," "laugh," "cough," "scoffed-at," and "Geoffrey".)

As a cunning statesman who disseminates his reputation over all England and most of Europe, Offa is the manager of a syndicate (like Jimmy Hoffa, whose name contains an obvious rhyme). He monopolizes the always available market for illusions and suspended disbeliefs by manipulating language; thus, he controls his people. As tyrant and demagogue, Offa is contemptible (he is "awful" and "offal"). As a bard, he is master of a specious fluency which possesses great emotive power and is entirely captivating. Hill compares the word forged in Offa's imagination and circulated among the crowd to his actual forgery of "Peter's Pence," which was the "specious gift" sent to Pope Hadrian. Hill acknowledges, with the ironic levity of Joyce, that all words are artificial forgeries and designed with great cunning. Hill frequently puns on "graft" and "craft" and "vice" and "device" in order to point out the collusion between the artist and the expert liar. Offa is the "starting-cry of a race" (the English race) and a "name to conjure with," a phrase which Hill redeems from cliché by using it literally. That Offa should amplify historical realities (as the Anglo-Saxon poets certainly did) is both the law and unlawfulness of his art.

Hill revealed his attitude towards Offa in an interview:

My feeling for Offa and Mercia can scarcely be disentangled from my mixed feelings for my own home country of Worcestershire. . . . Offa seems to have been on the whole a rather hateful man who nonetheless created forms of government and coinage which compel one's admiration. . . . The murderous brutality of Offa as a political animal seems again an objective correlative for the ambiguities of English history in general, as a means of trying to encompass and accomodate the early humiliations and fears of one's own childhood and also one's discovery of the tyrannical streak in oneself as a child. Here again one is speaking of those characteristics which one holds in common with one's fellow beings. (*VP*, p. 94)

Myths and mystiques in English culture which glorify childhood, as well as kingship, nature, and language, are the substances of *Mercian Hymns* and are what Hill, through the personality of Offa, continually deflates. Hill exposes kings for what they are and plays their tempestuous inner lives against their regal pomp and ceremony.

The year he commenced writing the *Hymns*, Hill reread Shakespeare's *Cymbeline* and, with regard to its myths of royalty and power, observed that "the world of common observation is one which disobeys at every turn the world of overriding mythology." In *Cymbeline*, Hill argues, Shakespeare opens the imperial palace for common inspection. The errors and sins of royalty (the lifeblood of tragedy) in *Cymbeline* resemble those of common humanity. Kings, both Hill and Shakespeare suggest, suffer ordinary foibles, but this affects how we react to traditional tragedies because "we are involved in a dualistic acceptance of things as they are. Such dualisms seem to avoid the chain of cause and effect which drives the tragedies. They avoid, also, the formal concept of Tragedy in which 'hamartia' indicates the irreparable severing of tragic experience from the normal conduct of life. . . . In the late plays hamartia appears as something integral to the human condition, innate, to be lived with" (*LL*, pp. 62–63). Hill's method of contrasting King Offa with himself and with the transcendent qualities of kings underlines, for satirical rather than tragic purposes, the "strange likeness" between regal and everyday "hamartia."

On Cultured Ground

In Christian hymns, similar events recur, accompanied by appropriate tones: villains harass the innocent; the afflicted plunge into gloom; God listens to their pleas and uplifts them. Laments tend to turn to songs of joy and praise. The *Mercian Hymns* comprise a series of movements which trace sinful falls, descents into underworlds of pain, and subsequent ascents towards redemption. As Aeneas guided Dante over the sloping ground of hell and purgatory towards paradise, illuminating the soul's topography as he went, so Offa leads Hill over the irregular ground of his culture. "Culture," for Hill, resembles the pharmacist's nutrient medium since from it grow both poisonous and healthy fruits. It is capable of both renaissance and decadence. It is a compost heap, full of moldy leaves and worms, a mound of offal (like "Offa" himself), a hoard of soiled coins and root words, but also a city and cultivated garden growing above it.

Among the most important sources of *Mercian Hymns* are T. S. Eliot's *Notes Towards a Definition of Culture* and Matthew Arnold's *Culture and Anarchy*. Hill's poem confronts these with a series of graphic and scurrilous repartees. With his usual avuncular wisdom Arnold recommends "culture as the great help out of our present difficulties; culture being a pursuit of our total perfection by means of getting to know, on all the matters which most concern us, the best which has been thought and said in the world; and through this knowledge, turning a stream of fresh and free thought upon our stock notions and habits."[8] Hill agrees, but his *Hymns* display culture travestied, turned into an avaricious pursuit of military supremacy and monetary gain, with the best minds traduced, the splendors of artifice attacked or decaying. Eliot defined culture in many ways: "the incarnation . . . of the religion of a people," a "way of thinking, feeling and behaving," and "the way of life of a particular people living together in one place,"[9] and maintained that family, school, language, and church were its principal oracles. He called for a stratified society but also for an "ecology of cultures" in which divergent groups "benefiting each other, benefit the whole."[10] He declared, pessimistically, that "our own period is one of decline; that the standards of culture are lower than they were fifty years ago."[11] Hill, however, alters Eliot's prognosis by finding in decadence the fertility for future renaissances.

As the guardian of the cultivated ground, of the enriching ruins and noxious fruits, Offa rises and falls vegetatively, appearing throughout the poem in many avatars. He is Christ, who dies in winter and resurrects in spring. He is Cernunnos, pagan god of the underworld, whose branching antlers symbolize new growth. He is the imaginative child burrowing into an underground shelter to cultivate fantasies of apocalyptic war planes. He is the poet who dies from society and nature in order to recreate them. In his many guises, he resembles Yeats's prophetic, Byzantine bird who tells "of what is past, or passing, or to come." But rather than perch on an emperor's golden bough, he struts over the ground like a raven. He is more akin to Joyce's "gnarlybird ygathering" the "bleakbardfields"[12] strewn with time's ruins, or a common gardener digging manure and spreading it over his vegetable patch.

If Christ was crowned for his exemplary reenactment of eternal rhythms, Offa is crowned because he imitates Christ. In the third hymn, "The Crowning of Offa," he officiates at an Easter ceremony with mythic significance and humorous irreverence. In a secular culture that worships kings by flaunting gift mugs and paper flags, Offa can only parody Christ's Eucharistic sacrifice by cooking and doling out sausages. He is chief priest, or at least chief of his tribe. With equal sanctimoniousness, he is chef at his barbecue. His church, if he has one, is his pub, "The Stag's Head" (mimicking Cernunnos's antlered head in "Hymn XV" and the "horned phonograph" of "Hymn II"), a place for the local community to communicate amongst themselves rather than to commune with (a dead) Christ. Christ's body, once transubstantiated into bread, wine, and communion wafer, is now the pig's body ground into sausage and garnished (charitably) with mustard. The chef's hat, to the congregation of screaming children and hungry adults, is the only meaningful symbol of the Easter rising. One of the children humorously recalls (like Eliot in "Coriolan," another poem of bizarre Easter festivities, sausage-eatings, and triumphal rituals):

> On the morning of the crowning we chorused our remission from school. It was like Easter: hankies and gift-mugs approved by his foreign gaze, the village-lintels curlered with paper flags.
>
> We gaped at the car-park of 'The Stag's Head' where a bonfire of beer-crates and holly-boughs whistled above the tar. And the chef stood there, a king in his new-risen hat, sealing his brisk largesse with 'any mustard?'

Like Christ at Easter, Offa's hat is "new-risen." Throughout the *Hymns*, Hill punctures the empty shells of ancient rituals and symbols.

He looks back at his home ground from realistic and mythical perspectives and juxtaposes them for hilarious contrasts. It is Adam's Eden as well as Christ's Golgotha. It is an inferno of Roman conduits, a heaven of Gothic cathedrals, the valley of Armageddon, and a pastoral field where the child lies down with the badger to learn his bestial ways. It is the womb of mother earth and the prison house of father time. It is Sisyphus's mountain and a mole's hill. Having burned up culture's refuse (holly boughs, beer crates) at the Easter coronation, in the second "Crowning of Offa," Hill plunges back into the heap. He recollects his childhood "investment" in history's cryptic caves and etymological catacombs and wonders whether scholarly withdrawals produced gain or pain.

> I was invested in mother-earth, the crypt of roots and endings. Child's-play. I abode there, bided my time: where the mole
>
> shouldered the clogged wheel, his gold solidus; where dry-dust badgers thronged the Roman flues, the long-unlooked-for mansions of our tribe.

Hill once said that "during the formative years of my childhood travel was very considerably restricted because of the war. We could not in any case have afforded a car on my father's pay, but even bus, coach and train journeys were something of a rarity in those days" (*VP*, p. 79). In Hill's early kigdom, he was like the mole, blind to the world outside but accustomed to the corridors of history beneath. Here he learned to "shoulder" the economic constraints of his family (the "gold solidus" is an actual coin from Roman Britain) and, through imaginative flights, transcend them.

Hill insists that art and economics are intertwined. When monetary circulation clogs, as Pound claimed, art may clog as well. But, as Hill remarks, "it is possible for serious artists to elicit a private freedom from the fact of not being received as they deserve" (*LL*, p. 55). To a degree, they must be self-sufficient, creating their own economies rather than being controlled by others'. The poet's words are his coins in *Mercian Hymns*, just as *koine* is a Greek word for the common idiom. The poet's business, like the minter's, is to coin new words from old ones, circulate them among the people, and restamp them when they get worn smooth.

If Offa sins by forging a gold solidus and sending it to Pope Hadrian, he makes up for it, one could argue, by commissioning some of the handsomest coins medieval England ever produced. Of his monetary graft and craftsmanship the historian Charles Oman remarks:

This donation [the gold "mancus" sent to Hadrian] was probably the origin of the well-known "Peter's pence" . . . which we find to our surprise was copied not from any late Roman coin, but from the *dirhems* of Saracen Caliphs. It bears on both sides a blundered Arabic inscription, across which the words Offa Rex are engraved in large characters. . . . There is nothing to compare it with in the Heptarchic age except a *solidus* of Archbishop Wigmund of York (837–54)—an equally rare issue.[13]

In an essay, Hill cited Dr. Johnson's remark that "no man but a blockhead ever wrote, except for money" and tailored it to imply "that all men write from impure motives" (*LL*, p. 7). Splendid artifice may rise, in fact must rise, from "a mound of refuse or the sweepings of a street."

In the third "Crowning of Offa," Hill examines the subliminal splendors of the Christian church, which, he points out, are prompted by perceptions of sin. What (spiritually, militarily) is a Christian culture worth when its elfish illusions die? Hill's first two words imply a quantity but also a grudging dismissal of that quantity:

> So much for the elves' wergild, the true governance
> of England, the gaunt warrior-gospel armoured in
> engraved stone. I wormed my way heavenward for
> ages amid barbaric ivy, scrollwork of fern.

Wergild, in the Middle Ages, was the value placed on a man's head and signified his rank in society. It was the price one had to pay for killing him. If the victim happened to be a churl rather than a noble, the murderer was not so heavily fined. In this hierarchical Christian society, a person was defined monetarily. Unlike Pound or Ruskin, Hill expresses little nostalgia for a feudal society based as strictly on money as modern society is on middle-class capitalism. But his tone acknowledges the enchantments that its trappings exerted on his youthful imagination.

His fall to earth, after scaling and transcending the gothic angelism of the church, is a painful blessing. Unearthly spirituality, he implies, is a sickness, an addiction which must be overcome:

> Exile or pilgrim set me once more upon that ground:
> my rich and desolate childhood. Dreamy, smug-faced,
> sick on outings—I who was taken to be a king of
> some kind, a prodigy, a maimed one.

In Malory's "Quest for the Holy Grail," which Hill alludes to, Percival is instructed "to anoint the Maimed King, both his legs and his body, and he shall have his heal."[14] Hill's heal (he was partially deaf) is contained in the poetic recollection of "familiar rhythms" in his past. "The Childhood of Offa" and "The Kingdom of Offa," appearing opposite one another, affirm continuities between the unconscious fallibility of childhood and the vocalized guilt of maturity. The child, Hill quips, is not so much father to the injudicious man as he is the injudicious man himself:

> 'A boy at odds in the house, lonely among brothers.'
> But I, who had none, fostered a strangeness; gave
> myself to unattainable toys.

The child does not father (foster) an urbane adult but rather a desire for strange gods. Hill's portrait of childhood is anti-Wordsworthian:

> In the schoolyard, in the cloakrooms, the children
> boasted their scars of dried snot; wrists and
> knees garnished with impetigo.

In medieval society (cf. *The Song of Roland*, whose motifs weave into "Hymn XVII"), relations between foster fathers and children were less pathological because 'it was the ancient custom to send a boy of good family to be brought up ("nurtured," or "fostered") in the household of one's over-lord. . . . Two boys thus bred up side by side from early youth, and competing together in their work and play, would become special friends, or "companions"; and this intimacy and friendly rivalry would be continued in after life."[15] In Hill's mid-twentieth-century world, chivalric companionship, once fostered by medieval culture, is dead. His school is Yeats's blind man's ditch, full of frog spawn and battering enemies. Ceremonial codes and heroic *gestes* are perversely supplanted:

> Ceolred was his friend and remained so, even after
> the day of the lost fighter: a biplane. . .
>
> After school he lured Ceolred, who was sniggering
> with fright, down to the old quarries, and flayed
> him.

Ceolred was an actual Anglo-Saxon king who ruled between 709 and 716 and who survives with character traits only slightly tempered. One historian states that he was "a dissolute youth, who oppressed monasteries, and according to St. Boniface died insane. He was the last descendent of Penda to rule in Mercia, and his death in 716 ends the first phase of Mercian history."[16] Ceolred is a grim distortion of Roland's companion Oliver, who helps him in the battle against the Saracens. When Oliver is about to die

> Then each to other bows courteous in his place.
> With such great love thus is their parting made.
> (sec. 149)

Offa's attitudes towards civilities are more like Freud's than the poet's in *The Song of Roland*. To restrain childlike instincts, Offa finds, only exacerbates his irrepressible instinct for murder. The chivalric view of the Middle Ages was that violent passion could be gracefully stylized into decorous patterns. Offa recoils from the violence of contemporary and medieval cultures and, in "Offa's Leechdom," proposes to expunge it. His "Leechdom," however, is very different from medieval books filled with bizarre cures for ordinary ailments, which took their names from the leeches who were ancient physicians. Doctors of leechcraft might recommend eye of newt, toe of frog, and tail of lizard stirred in bat's blood to remedy toothache. Offa's leechdom, however, is a manual of psychological and military strategy, which he used to cure anarchy festering inside and outside his borders.

One prescribed method was principled obstinacy. Offa's diagnosis begins:

> The mad are predators. Too often lately they harbour
> against us. A novel heresy exculpates all maimed
> souls. Abjure it! I am the King of Mercia, and
> I know.
>
> Threatened by phone-calls at midnight, venomous letters, forewarned I have thwarted their imminent
> devices.
>
> Today I name them; tomorrow I shall express the new
> law. I dedicate by awakening to this matter.

Menaced by fears and divisions, Offa musters his leeches (his authoritarian words and laws) to repulse the demons and drain the poison from his state.

The ditch where Offa conducts his battle for culture signifies many things. It is the place where he gathers leeches, the "historic rampart and ditch" which divides Mercia from Wales, the ditch around a contemporary Englishman's garden, an archaeological dig full of Anglo-Saxon relics, and a grave of innumerable victims. It is fertile ground for plants and investigative foragers:

> Heathland, new-made watermeadow. Charlock, marshmarigold. Crepitant oak forest where the boar
> furrowed black mould, his snout intimate with
> worms and leaves.

Here dead forms are continually dug up, polished, and recirculated. "Kingship, in the domain of matter and energy, is nothing other than the power to amass and distribute," Ezra Pound wrote in his *Guide to Kulchur*.[17] The various coin collectors and word hoarders in the *Hymns* demonstrate a boarish bravado and irreverence for sacred ground but also a noble effort to circulate what has been buried in the ground. If they steal from tradition like grave robbers (as Eliot said good poets do), they also graft new life onto the dead forms they dig up.

This is the gist of "Hymn XII." Hill may be referring to *Beowulf* scholars, Anglo-Saxon archaeologists, and to himself:

> Their spades grafted through the variably-resistant
>   soil. They clove to the hoard. They ransacked epi-
> phanies, vertebrae of the chimera, armour of wild
>   bees' larvae. They struck the fire-dragon's fac-
> eted skin.

Beowulf recounts similar pilferings of a hoard guarded by a fire-drake (lines 2082–91) although for the modern source hunters, the treasure trove *is Beowulf* and the Anglo-Saxon and Scandinavian word hoard beneath the strata of the English language. The contemporary Mercian workman, plunging his spade into the barrow and desecrating past treasures, offends the dragonlike guardian, which for Hill, among other things, is the scholar's conscience. Unlike the excavators at Sutton Hoo in 1939 (whose findings contributed much to *Beowulf* scholarship),

> The men were paid to caulk water-pipes. They brewed
>   and pissed amid splendour; their latrine seethed
>   its estuary through nettles. They are scattered
>   to your collations, moldywarp.

Hill relishes the workers' iconoclastic energy but at the same time despairs of their plunderings. They are "wild bees," soldiers and workers repairing the hive, just as the larvae they dig up are Anglo-Saxons (in embryo) from whom later come the beelike "White Anglo-Saxon Protestants" of England.

This archaeological plumbing is a synecdoche for all the excavations in *Mercian Hymns*, just as the digger is a paradigm for all the artists. Hill's workman resembles the Anglo-Saxon scop, amasser and distributor of the tribe's records, who restores the circulatory systems of the community. Michael Alexander observes that "in such a society the poet is the keeper of the traditions which hold the *cynn* (kin) together, just as the king (*cyn-ing*) is the keeper of the treasure which is the *cynn's* only possession and defence. The older a sword was, the older a word was, the more it was valued by the *cynn*. In a primitive society the poet is historian and priest, and his songs have ritual signficance."[18] If the king's burden is to organize his people, the poet's is to organize and circulate his words. The poet bears the responsibilities of any nation's treasurer. According to the *Beowulf* poet, he is

> a fellow of the king's
> whose head was a storehouse of the storied verse,
> whose tongue gave gold to the language
> of the treasured repertory, wrought a new lay
> made in the measure. (865–869)

But if Hill is the historian of the tribe, he possesses much more anxiety over "word-changes" than his Mercian forbear. His lengthy notes to the poem attest to his care for scholarly exactitude. While the Anglo-Saxon poet extemporized, Hill scrutinizes with methodical rigor. He confesses in an essay that "it is perhaps fitting that a debate such as this should convey an apprehension of its own trespass; a trespass inextricably involved with tradition and decorum. . . . I am a mere stumbling latecomer to a field . . . traversed by distinguished scholars" (*LL*, p. 14). In *Mercian Hymns*, Hill apologizes for his trespass in many ways, one of which is by intimating that he is just another workman disturbing sacred ground.

In self-chastisement, he also depicts himself as a molelike scholar compiling collations, battering blindly through culture's relics and heaping them up like "moldywarp," the mole that warps mold (as Shakespeare uses the term in *Henry IV*, part I, III, i). The scholar's treasure hoard, Hill states with sardonic glee, is a splendid dump, a garden rich in excrescent growths and decayed fruits:

> It is autumn. Chestnut-boughs clash their inflamed
>   leaves. The garden festers for attention: telluric

cultures enriched with shards, corms, nodules, the
sunk solids of gravity. I have accrued a golden
and stinking blaze.

To this rotting garden, Hill's scholar does not show a dragon's fiery possessiveness so much as a janitor's ambivalence.

It is the writer, the bibliographical collator, in Hill's myth, who aerates and catalogs the moldy hoard. He rescues language and myth just as the mole, spade, farmer's plow, and boar's snout dig up fallen objects from the ground. His verse, as its Latin root denotes, is agricultural. It works against the density of the earth, its "sunk solids of gravity," and makes them fertile. Hill explains in an essay that "Karl Barth remarked that Sin is the 'specific gravity of human nature as such'. I am suggesting that it is at the heart of this 'heaviness' that poetry must do its atoning work, this heaviness which is simultaneously the 'density' of language and the 'specific gravity of human nature' " (*LL*, p. 15). The poet is an "etymologist of roots and graftings," as Seamus Heaney declares in "Glanmore Sonnets." He works close to language's grave, its buried hoard. A network of word roots (the underground stems, which are "corms"), in fact, extends under the surface of Hill's poem. Spades "graft" the soil like a small pencil (Latin *graphiolum*). From the Latin comes the Old French *graffe*, also a sort of pencil, and the Middle English *graffen*, meaning to join illicitly. Etymologically, as Hill subtly observes, the soil cutting of spades and curative binding of pens are related. "Grafting" may be sinful grave digging, but it is also redemptive engraving. In Hill's fable, Offa is the archetypal writer; he is full of graft but uses his cunning to make a great poem, which is his Mercian kingdom. He inscribes ditches and dikes into the English landscape, grafts new estates to his kingdom, digs graves for his murdered enemies, and engraves laws in the hearts of his people. The poet writes "not merely with his own generation in his bones, but with a feeling that the whole of the literature of Europe from Homer and within it the whole of the literature of his own country has a simultaneous existence."[19] He plows a field of artifacts and word roots interred from many cultures and attempts (by warping furrows in the mold) to make them new.

From a well—a favorite Anglo-Saxon dumping place and thus a good site for archaeologists to begin investigations—Hill retrieves more "sunk solids of gravity," this time one of Offa's coins:

> Ringed by its own lustre, the
> masterful head emerges, kempt and jutting, out of
> England's well. Far from this underkingdom of crin-
> oid and crayfish, the rune-stone's province, *Rex
> Totius Anglorum Patriae*, coiffured and ageless,
> portrays the self-possession of his possession,
> cushioned on a legend.

Of Offa's coins, with their magisterial bust and inscription, one historian writes that "there is no revolution in the demonstrable history of the English currency comparable to the passage from the unsigned coinage . . . to the signed currency bearing the name of King Offa."[20] Pound celebrates Offa's coinage in "Canto XCVII." For Hill, Offa's coins approximate runes in an underground kingdom of fossil-like crustaceans and fossilized flowers (crinoid). Runes to a largely illiterate populace became images of deceptive power, like Offa's coins, of which R. H. M. Dolley in his *Anglo-Saxon Coins* says that "although Offa employed the regnal style *rex totius Anglorum patriae*, he never went further on his coins than to describe himself *Rex Merciorum*."[21] Hill has minted a new coin in his poem, engraved with *Rex Totius Anglorum Patriae*, a forgery which attests to his artistic cunning.

In "Offa's Bestiary," political Offa appears in the guise of an uncultured Adam who attains the painful boons of culture by tearing up an apple tree by its roots, as if the forbidden knowledge he craves resides in the root rather than in the fruit. He suffers a concussion and recognizes, ironically, that now he *is* the uprooted tree, the "branched god" who has been torn to pieces, wounded like the crucified Christ on his cross-tree. He is also Cernunnos, the vegetation god, symbol of autumnal falls and vernal resurrections, who held a rootlike serpent in his hand and sprouted branchlike antlers from his head. In Hill's polymythic tale of digging, writing, and culture, he is any god and any man sacrificing "unity of being" in his quest for and conquest of civilization:

> Tutting, he wrenched at a snarled root of dead crabapple. It rose against him. In brief cavort he was Cernunnos, the branched god, lightly concussed.
>
> He divided his realm. It lay there like a dream. An ancient land, full of strategy. Ramparts of compost pioneered by red-helmeted worms. Hemlock in ambush, night-soil, tetanus. A wasps' nest ensconced in the hedge-bank, a reliquary or wrapped head, the corpse of Cernunnos pitching dayward its feral horns.

Like Joyce's uncommonly common Irishman, Humphrey Chimpden Earwicker, Hill's Englishman must fall in his struggle to discover genealogical roots and buried sins. Only then will he be sufficiently moved to redeem them.

Hill's garden, with all its agricultural metaphors, is more symbolic than bucolic. It is the small plot of ground behind any number of English houses, safely divided from the neighbor's plot by a high wattle fence or hedge bank, but it is also Eden, the landscape of a dream, Offa's ancient Mercia strategically divided from Wales by the rampart posted with satanic (wormlike) soldiers, a nest of English wasps (WASPs). It is also a metaphor for the mind of England, full of devisive strategies and poisonous growths (hemlock, tetanus). The savage (feral), mummified head of Cernunnos is the "horned phonograph" and scapegoat poet of "Hymn II," as well as the ground of preserved records.

The rhythms of culture are cyclical and seasonal in Hill's Mercian garden. Cycles may "mitigate the terror of history" by showing event and decision to be part of an "irreversible pattern,"[22] but in *Mercian Hymns*, mythic ritual reveals history for what it is, irrevocable and without mitigation. Cycles appear so frequently in Hill's poem that they become a law of both the poem and the universe of which it is a part. Birds and bees, mice and snakes, walls and houses, Wales and Mercia, rise and fall to the same inevitable tune. As Spengler insisted, natural and political history, although apparently distinct, are guided by the same seasonal and vegetative laws. When one cycle ends with "primeval heathland spattered with the bones of mice and birds," another begins, like the symbolic snake that swallows its tail. Hill portrays Anglo-Saxon political animals with Aesop's terse, fanciful wit:

> adders basked and bees made pro-
> vision, mantling the inner walls of their burh:
>
> Coiled entrenched England: brickwork and paintwork
> stalwart above hacked marl.

In Hill's fable, adders are lax English vacationers sunning themselves, while wasps are their industrious, visionary compatriots, who prophesy future troubles before they arrive and store up provisions for hard times. The bees may be inner-light Protestants, walling out the world (mantle is also the luminous sheath of a lamp), by constructing *burhs* (Anglo-Saxon fortified towns) to hive their warriors and workers. On their wall is a mural which mirrors their colorful, violent battles:

> The clashing prim-
> ary colours—'Ethandune', 'Catraeth', 'Maldon',
> 'Pengwern'. Steel against yew and privet.

These, Hill says in his notes, are "supposedly the names of English suburban dwellings" (*MH*). They are also sites where Offa and other early English warriors battled. At Ethandune, in 878, King Alfred decisively defeated the Danish army and afterwards incorporated them into English culture, forming the Danelaw. Aneirin, the famous Welsh poet, recalls that at Catraeth, in the late sixth century, Mwynfawr lost all but one of his soldiers in a fight for an English stronghold. "The Battle of Maldon," the Old English poem, describes a battle lost by the English against a Viking invader: "Whereat one of Offa's kin, knowing the Earl . . . stepped to battle." Pengwern or Shrewsbury, the capital of the Princes of Powys, was captured and destroyed by Offa in 779.

With regal exploits on his mind, Hill recalls Milton's two long prose works in *Defence of the English People*, which argue that kings should be done away with. Milton's first *Defence* apologized for Cromwell's action against Charles I and with impassioned rhetoric and blasphemous invective attacked Salmasius, the author of *Defensio Regia* (1649), an expatriate Englishman, who condemned the English people for their regicide. Salmasius argued that the people were natural subjects of governing sovereigns. Milton repudiated this, contending that people were answerable only to God and must serve "higher laws" rather than the ones promulgated by kings. Hill's "Defence," however, takes elements from both defences and satirizes them. Hill does not advocate the beheading of King Offa, as Milton did with Charles, but neither does he share Milton's sanguine faith in the English people.

For Milton, Cromwell's England is paradise regained; Royalist England is paradise lost. Once the satanic kings are deposed, original freedom and justice flourish. In his childhood Eden of meadow and apple tree, Hill has simply to turn on the radio to find tyrannical wars raging around the world. If apples and angels conduct news of future wars to Adam, the wireless delivers them to Hill:

> At home the curtains were drawn. The wireless boomed
>   its commands. I loved the battle-anthems and the
>   gregarious news.

> Then, in the earthy shelter, warmed by a blue-glassed
> storm lantern, I huddled with stories of dragon-
> tailed airships and warriors who took wing im-
> mortal as phantoms.

Hill, as a child, indulges in romanticized fantasies of war projected by Gothic panels on his lamp. He knows little of war's pain and remorse. His "Defence of the English People" is a paradoxical one; it indicts England and his childhood for their insularity. To thrive, Hill asserts throughout *Mercian Hymns*, English culture must return to its European roots, recognize its graftings, revise its aims.

Offa, the Political Artificer

In *Mercian Hymns*, all people, in one way or another, are political. The "true governance of England," in which they participate, is an indefinite quantity that Hill intends to define. To his "Opus Anglicanum", he invites all masons, weavers, nailers, painters, soldiers, minters, poets, philosophers, archaeologists, and politicians to demonstrate how their arts are governed by similar laws and conventions. His desire to find in all aesthetic preoccupations a teleological unity may be traced to Aristotle's *Nicomachean Ethics*, which state that "every art and every inquiry, and similarly every action and pursuit, is thought to aim at some good; and for this reason the good has rightly been declared to be that at which all things aim."[23] For Aristotle, the master art subsuming all others is politics. The well-governed state is the highest end of both public and private man, just as "the conscious mind's intelligible structure," for Hill, is the highest end of the poet.

Hill also finds cogent political allies in the contemporary writer C. H. Sisson, and the eighteenth-century jurist William Blackstone. The paragraph from Sisson that serves as the poem's epigraph states that private persons and public governments direct themselves towards similar ends but employ different means to do so. Between public and private man, Sisson claims, "there is all the difference which separates . . . the man acting on behalf of himself from the man acting on behalf of many."[24] The statesman who sacrifices an unwilling population in order to create a superstate (as Hitler tried to do) is in a very different moral position than the poet who wants to sacrifice himself to write great poetry. What laws govern the decisions of public and private men? Sisson's quotation from Blackstone provides grist for the inquiry: "Upon 'the law of nature and the law of revelation . . . depend all human laws' " (*MH*). That humans kill and die, for instance, is a law of nature. That they should kill and die less frequently, or never, is a law of revelation. Human laws attempt to reach reasonable compromises between the exigencies of human nature and the ideals of imagination.

To learn the laws of nature, Offa burrows into earth like a mole or roams over it with the attentiveness of a botanist. Too often, however, his egocentricity blinds him to everything but his moods. The world becomes a forest of symbols in which he reads of nobody but himself. As he retreats into the "egotistical sublime," nature loses its status as a separate entity. Judicious politics are abandoned. In "Offa's Laws," Hill describes, in a beautiful but chilling vignette, the failure of Offa to unify his revelations with nature:

> When the sky cleared above Malvern, he lingered in
> his orchard; by the quiet hammer-pond. Trout-fry
> simmered there, translucent, as though forming the
> water's underskin. He had a care for natural min-
> utiae. What his gaze touched was his tenderness.
> Woodlice sat pellet-like in the cracked bark and
> a snail sugared its new stone.

Offa sees in nature only what he wants to see. When he touches the world, he touches his own skin. His "care for natural minutiae" is largely a pretense for finding symbols which reflect, like the mirror image of Narcissus in the pool, his own face. As a result, he is more nature's oracle and puppet than her civil diplomat. Although the historical Offa drafted codes of laws, his treachery persistently made shreds of them. In *Mercian Hymns*, he brandishes the peremptory contempt for humanity of a Shakespearean villain or Mafioso godfather. His antagonistic poses, as Hill delights to reveal, are frequently absurd and grandiose:

> Dismissing reports and men, he put pressure on the
> wax, blistered it to a crest. He threatened male-
> factors with the ash from his noon cigar . . .
>
> At dinner, he relished the mockery of drinking his
> family's health. He did this whenever it suited
> him, which was not often.

Fond of nature's lice and snails (they reflect his reptilian ways), Offa shows little sympathy for his family or human compatriots.

But Offa is more than a pelletlike louse or hideous dragon terrorizing England's kingdom. Continually skirmishing with barbarous instincts, he makes genuine efforts to conform with tradition and community, to learn temperance from its artifice and rituals. He possesses some of the contradictions that inflamed Jonathan Swift, whose poetry and politics Hill was studying when he began the *Hymns*. Conservative and ceremonious, Swift was also pig-headed, reactionary, and scurrilous. Entrenched in religious and artistic tradition, he reveled in a satirical animosity towards everything traditional. Between his public duties and private abandonments, he skilfully cut a path, and Hill honors him for his accomplishment:

> In Swift a sense of tradition and community is challenged by a strong feeling for the anarchic and the predatory. A necessary qualification is that the appeal of Community exists not as a fine Platonic idea but as something soberly lived, taken into the daily pattern of conduct and work. A reader of his correspondence . . . comes to accept the real presence, as well as the ritual, of his friendships. This affects the poetry, in particular its power to move with fluent rapidity

from private to public utterance and from the formal to the intimate in the space of a few lines. (*LL*, p. 68)

No high-minded Platonist, Offa is also no church dean, but rather a cunning politician and civil engineer trying to bridge (with "the Welsh Bridge and the Iron Bridge") warring factions in his kingdom and self.

When Offa is not fleeing from tradition's habitations (nation, church, school, office, home), he is vigorously seeking to reenter them. In these human enclosures he attempts to take on more of revelation's strictures. But if "a civilization is a struggle to keep self-control,"[25] as Yeats said, Offa is a heroic failure. The rubble of his impudent and indulgent life style surrounds him. Revelation, in fact, makes Offa even more violent and intolerant than he already is. In "Hymn XXVI," another part of "Offa's Bestiary," rituals celebrating God's incarnation (as they often happened in medieval England) turn a Christmas party into a barbaric carnival:

> Fortified in their front parlours, at Yuletide men
>   are the more murderous. Drunk, they defy battle-
>   axes, bellow of whale-bone and dung.

Hill's master mason, in an earlier hymn, depicts similar collusions between natural and apocalyptic violence:

> Itinerant through numerous domains, of his lord's
>   retinue, to Compostela. Then home for a lifetime
>   amid West Mercia this master-mason as I evisage
>   him, intent to pester upon tympanum and chancel-
>   arch his moody testament, confusing warrior with
>   lion, dragon-coils, tendrils of the stony vine . . .
>
>   Easter sunrays catch the ob-
>   lique face of Adam scrumping through leaves; pale
>   spree of evangelists and, there, a cross Christ
>   mumming child Adam out of Hell . . .

Medieval stone masons often traveled from England to the continent to copy church sculpture into pattern books. One of the great pilgrim roads led to the shrine of St. James of Compostela, and it was on this road, in the pass between the Pyrenees, that Charlemagne's rear guard, led by Roland, made its bloody stand for Christianity against Saracen Moslems. Offa's mason incorporates that violence, and the complicity of all political and spiritual wars, into the design of his "moody testament."

Remembering church sculpture, Hill remembers medieval embroidery as well, rhyming the two through his title "Opus Anglicanum." Originally, "Opus Anglicanum" referred to tapestry woven during the great period of embroidery between 1250 and 1350. *Mercian Hymns*, with its panels of statuesque poses meticulously carved, its scrollwork and vines, fantastic beasts and angels, armored warriors and wounded artists, assimilates many techniques and motifs from this early art. The poem, in fact, resembles the Bayeux tapestry which depicts the Norman Conquest.

One law which pervades Hill's work is close to Newton's: for every action there is an equal and opposite reaction. When the natural world is repressed, the supernatural world surges up to fill the vacuum. Forcefully unleashed, the mind's energies soar into a manic (and mantic) empyrean of warrior angels and dragon-tailed airships. The laws of grammar and syntax, for the poet, are like gravity; they pull him back to the human world of intelligible discourse. In an oblique reference to the moon flight, Hill makes the reentry of the rocket into the earth's gravitational field representative of all descents. Hill wittily conjoins the astronauts and embroiderers in order to press his point that all journeywork is treacherous but, when properly executed, a triumph over "riddling" difficulties.

> In tapestries, in dreams, they gathered, as it was enacted, the return, the re-entry of transcendence into this sublunary world. *Opus Anglicanum,* their

> stringent mystery riddled by needles: the silver
> veining, the gold leaf, voluted grape-vine, master-
> works of treacherous thread.

A passage from "Poetry as 'Menace' and 'Atonement' " could act as a gloss: "one does not regard it as at all eccentric to endorse the view that grammar is a 'social and public institution', or to share W. K. Wimsatt's belief in 'the fullness of [the poet's] responsibility as public performer in a complex and treacherous medium' " (*LL*, p. 8). The writer works on similarly treacherous looms, weaving texts with the care once devoted to textiles.

Unlike Ruskin and Pound, who blamed the breakdown of the medieval devotion to craft ("All noble art is the expression of man's delight in God's work,"[26] Ruskin said) on the deplorable conditions of workers in the industrial age, Hill sees the risk of breakdown implicit in all artistic and political endeavours. In "Hymn XXV," the last of the "Opus Anglicanum" sequence, he ponders Ruskin's letter on English nail making in the context of his grandmother, who worked as a nailer:

> Brooding on the eightieth letter of *Fors Clavigera,*
>   I speak this in memory of my grandmother, whose
>   childhood and prime womanhood were spent in the
>   nailer's darg.
>
> The nailshop stood back of the cottage, by the fold.
>   It reeked stale mineral sweat. Sparks had furred
>   its low roof. In dawn-light the troughed water
>   floated a damson-bloom of dust—
>
> not to be shaken by posthumous clamour. It is one
>   thing to celebrate the 'quick forge', another
>   to cradle a face hare-lipped by the searing wire.

Like Eliot in "Burnt Norton," Hill addresses the dust on ruined flowers (which he connects with his grandmother's ruined womanhood), but with angrier persistence. If Eliot ruminates at the gate to the past, which he did not open, Hill applies to it a more forceful key, as Ruskin's *Fors Clavigera* implies. In 1877, Ruskin traveled to Bewdley, Worcestershire, (close to Hill's home, where his grandmother worked in a nailer's cottage under a damson tree) and on July 16 wrote his letter to the working men of England, complaining of two women ruining their youth in a twelve-hour "darg" or day's work. Among quietly articulated details, Ruskin perceives the English class system and the usurious practices that perpetuate it. In a later depiction of the nail-shop, Hill bears witness to the afflictions of Offa's cruel, patriarchal institutions, which are another root of English society.

Hill never foregoes judging the past with radical fierceness. Bewigged for court, loaded with legal documents and plentiful evidence, Hill is also the dragon squatting on time's hoard and examining all the sins beneath him. If he finds Offa's "coins handsome as Nero's," he also implies that Offa is as egregiously inhuman as Nero. If he finds Offa's charters paradigms of draftsmanship and political ingenuity, he also compares their efficiency to that of modern totalitarian governments. Stenton tells us of the charters that "the contrast between the crude provisional script of the text and the practised, almost official, hand of the endorsement represents a real distinction between the primitive government of the local kingdoms and the beginnings of administrative routine in a court which had become the political center of England south of the Humber."[27] In "Offa's Laws, Hymn X," Hill provides an ironic counterpoint to Offa's "administrative routine" by equating it to the officious games of a child:

> He adored the desk, its brown-oak inlaid with ebony,
>   assorted prize pens, the seals of gold and base
>   metal into which he had sunk his name.
>
> It was there that he drew upon grievances from the
>   people; attended to signatures and retributions;
>   forgave the death-howls of his rival.

Offa treats the people, with their affixed *wergilds*, the way he treats his coins and charters. He stamps them with his image or stamps them into oblivion, then pretends to forgive their cries of pain. Safely sequestered behind desk and walls, he enjoys a sense of illusory power. He engages with his muse (Mnemosyne) in an exchange which is at once Oedipal, economic, and confessional. He acknowledges his sins and expects history to grace him with immortality. As legend has it, one of his more egregious sins was the murder of Ethelbert, after which he took a penitential journey to Rome. As private and public man, he lapsed repeatedly into childlike indiscretions. Like a schoolboy trying to discipline his sexuality and learning, Offa is partially enslaved by what he would prefer to master.

> He swayed in sunlight, in mild dreams. He tested the
> little pears. He smeared catmint on his palm for
> his cat Smut to lick. He wept, attempting to master *ancilla* and *servus*.

In this womb of opiates and dreams, vigorous perception and action dissolve into a syrupy eroticism.

The same sort of drowsy sensuality clouds the church in "Offa's Book of the Dead," where, Hill says, "the strange church smelled a bit 'high', of censers and polish." The schoolboy's study, the politician's office, and the priest's "high" church (High Anglican, where the congregation is "high" on the "opiate of the masses") are places where the meditative mind apprehends laws of revelation. But Hill chastises this "higher" consciousness for its otherworldliness. The curate at the funeral of Hill's grandmother, he implies, shepherds the living and dead into artificial paradises just as demagogues seduce whole populations into absurdly impractical utopias:

> Then he dismissed you, and the rest of us followed,
> sheepish next-of-kin, to the place without the
> walls: spoil-heaps of chrysanths dead in their
> plastic macs, eldorado of washstand-marble.

As the tyrant dismisses reports and men in "Hymn XIV," the curate dismisses the "sheep" in the funeral. In an apostrophe to his grandmother, Hill says: "I unburden the saga of your burial," and it is the saga of her travail as well as the travail of the common worker throughout English history which he redeems from the past.

The best example of the treachery implicit in politics and artifice, and the diplomacy needed to curb it, exists in *Mercian Hymns* in the fanciful meeting between Offa and Charlemagne on the shores of the English Channel:

> Clash of salutation. As keels thrust into shingle.
> Ambassadors, pilgrims. What is carried over? The
> Frankish gift, two-edged, regaled with slaughter.
>
> The sword is in the king's hands; the crux a crafts-
> man's triumph. Metal effusing its own fragrance,
> a variety of balm. And other miracles, other
> exchanges.

The exchange of a sword, "emblematic of love and war," to borrow Yeats's phrase, is a synecdoche for the history of Anglo-French quarrels, from Offa's day to the Norman Conquest and the present. Charles Oman writes that Charlemagne, in 786, after defeating the Avars on the Danube, "sent to Offa some of his trophies, gold, swords, and embroidered garments, as testimonies of his regard and friendship."[28] Hill's clash between French and English, however, is archetypal and anachronistic. It includes all fruitful meetings from incarnation ("Christ's mass") to photosynthesis ("the flickering evergreen fissured with light.") Over a terrain of conflict Hill travels in his car with sardonic awareness. His car radio crackles with static from electrical storms, just as his conscience winces from painful memories:

> He drove at evening through the hushed Vosges. The
> car radio, glimmering, received broken utterance
> from the horizon of storms . . .

Near the Vosges mountains in France, ghosts of Charlemagne's battles mix with those of World War I (the Vosges marked one boundary of the western front) and those of childhood accidents.

Hill's collage of anxieties is both comic and tragic. He travels in his "maroon GT," as in a time machine, back to one of the origins of western civilization, Rome. A vacationer with a well-fueled imagination, he follows an itinerary which knows no bounds in space or time. He returns to the declining Roman Empire, not for Catholic communion but to bear secular witness to the imprisonment and torture of Boethius by Theodoric in A.D. 524. Boethius, in his *Consolation of Philosophy*, wrote a meditation, interspersed with poems, on the vacillations of fortune. For Hill, Boethius becomes a symbol of all martyrs, including Christ, who die under imperial rule. He seems to recall Gibbon's description of Boethius's torture; Gibbon wrote that "a strong cord was fastened round the head of Boethius, and forcibly tightened till his eyes almost started from their sockets; and some mercy may be discovered in the milder torture of beating him with clubs till he expired."[29] Hill writes:

> At Pavia, a visitation of some sorrow. Boethius'
> dungeon. He shut his eyes, gave rise to a tower
> out of the earth. He willed the instruments of
> violence to break upon meditation. Iron buckles
> gagged; flesh leaked rennet over them; the men
> stooped, disentangled the body.

As in the "composition of place" in a Loyolan spiritual exercise, Offa imagines the scene of Boethius's execution in graphic detail so that in the end he may "wipe his hands" of his own sin and guilt. Hill's meditation ends with a grim parody of a visionary sightseer collecting souvenirs:

> He wiped his lips and hands. He strolled back to the
> car, with discreet souvenirs for consolation and
> philosophy. He set in motion the furtherance of
> his journey. To watch the Tiber foaming out
> much blood.

He alludes to Virgil's *Aeneid* and agrees with the Sibyl's prophecy delivered to Aeneas at Cumae, that "war, terror, war" awaits him "and Tiber foaming red with blood." From the reddened waters, the towers of Rome will rise.

In the last section of *Mercian Hymns*, Hill commemorates Offa, who, like Aeneas, must be brutal to father an impressive culture. But Hill does so with delicious irreverence. When Offa dies, his funeral is not like Sir Winston Churchill's but like Earwicker's in *Finnegans Wake*, a comic testimony to a great man's ambiguous accomplishments. Joyce described Earwicker's funeral as an uproarious holiday during which all the nation congregates to desecrate its primordial leader. A motley bunch attends Offa's wake with similar gleeful carousings:

> 'Now when King Offa was alive and dead', they were all there, the funereal gleemen: papal legate and rural dean; Merovingian car-dealers, Welsh mercenaries; a shuffle of house-carls.
>
> He was defunct. They were perfunctory. The ceremony stood acclaimed. The mob received memorial vouchers and signs.

In this mélange of sacred and profane denominations, Hill deflates any sanctimonious keening. The gleemen (medieval itinerant singers) and dissolute, long-haired Merovingian kings (who reigned in France before Charlemagne's times) stand beside papal legates (who came from Rome in 786 to help Offa supervise his ecclesiastical affairs) and English church deans (who by medieval laws were forbidden to be gleemen). Among other things, Offa's wake is a ceremonious game, like a game of cards in which all suits are shuffled together. It is also a game of puns, in which different factions are unified in a democratic melee. In Hill's language game, a "shuffle of house-carls" can be a shuffled pack of cards, a pack of shuffling churls, or a shuffled band of carls (Carolingians) from Charlemagne's France. The game subsumes politics and art, which are similar games, played according to set laws and unpredictable circumstances.

The cosmic game in *Mercian Hymns*, as Hill delineates it, is the mythical dream of the archetypal father, Offa. Hill compares it to the English game of ludo (from the Latin meaning 'game'), in which a cup of dice, rolled and spilled on a board, determines a player's movements along an established path. Hill's grandmother presides at the game, a referee to whom he continually refers. Hill said to Haffenden: "I felt very close to her; I realize retrospectively how close the attachment was" (*VP*, p. 76). In the penultimate "Hymn" he writes:

> Gran lit the
> gas, his dice whirred in the ludo-cup, he entered
> into the last dream of Offa the King.

Like Joyce, Hill envisions his game in ever-widening contexts of self, family, city, nation, culture, world, and cosmos. But Hill's ritualistic "at-one-ment" between many times and places also establishes differences, among them the game's winners and losers. He tabulates with mock seriousness a hierarchy or score card. His competitive game is partly played against his family:

> 'Not strangeness, but strange likeness. Obstinate,
>   outclassed forefathers, I too concede, I am your
>   staggeringly-gifted child.'

A competitive urge to excel is grounded in English class warfare. In his interview with Haffenden, Hill reveals more about his "outclassed forefathers" and their composite ghost—the law-making, law-enforcing Offa:

I was an only child. My father was a police constable and remained so throughout his career; I believe that my father's father started work as a stoker on the Great Western Railway. He afterwards joined the police force and rose to be Deputy Chief Constable of Worcestershire, which was the highest position one could then rise to from the ranks.

He was an impressive man. I felt considerably in awe of him, without feeling particularly close. (*VP*, p. 76)

Mercian Hymns maps the dialectical track of English generations. It documents Adam's legacy (wages of sin—coins, "traces of red mud") as if its genetic code were deeply imprinted in Offa's and Hill's personality.

Although the final *Hymns* offer uproarious parodies of birth ceremonies and funerals, the festive lights blaze only momentarily. Lengthening shadows contribute to a sense of tenebrous gloom:

> After that shadowy, thrashing midsummer hail-storm,
> Earth lay for a while, the ghost-bride of livid
> Thor, butcher of strawberries, and the shire-tree
> dripped red in the arena of its uprooting.

After this final mythic consummation (Offa was supposedly descended from Thor), the poet returns once again to Worcestershire, from which he was uprooted twenty years before. He meditates on his lost heritage:

> Tracts of ancient occupation. Frail ironworks rusting in the thorn-thicket. Hearthstones; charred lullabies. A solitary axe-blow that is the echo of a lost sound.

In the middle of the poem, Hill thought of his past as a compost heap rotting and festering. Now, more gently, he imagines it charring and rusting. He finishes the poem with Offa's spirit, like the echo of the axe blade, vanishing into air.

5 / PASSION RITUALIZED

Tenebrae

After retrieving an ancient Anglo-Saxon king from the shadows of myth and history, Hill moves to a ritual that is specifically Christian. *Tenebrae* commemorates Christ's Passion, His descent from the cross into hell, and His resurrection. It is one of the oldest and most impressive ceremonies of the church, but it is rarely performed now. When first practised, it included the matins and lauds recited during the last three days of Holy Week. The matins were said during the night and the lauds at cockcrow. When people found it difficult to rise in the middle of the night, matins were recited before bed. Now they are often performed in the later part of the afternoon. The principal symbolic act of Tenebrae is the lighting of fifteen candles on a triangular "hearse" and the gradual extinguishing of the candles, one by one, after each psalm is read until total darkness fills the church. One candle is hidden and at the crucial moment restored to the hearse to allow the celebrants to depart. This one light symbolizes Christ's resurrection from the darkness or *tenebrae* of hell.

The matins are divided into three nocturns, which are divided further into three psalms and several lessons, and along with the lauds (five psalms and a Benedictus) form a liturgy of despair and supplication for divine solicitude. The sixty-eighth psalm recited in the matins for Maundy Thursday exemplifies the ritual's mood of dolorous lamentation: "Save me from sinking in the mire, rescue me from the enemies, from the deep waters that surround me. Let me not sink under the flood, swallowed up in its depths, and the well's mouth close above me." Besides the psalms, there are lessons taken from Jeremiah's lamentations, Augustine's commentaries on the Psalms, and St. Paul's Epistles, which constitute the present ceremony, as they did the original ceremonies of the eighth century.

Tenebrae, Hill said in an interview with Blake Morrison, "is a ritual, and like all rituals it obviously helps one to deal with and express states which in that particular season of the church's year are appropriate—suffering and gloom. *Tenebrae* does at one level mean darkness or shadows; but at another important level it clearly indicates a *ritualistic*, formal treatment of suffering, anxiety and pain."[1] In returning to ballad and sonnet forms after mining traditions of prose poetry in *Mercian Hymns*, Hill achieves a new succinctness and gentleness of tone. If before he shaped his poems like a medieval sculptor hammering a "moody testament" of Christian warriors and pagan beasts into churchstone, now, as "An Apology for the Revival of Christian Architecture in England" demonstrates, he infuses his poems with the lightness and delicacy of rose windows. Although still iconoclastic, he is less stentorian in his attacks. He finds the passion of the artist and lover crucifying, but his reaction is now more quietly modulated, twilit.

Tenebrae, like Hill's other books, traces the creative mind's wintry descent and vernal resurrection but provides the journey at all points with plangent music, roseate imagery, and guiding lights. It takes as its subject the suffering inflicted by those who betray humanistic ideals of civilization and compares their acts to Judas's betrayal of Christ. But if one theme predominates, it is the difficult voyage towards love, its attendant passions and nightmares. The knight of chivalric love martyrs himself as he quests for requital in "The Pentecostal Castle." In "Lachrimae" he weeps in darkness over rituals and symbols that no longer offer consolation. In "An Apology" his tears are more political; he laments the history of betrayals in the governance of England and its Empire. In "Tenebrae," the last poem, he diagnoses the heart-rending travail of sexual and innocent love and searches for a cure. But amid the gloom come glimpses of rapprochement. The poet achieves a marriage between symbols and passion in the "tremulous boudoirs where the crystals kissed / in cabinets of amethyst and frost." Such crystalline images allay the perplexities of the amorous soul. In patterning chaos, they effect a tentative redemption.

"The Pentecost Castle": Ritual and Romance

Yeats in old age modeled many poems on ballads in order "to think like a wise man, but to express oneself like the common people."[2] So Hill in "The Pentecost Castle" imitates ballads written during the Spanish Renaissance. He came to these Spanish ballads by way of a harpsichord recital by Rafael Puyana, which included Antonio de Cabezón's sixteenth-century composition "Diferencias sobre el canto del Caballero":

It struck me as a piece of such stunning power and beauty that from then on I was entirely enthralled by it, and I struggled until I could make some competent show of it on the piano. I then discovered that the theme for these magnificent variations was a little folk tune which gave Lope de Vega the motif for his play *El Caballero de Olmedo*. Again, by a lucky accident, I had been browsing through the *Penguin Book of Spanish Verse* and had discovered one of the religious sonnets of Lope de Vega which enchanted me so much that I began to try to translate it. These two figures, Cabezón and Lope de Vega, were united by this tiny thread of folk song. I began to read my way into Lope de Vega's work—that play in particular—and I pursued every clue I could between the Cabezón piece and that snatch of folk song. The words of the little folk song became the first lyric of the "Pentecost Castle" sequence. (*VP*, pp. 91–92)

The love song of Hill's *caballero*, with its delicious ecstasies and nocturnal woundings, resembles "The Songbook of Sebastian Arrurruz." Indebted to Spanish Renaissance ballads, both belong to a more general European tradition of biblical, Troubadour, and Petrarchan love poetry, in which sacred and profane love coexist in uneasy proximity. The simple, passionate sensuality of these poems catches experience at the nerve tips rather than in the abstract mind and expresses it in a rhetoric of paradox and oxymoron.

According to Pound in *The Spirit of Romance*, "though the servants of Amor went pale and wept and suffered heat and cold, they came on nothing so apparently morbid as the 'dark night.'"[3] In Hill's "Pentecost Castle," as the title implies, the Provençal *chanson* and the mystic's love lyric stand side by side. The castle to which the *caballero* rides contains both a real and imaginary lady. It promises both the fire of mundane sexuality and the pentecostal fire of ascetic inspiration. It is both the medieval knight's fortress and the Christian temple into which the resurrected Christ spoke with tongues of flame. Although Pound and Hill diverge on the role of the sacred they do not on the romantic spirit's need for ritualistic discipline. In his discussion of Provençal verse, Pound wrote that "the electric current gives light when it meets resistance. I suggest that the living conditions of Provence gave the necessary restraint, produced the tension sufficient for the results, a tension unattainable under, let us say, the living conditions of imperial Rome."[4]

If ritual is defined as the "ceremonious performance or recreation of a crucial, sanctified action,"[5] its purpose is to guide the impassioned soul not with Christ into heaven but back into human community. Instead of following the grand narrative sweep of Christ's descent from the cross into the inferno and His ascent into transcendent paradise, Hill's *caballero* follows endless cycles. He enters and abandons the "Pentecost Castle" as many times as the lover falls in and out of love. For this reason, as Hill explains, "Pentecost Castle" is a "hinted drama": "One or two critics have suggested that a coherent, consecutive drama is being conveyed: I don't think it's so. I had no such intention; there's no plot but there are little shadowy hints of one" (*VP*, p. 92). Unlike Auden, who felt that poetic rituals "must be beautiful, exhibiting, for example, balance, closure and aptness,"[6]

Hill believes that if they represent contemporary experience, they must by asymmetrical and unclosed.

Some lines from Sidney Keyes, the young English symbolist poet who died in World War II, serve as *Tenebrae's* epigraph and further define Hill's chivalric journey towards love. If young questers fear sexual love, represented here by the seductive islands of Circe's Aiaia and Aphrodite's Cythera, Keyes believes that older poets, having grown tired of imagined and solitary love, seek out seductive entrapments and amorous ordeals:

> This is a very ancient land indeed;
> Aiaia formerly or Cythera
> Or Celidon the hollow forest called;
> This is the country Ulysses and Hermod
> Entered afraid; by ageing poets sought . . .

Hermod, the Norse god, achieved notoriety by journeying to Hela, the Scandinavian hell, to resurrect Balder, one of the most beloved of Norse gods, who had the misfortune to be killed by Loki's mistletoe spear, which pierced his heart. Hela promised to release Balder if Hermod could prove that all living creatures wept for him. All cried but one, and he kept Balder imprisoned in hell. Weepings, heart wounds, and descents to hell are common fare for Hill's lovers. Hill, approaching the age of fifty when he finished *Tenebrae*, expresses the older man's discontent with the sugary romance of youth and partial acceptance of the lover's trials. Shortly after finishing "Pentecost Castle," he wrote that "however much and however rightly we protest against the vanity of supposing it to be merely the 'spontaneous overflow of powerful feelings', poetic utterance is nonetheless an utterance of the self, the self demanding to be loved, demanding love in the form of recognition and 'absolution' " (*LL*, p. 17). The poet erects his "Pentecost Castle" so that others may travel there to offer absolving love.

In Spain, during its Counter-Reformation, as R. O. Jones points out, there was an "ecstatic interfusion of the secular and divine."[7] Sections of "The Pentecost Castle" when they first appeared in *Agenda* provided an epigraph from R. O. Jones which freely celebrated this commingling of oppositions: "San Juan de la Cruz sang, as he danced holding in his arms an image of the infant Jesus snatched from a crib, the words of an old love song: "Si amores me han de matar / agora tienen lugar."[8] Throughout *Tenebrae*, the lover's passion is similarly, but not always harmoniously, sacramental and secular.

Like St. John of the Cross and St. Teresa in their poetry and meditations, Hill conjoins the disparate aspect of passions in the image of "the wound of love." In St. Teresa's *Interior Castle*, a book which may have suggested the title, "Pentecost Castle," the spiritual bridegroom, Christ, is imagined as ravishing the contemplative soul and the soul as relishing its hurt. At this stage (the sixth mansion), the soul is "conscious of having received a delicious wound but cannot discover how, nor who gave it, yet recognizes it as a most precious grace and hopes the hurt will never heal."[9] Wounds of love abound in St. John's verse as well. The bridegroom in his "Spiritual Canticle" enjoys the same sanctified masochism:

> And in solitude He guides her,
> He alone, who also bears
> In solitude the wound of love. [10]

Ecstasy in any form, whether it be divine grace, poetic inspiration, or sexual passion, according to Hill and the mystics, almost requires a breakdown of ordinary health and a reverence for wounds. For Hill, this comes with exhaustion, as he told an interviewer: "I think exhaustion is a great begetter of inspiration: sheer tiredness breaks down certain barriers of the conscious mind."[12] The pentecostal wound, he writes in "Funeral Music," is inflicted by either axe or seraph. It is a composite affliction, both debilitating and energizing. Christian rituals, or at least the vestiges of rituals, throughout "The Pentecost Castle" seek to express and control this romantic agony. In no other poem does Hill articulate his quest for reciprocity between lovers with the same pared-down, unpunctuated clarity.

The Journey to Love

An ill-advised journey through a dark night, culminating in death, begins the sequence forebodingly.

> They slew by night
> upon the road
> Medina's pride
> Olmedo's flower
>
> shadows warned him
> not to go
> not to go
> along that road
>
> Weep for your lord
> Medina's pride
> Olmedo's flower
> there in the road

In most journeys, the hero dismisses warnings and trespasses on dangerous ground in order to capture his prize. He dies from ordinary society, but here he seems to die completely. Hill appropriates from Spanish poets, such as Lorca and Lope de Vega, a figurative language delimiting love's life and death. He uses polyptoton (the repetition of word or phrase) and a two- or three-beat line to articulate love's ambiguities. But, besides these, he also borrows from de Vega many of his original lines. Lope de Vega's lyric, composed around 1600, is altered in Hill's version, so that "lord" replaces "caballero" or "knight," and Christian and chivalric figures stand together. Weeping can be either sacred or profane in Hill's poem: Mary Magdalen's lament for her slain Lord, a Spaniard's lament for his feudal lord, or any person's lament for St. John of the Cross, who journeyed through similar dark nights, suffered wounds, and came from Medina.

In the second section, Hill elaborates on the theme of love's death in fulfillment. If Adam is the primordial lover, mingling with Eve among Eden's orchards and flowers, he is also a prefiguration of Christ, who suffers a crown of thorns in his love for humanity. Hill evokes traditional associations of the rose with love to intimate both the thorniness of amorous relationships and the fact, expressed earlier in the epigraph from Yeats, that desire and possession can be equally unsatisfying:

> Down in the orchard
> I met my death
> under the briar rose
> I lie slain
>
> I was going
> to gather flowers
> my love waited
> among the trees
>
> down in the orchard
> I met my death
> under the briar rose
> I lie slain

In "Tenebrae Responsories," composed by Tomás Luis de Victoria about the same time Lope de Vega lived, one can find the correlative for this descent into the orchard of death, framed by Catholic ritual. In the seventeenth and last responsory, Christ and communicant declare:

> I am counted among those
> that go down to the depths:
> I am as a man without help,
> free among the dead.
> They have laid me in the lower pit,
> in darkness, and in the shadow of death.

Hill makes the descent in his poem archetypal; it is not only Christ's but any man's who falls in love. "We must love one another or die," Auden wrote in "September 1, 1939." Hill would retort that we figuratively die when we love and figuratively live because we die.

Although Hill borrows from the Spanish traditions of romance poetry, he also returns to its principal source, the Bible, and its "Song of Solomon." There, requited and unrequited love are expressed in a natural imagery of flowers, trees, and stones. Many of Hill's lines read like sentences taken from the "Song" and are broken into two- or three-beat lines. A verse from the "Song" begins:

> My beloved is gone down
> into his garden,
> to the beds of spices,
> to feed in the gardens,
> and to gather lilies.
> (6.2)

But Hill's insistence that love is a wound to the sensitive, withdrawn mind is characteristic of the Spaniard's "dark night" rather than of Solomon's "Song."

Darkness is never really dispelled in Hill's poem, however, as it is in St. John of the Cross's "Dark Night." After lover and beloved make contact ("He wounded my neck / With his gentle hand"), St. John tells us that the soul forgets its nocturnal anguish and enjoys ecstatic forgetfulness. He describes his ecstasy as, literally, a "standing outside oneself":

> I abandoned and forgot myself,
> Laying my face on my Beloved;
> All things ceased; I went out from myself,
> Leaving my cares
> Forgotten among the lilies.[12]

Although dawn light rises with Christ's resurrected body in the fourth section of Hill's poem, journeys through the dark are not over.

As season follows season, and one year's Easter another year's Tenebrae, emotions of love rise and fall as naturally as leaves on a tree. Hill catches the organic nature of the spirit in his figure of the Jesse tree:

> At dawn the Mass
> burgeons from stone
> a Jesse tree
> of resurrection
>
> budding with candle
> flames the gold
> and the white wafers
> of the feast
>
> and ghosts for love
> void a few tears
> of wax upon
> forlorn altars

In his prophecy of Christ's peaceable kingdom, where wolf shall dwell with lamb and a little child lead them, Isaiah says:

> And there shall come forth a rod
> out of the stem of Jesse,
> and a Branch shall grow out of his roots:
> And the spirit of the LORD shall rest upon him. . . .
>   (Is. 11. 1-2)

In Hill's vision, Jesus is the tree, the Tenebrae candle, the Holy Ghost, the spirit of love, but most importantly an image of the hurt, weeping lover. Gradually, as the darkness of Tenebrae lifts on Easter morning, the lit candles symbolically dispense love and grace to the shadowy communicants.

In the first version of "The Pentecost Castle," the sections of the poem describing the night journey, garden descent, and Easter resurrection appeared in orderly succession, followed by a section about the spirit's journey up a purgatorial mountain,

Tenebrae

in which a heron pierced by a blade and flying heavenwards symbolized the wounded, ascending spirit of the lover. The bird could be Christ resurrected, although it could just as well be anyone searching for blissful transcendence in love:

> Slowly my heron flies
> pierced by the blade
> mounting in slow pain
> strikes the air with its cries
>
> goes seeking the high rocks
> where no man can climb
> where the wild balsam stirs
> by the little stream
>
> the rocks the high rocks
> are brimming with flowers
> there love grows and there love
> rests and is saved

Completely spiritualized love, Hill interposes ironically, is attained by no man. It attracts those who suffer, but its promises of tranquillity, in the end, are illusory and often fatal.

Transcendence is not Hill's way, at least not for very long. Even as a child, he remembers humorously, he resisted the seduction of Christian otherworldliness (although not always successfully). Like Roethke, to whose book *The Far Field* Hill alludes, he climbs rarefied summits only to return to visceral realities, loving them as much as he hates them. His tenderness is always undergirded by a knowing sarcasm:

> I went out early
> to the far field
> ermine and lily
> and yet a child
>
> Love stood before me
> in that place

> prayers could not lure me
> to Christ's house
>
> Christ the deceiver
> took all I had
> his darkness ever
> my fair reward

The child's hostility towards Christ is like his adolescent reaction towards his parents, but in this case it is surprisingly high-principled. To keep in touch with his natural environment, he leaves parental home and Christian church.

Christ's spiritual darkness, the poem contends, is both reward and punishment, just as Adam's sin (a *felix culpa*) can be felicitous because it makes Christ's redemption possible. "The Pentecost Castle" is a series of transfigurations or redemptions in which dark turns to light and light to dark. Like Peter, James, and John, who witnessed Christ's transfiguration, Hill's wounded lover finds his love transfigured on the mountain top. The tenth section remembers this and, in so doing, recalls many other metamorphoses as well. These are condensed into one of the poem's more allusive vignettes:

> St James and St John
> bless the road she has gone
> St John and St James
> a rosary of names
>
> child-beads of fingered bread
> never-depleted heart's food
> the nominal the real
> subsistence past recall
>
> bread we shall never break
> love-runes we cannot speak
> scrolled effigy of a cry
> our passion its display

Hill makes St. James and St. John engage with other literary and religious figures. James, for instance, was the patron saint of pilgrims, and his relics were entombed at Compostela in Spain. Many medieval Europeans traveled along pilgrim routes to pay homage to him and brought with them remnants of Troubadour love songs, which later transformed Spanish poetry. J. M. Cohen, the editor of the anthology of Spanish verse which Hill used when writing his poem, explains that the lyrical poets of the fourteenth century modeled their poems on the style of the Galicians, "whose songs were a last offshoot of the Troubadour tradition, carried along the pilgrim road to Galicia's shrine, the tomb of St. James at Compostela, after the destruction of Provençal civilization in the Albigensian wars."[13] Along the pilgrim road traveled the spirit of romance, which Hill imagines as a symbolic Mary ("bless the road she has gone"). Later poets like St. John of the Cross transfigured profane beauties through a Catholic rosary into spiritual ones (the rosary is devoted to Mary). Hill communes with his ideal lover through a rosary compiled of saints' names. Both poet and saint celebrate images of the eternal feminine. But for Hill, symbolic language, whether it belongs to devotional love poetry or Catholic ritual, is now a scroll of "nominal" runes and effigies. Christ has become a dead word, his communion a feast of clichés.

Transfiguring Christ from a mystifying effigy into a figure of vital significance is Hill's goal, just as it was St. Teresa's to apprehend God in a "clearness of language."[14] When language is purged of atavistic obscurities, communion once again becomes possible. Hill prays for contact between words and realities, lovers and beloveds. He calls for an enlightenment of language's dark night. But in the end no contact occurs.

> If the night is dark
> and the way short
> why do you hold back
> dearest heart

> though I may never
> see you again
> touch me I will shiver
> at the unseen
>
> the night is so dark
> the way so short
> why do you not break
> o my heart

Although the way to the heart may be physiologically short, a tryst is a long way off, as in the anonymous song from fifteenth- or sixteenth-century Spain,[14] which the poem copies:

> Si la noche hace escura
> y tan corto es el camino,
>   cómo no venís amigo?
>
> (If the night is dark
> and the way is so short
> why do you not come, friend?)

Love fails because lovers fail to find a common language.

Drawing on Petrarchan conventions which entered Spanish love poetry with Boscán and Garcilaso de la Vega in the early sixteenth century, Hill analyzed love as an economy of loss and gain, dispossession and possession, and maddening dreams. Failing to repossess the image of Christ as an exemplary lover, Hill's chivalric knight is equally unsuccessful in his pursuit of women. The mystical marriage prescribed by St. John and St. Teresa, as well as the secular marriage, is in ruins. His knight's amorous adventures go on like Don Quixote's, his countryman's, in a spirit of heroic futility. His *amor herido*, or love wound, will never heal, and he does not want it to. He would rather chase specters through fire and ice, with death always looming on the horizon. With this in mind, Hill ends with a question and an assurance of future quests rather than an affirmation of happy resolutions in sanity and sanctity:

beloved soul
what shall you see
nothing at all
yet eye to eye

depths of non-being
perhaps too clear
my desire dying
as I desire

The knight at the end does not find a fiery tower filled with lovers and answers to his metaphysical questions but its opposite, a dark well. He does not experience a still point of renounced desire but its entropy, a gradual dying of energy into the void.

Love, Death, and the Mystical Marriage

For St. John of the Cross and St. Teresa, the goal of meditation is a sacred marriage of the soul to Christ. In the last mansion of *The Interior Castle*, St. Teresa says that Christ "has spiritually taken for His bride [the soul, and] before consummating the celestial marriage, He brings her into this His mansion in a dwelling place in heaven."[16] In St. John's "Spiritual Canticle," a dialogue between spiritual bride and bridegroom, the poet declares:

> The bride has entered
> The sweet garden of her desire,
> And she rests in delight,
> Laying her neck
> On the gentle arms of her Beloved. [17]

"Pentecost Castle" reflects on these moments of unity but from the vantage of a tough, sceptical intellect all too familiar with divorce and disillusionment. Hill wonders whether mystical trysts in remote mansions and gardens are merely fanciful flights, forms of sleep and death, seductive to those who find themselves crucified in the world.

When asked by John Haffenden whether his fascination with mystical experience arose from a belief that "the possibilities of faith and doubt form a crux of the human condition," Hill responded:

> I am interested in mysticism as an exemplary discipline, and I'm also interested in the psychopathology of the false mystical experience. Of course no one has been more accurate in defining and warning against the perils of false mysticism than the medieval mystics; the genuine mystic is usually a tough, practical, level-headed man, and I think those iron-disciplined mystics—unless their charity overcame their scorn—would have hard things to say of the more self-indulgent mystical cults of the present day, (VP, pp. 89–90)

True mystical experience depends upon an intensification of ordinary perception and memory, whereby the mind grows luminous with palpable images. Pleasures and pains, taken in stride by the ordinary man, affect the mystic like lightning bolts. If he does not renounce the normal turbulence of society, as Hill's mystics do not, then he seems condemned to a cycle of mania and despair.

Often Hill appears as a discriminating spectator looking down on martyr and mystic from a great height. Since one of the Christian mystic's principal goals is the recollection and imitation of Christ's martyrdom, his desire for "spiritual marriage" can be obsessive, voyeuristic, neurasthenic. If mystics are guardians of an "exemplary discipline," they can also resemble satanic birds perched on Eden's walls, relishing self-chastisement. They "watch" their own and others psychopathology:

> You watchers on the wall
> grown old with care
> I too looked from the wall
> I shall look no more

> tell us what you saw
> the lord I sought to serve
> caught in the thorn grove
> his blood on his brow

To the martyr, destruction is both a friend and an enemy:

> What friend or enemy
> sets free the cry
> of the bell

Because the cry of pain or death releases the cry for redemption and the cry of sexual distress sets the bell of mystical marriage ringing, Hill accepts what at first would seem unacceptable.

The ninth section best illustrates Hill's complex attitudes towards sleep, death, sexual passion, and the mystical marriage. At first, it would seem that the soul yearns for annihilation and that love and sleep provide therapeutic tranquility. Christ here is both Eros and Thanatos, and, shockingly, he is also a card dealer dealing out wounds for those who sadistically or masochistically relish them.

> This love will see me dead
> he has the place in mind
> where I am free to die
> be true at last true love
>
> my love meet me half-way
> I bear no sword of fear
> where you dwell I
> dwell also says my lord
>
> dealing his five wounds
> so cunning and so true
> of love to rouse this death
> I die to sleep in love

Imitating Christ by dying from life, the meditating soul puts down its "sword of fear" and enters into a mystical marriage with its beloved lord. As if to repudiate the warning in the famous *Imitation of Christ* that "spiritual armour shall always, as long as thou livest, be necessary for thee,"[18] the meditator discards his armor to love Christ as purely as he can. Through his and Christ's sacrifice he achieves Eucharistic "at-one-ment": "For whoso eateth my flesh and drinketh my blood, he shall dwell in me and I in him."[19] The colloquial stress on "die" at the end of Hill's poem, however, indicates that the meditator's desire has not died at all but passed through death into a greater intensity. The love he seeks through crucifixion is not eternal sleep or bodily annihilation, although it may come to that, but a new dispensation, a burst of pentecostal energy. The poem, like so many of Hill's, is in Merle Brown's phrase a "double lyric." It can be read in two ways, depending on which connotations are chosen for the polyvalent words.

Paradoxes run rampant through "Pentecost Castle" as Hill shows how losses in sexual love are compensated by gains in spiritual love, and vice versa. He twists and turns, like Petrarch recording his tormenting chills and heats for Laura:

> And you my spent heart's treasure
> my yet unspent desire
> measurer past all measure
> cold paradox of fire
>
> as seeker so forsaken
> consentingly denied
> your solitude a token
> the sentries at your side
>
> fulfillment to my sorrow
> indulgence of your prey
> the sparrowhawk the sparrow
> the nothing that you say

In this economy, the heart's treasure of desire appears spent but then produces more desire, as if no measurer could ever deplete or fill it. Sexual desire is burned or fended off by sentries so that the mystical marriage can occur. The poet converts his losses and sparrowlike humiliations into words, his sexual losses into spiritual gains.

Like Robert Lowell in his first book, *Land of Unlikeness*, Hill wanders through a spiritually divided land and borrows a phrase which Etienne Gilson applied to St. Bernard (who in turn took it from Augustine's *regio dissimilitudinus*): "Such is the condition of those that live in the Land of Unlikeness. They are not happy there. Wandering, hopelessly revolving, in the 'Circuit of the impious' those who tread this weary round suffer not only the loss of God but also the loss of themselves."[20] Only paradoxical poems, it would seem, can capture the unlikenesses of this lost land. Encastled, the haunted lover transcends his dark night only by fastidiously recording the conflicts within:

> Splendidly-shining darkness
> proud citadel of meekness
> likening us our unlikeness
> majesty of our distress
>
> emptiness ever thronging
> untenable belonging

The romantic mania that descends on inhabitants of the "Pentecost Castle" makes it impossible for them to abide there. The castle promises transient, untenable bliss rather than the kind of eternal fulfillment that the lover, in moments of isolation, longs for:

> how long until this longing
> end in unending song
>
> and soul for soul discover
> no strangeness to dissever
> and lover keep with lover
> a moment and for ever

PASSION RITUALIZED

It is one of Hill's most eloquent moments. The actual end of Hill's song occurs after two more sections, but Hill's question applies not only to his poem but to all human desires. Like Baudelaire, another poet of tenebrous longings and melancholy disillusionments, Hill finds great pathos in the lover's inability to quell his longing. What Eliot said of Baudelaire's romanticism applies equally to Hill's, namely that "in much romantic poetry the sadness is due to the exploitation of the fact that no human relations are adequate to human desires, but also to the disbelief in any further object for human desires than that which, being human, fails to satisfy them."[21] This constitutes the romantic *caballero's* damnation.

"Lachrimae"

"Lachrimae" is another tortuous but splendidly wrought meditation on the suffering inherent in passion and the traditional means of alleviating it. Hill examines dreams, rituals, symbols of the church, secular artifice, and techniques of Christian meditation and martydom as possible cures. No sooner has the poet constructed a stay against confusion than, as he gloomily remarks, "all that he has made / vanishes in the chaos of the dark." Hill imagines the poet as a frantic Christ who has been oddly transported to or transformed into a leaking boat on a flood of tears. He bails out the water rushing in, knowing that if he stops for a moment he will drown (and drown all those seeking salvation) and if he continues he may die of exhaustion. The poem also rings several symbolic changes, often blasphemously funny, on Christ as a swimmer (with a glance at Allen Tate's "The Swimmers") who treads water and teaches life's castaways to do the same.

In the postdiluvian world, Christ embodies some of the futility of penitential exercises. As Eliot says in "The Dry Salvages": "We have to think of them as forever bailing . . . / In a drifting boat with a slow leakage," and think of Christ as the "salvager." Hill makes use of Eliot's imagery in his first sonnet:

> Crucified Lord, you swim upon your cross
> and never move. Sometimes in dreams of hell
> the body moves but moves to no avail
> and is at one with that eternal loss.

Hill's swimmer may be compared to Yeats's dancer in "Among School Children." But Hill emphasizes how all ceremonious ritual or artifice is skillfully and perhaps perversely designed to inflict pain and habituate one to it. Hill addresses Christ as well as himself in an ironic meditation on the artificer's "at-one-ment":

> you are the world's atonement on the hill.
> This is your body twisted by our skill
> into a patience proper for redress.

Thinking of the crucifixion on tear-swept Calvary and of Noah's ark wrecked on Ararat, Hill excoriates rather than worships images of Christ's patient suffering. The religious imagination, Hill observes, twists the historical event of Christ's crucifixion into artifice for its own rhetorical purposes and psychological needs. Christ is thereby made to suffer, twisted, paradoxically, to "straighten out" humanity (*redresser,* from Old French *dresser,* means to make straight), only because humanity has tortured itself and Christ.

Critics anxious to link Hill's "Lachrimae" to traditions of Christian devotional poetry fail to notice Hill's criticism of Christian devotion. Although his epigraph refers to St. Robert Southwell's meditation on Christ's crucifixion in *Mary Magdalen's Funeral Tears,* Hill reverses Southwell's assertions. His epigraph reads: "Passions I allow, and loves I approve, onely I would wish that men would alter their object and better their intent." Hill's fifth sonnet begins: "Loves I allow and passions I approve." He uses the "composition of place," made famous by *The Spiritual Exercises of St. Ignatius* with similar insubordination. He imagines Christ on the cross so he can heckle and interrogate Him. When

Hill addresses Christ, he immediately recognizes differences rather than similarities. If the Christian mystics and devotional poets of the English Renaissance believed in Christ and His salvation, Hill is never more than passionately ambivalent.

In "Lachrimae," Hill is a historian and psychologist of meditation rather than its propagandist. He comments on and dramatizes religious experience without ever affirming belief. His concerns are more with poetic technique than with dogmatic exegesis. He said in an interview:

> Paradox, and the closely related oxymoron, belong both to the tradition of mystical poetry and to the tradition of Petrarchan poetry, which are the main models for "The Pentecost Castle" and "Lachrimae." Certain kinds of poetry contain certain kinds of in-built problems to be solved. How, for instance, do you cope with this volatile and very treacherous instrument, paradox? How do you enter that strange relationship with form and language in which you partly guide them, and they partly guide you?[22]

As in "The Pentecost Castle," Hill finds models for "Lachrimae" in the sacred and profane love poetry of the Spanish Renaissance. Hill's fourth poem alludes to an anonymous "Soneto a Cristo Crucificado"[23] about a man's love for Christ on the cross, but Hill contradicts the Spanish poet by declaring that he cannot be enamored of Christ, however much he tries. Hill's second poem borrows motifs from Francisco de Quevedo's sonnet portraying a lover locked in a ring. But if Quevedo boasts of possessing the lover and, in fact, the whole cosmos of love, Hill writes despairingly of his dispossession and the collapse of a cosmos. Hill's last poem offers a close translation of a sonnet by Lope de Vega,[24] which describes an unrequited alliance with Christ. Hill deviates only slightly from the original because, in de Vega, he finds a disillusionment similar to his own.

Not only does Hill develop motifs from the Petrarchan tradition, but, like the French Symbolists, he also constructs his sonnets according to Petrarch's demanding rhyme scheme (abba

abba cde cde). The ability to transfigure splenetic, tenebrous dissipations into opulent, intricately-designed artifice and to chart the paradoxes of the passionate lover makes Baudelaire or Rimbaud as attractive to Hill as Petrarch or de Vega. At the root of "Lachrimae" is the symbolist conviction that poetry is a substitute religion. But, for Hill, the substitute religion is also flawed. After the gods have died, as Stevens said, poetry's supreme fictions will take their place. Hill, however, would like to think that all the arts and not just poetry will take religion's place, and "Lachrimae" offers a museum of tapestries, old poems, Renaissance dance music (John Dowland's and Peter Philips's pavans for lute or viol), masques (Ben Jonson's *Masque of Blacknesse*), and icons as possible antidotes.

In Hill's world, artifice patterns and checks the poet's "spontaneous overflow of powerful feelings," which in "Lachrimae" takes the form of a gush of tears. It is as if Mary Magdalen in Southwell's *Funeral Tears* had no angels to dampen her sobs and assuage her fears. Even with them, she is nearly unconsolable: "I will live out my living death by his grave, and dye on my dying life by his sweet tombe."[25] His goal is the same as John Dowland's in his dance music, elaborately entitled "Lachrimae or Seven tears figured in seven passionate Pavans with divers other pavans, galiards, and almands, set forth for the lute, viols, or violins, in five parts" (1605). Dowland's music, like Hill's poem, is a combination of self-revelation and self-renunciation, not an escape from remorse and despair but a fusion of explosive emotion with image and ritual pattern.

With their armor of Latin titles and allusions to Catholic rituals and Renaissance musicians, Hill's meditative lyrics are about the pastness of the past as well as about its relevance to the present. They never glorify the past. What Southwell found invidious in Renaissance society Hill finds invidious in modern society. Southwell complained that "for as passion, and especially this of love, is in these daies the chief commaunder of most men's actions, and the Idol to which both tongues and pennes doe sacrifice their ill bestowed labours: so is there nothing nowe more needefull to bee intreated, then how to direct these humors into their due courses, and to draw this floud of affections into the righte chanel."[26] Hill's sonnets, in compliance with Southwell, map out intricate networks of channels to drain and guide the lachrymose flood.

Rituals of Meditation

"Lachrimae," as the poet John Peck has observed, "scourge[s] the traditions of meditation and of meditative verse,"[27] in order to test their contemporary and historical validity. The traditional reunion of the alienated soul with Christ is chronically perplexed. "I will tell you plainly," says Lorenzo Scupoli in a recension of the *Unseen Warfare*, "the greatest and most perfect thing a man may desire to attain is to come near to God and dwell in union with Him."[28] Scupoli exuded the confidence his medieval faith allowed. Hill retracts traditional paradigms. Louis Martz argues that "without expecting any hard and fast divisions, then, we should expect to find a formal meditation falling into three distinguishable portions, corresponding to the acts of memory, understanding, and will—portions which we might well call composition, analysis, and colloquy."[29] So Hill broods repeatedly on the "Crucified Lord," analyzes his love and hostility towards Christ, and gives to his feelings of estrangement a secular emphasis. His sequence ends:

> So many nights the angel of my house
> has fed such urgent comfort through a dream,
> whispered 'your lord is coming, he is close'
>
> that I have drowsed half-faithful for a time
> bathed in pure tones of promise and remorse:
> 'tomorrow I shall wake to welcome him.'

The traditional end of a meditation, the colloquy, for Hill is a possibility repeatedly postponed.

As both memorial and valediction to Catholic meditation, "Lachrimae" appropriately chooses Southwell as its patron Saint. He was the first to introduce Continental practices of meditation successfully into English Renaissance poetry. "In establishing these arts on English soil, Southwell became the first significant writer of a new kind of English poetry, a kind which at its best blended religious meditation with Elizabethan lyric."[30] Because he traveled to England from Rome to serve the Catholic church during Elizabeth's reign, Southwell was hunted, captured, tortured and finally hung, quartered, and burned. For Hill, Southwell's insensitivity to pain and pursuit of self-immolation is frightening as well as extraordinary. He told John Haffenden that "to take the group who have most interested me in recent years, the Catholic martyrs of the age of Elizabeth I, there seems there to have been what I might call a pedagogy of martyrdom, a scholastic process of training towards that deliberate goal. I do find the psychology of that kind of procedure fascinating, and of course chilling in many ways" (*VP*, pp. 90–91). Faced with crucifixion, Hill's meditating persona copies Southwell's Magdalen, suffering in a "perplexed manner, now falling, now rising in her owne uncertainties." But Magdalen affirms: "If hee bee not within thee, stand weeping without, and seeke him in other creatures, sith being present in all, hee may bee found in any."[31] Hill's meditator is similarly dispossessed, but, while he dreams of embracing Christ, he never actually does so.

Hill is as insubordinate with the order of traditional spiritual exercises as he is with the order of Dowland's dance music. Dowland ends his sequence with "Lachrimae Verae." Hill places his "Lachrimae Verae" first. To counter St. Ignatius, Hill opens his meditation with a grotesque vision of Christ on the cross. In Loyola's four-week and four-part meditation, crucifixion is the topic of the third week. The first week is devoted to searching the soul for private sins. In Southwell's meditation, Magdalen weeps at Christ's tomb; Hill's meditator weeps at Christ's crucifixion. If this is a composition of place, it is a strange one, although Hill finds precedents in Donne and Crashaw, who also imagined Christ bizarrely swimming on the cross. In "The Crosse," Donne declared:

> Who can deny mee power, and liberty
> To stretch mine arms, and mine owne Crosse to be?
> Swimme, and at every stroake thou art the Crosse.

In Crashaw's "Sancta Maria Dolorum," similarly, Christ appears to Mary as a swimmer:

> She sees her son, her God
> Bow with a load
> Of borrowed sins; And swimme
> In woes that were not made for Him.

Hill's Christ swims in tears shed by mourners and tries to account for them on his cross.

After an analysis of the scene of Crucifixion, which considers the martyr's reconciliation with hellish torment, the poet utters his derisive colloquy. In order to mediate between anguished mind and torturous world, Christ, poet, and artifact are turned (twisted) purgatorially, like Eliot on his staircase, but never manage, in the end, in turn away from the omnipresent fact of failure and pain. The poet declares:

> I cannot turn aside from what I do;
> you cannot turn away from what I am.
> You do not dwell in me nor I in you
>
> however much I pander to your name
> or answer to your lords of revenue,
> surrendering the joys that they condemn.

In "Ash Wednesday," Eliot despairs of heroic ascents but continues to ascend. For Hill, rest and passive acceptance are impossible, but so is grace. He turns in pain but cannot cease to turn. He cannot evade the writhing of others or the writhing of Christ but confronts and vicariously suffers them. Although he renounces joys and pays the "lords of revenue" the standard wages of contrition, at the end he appears bankrupt. Ironically, he only possesses his losses, futile strivings for salvation, and wounds.

Somewhat like Simone Weil, who, as Hill has said, "devoted a good deal of 'wistful attention' to the Church but . . . was unable, finally, to assent,"[32] Hill remains distant, sceptical, drawn to Christian devotion only to find himself repelled by it. In the fourth section, "Lachrimae Coactae," a poem of "forced tears," Hill speaks further of his futile effort to imitate Christ and accept Christian dispensations:

> Crucified Lord, however much I burn
> to be enamoured of your paradise,
> knowing what ceases and what will not cease,
> frightened of hell, not knowing where to turn,
>
> I fall between harsh grace and hurtful scorn.

His painful brooding winds tortuously through ironies and paradoxes:

> You are the crucified who crucifies,
> self-withdrawn even from your own device,
> your trim-plugged body, wreath of rakish thorn.
>
> What grips me then, or what does my soul grasp?
> If I grasp nothing what is there to break?
> You are beyond me, innermost true light,
>
> uttermost exile for no exile's sake,
> king of our earth not caring to unclasp
> its void embrace, the semblance of your quiet.

Hill imagines Christ as an unacknowledged legislator of the world, whose covenant or word still abides (in language if nowhere else). But he mocks Him as a rakish, debauched libertine who indulges in flamboyant suffering so that his communicants can indulge vicariously. He may be either the inner light of the Protestant or the sacramental bread of the Catholic. His spirit is absent from the contemporary world but also accessible to it. His fate is to be guided by forces of attraction and repulsion like a satellite orbiting invisibly through heaven.

The crux of Christ's presence and absence forms the background of Hill's last meditation on the "Crucified Lord," "Lachrimae Antiquae Novae." Hill again looks at an icon of Christ (the imagistic "device" mentioned in Sonnet 4) and mulls over the linguistic connotations of the Christ Word. As a signifier, the Word makes present what is absent, but as an "emotive cliché" (as Hill calls "the Word" in his gloss to "Annunciations"), it no longer communicates vital significance. But is that because the modern mind has betrayed the Word by consigning it to a dusty museum?

> Crucified Lord, so naked to the world,
> you live unseen within that nakedness,
> consigned by proxy to the judas-kiss
> of our devotion, bowed beneath the gold,
>
> with re-enactments, penances foretold:
> scentings of love across a wilderness
> of retrospection, wild and objectless
> longings incarnate in the carnal child.

Bowed beneath His halo, in this oblique portrait, Christ is bowed beneath the weight of tradition's and humanity's impure motives, which Hill symbolizes as "gold." He admonishes humanity to reenact personal sins and accept penitential punishment. But what is remembered, besides the romantic, saintly love which the naked Christ represents? If Christ is the innocent, natural child in the wilderness, an incarnation of otherworldly ("objectless") love, what does he have to say to modern man? Pound lambasted the Christian and romantic "abstract love of mankind at large regardless of his abstract and collective infamies and imbecilities."[33] Hill finds in Christ a cherishable emblem to elegize.

As an iconoclast half in love with what he destroys, Hill observes with sad magniloquence:

> Beautiful for themselves the icons fade;
> the lions and the hermits disappear.
> Triumphalism feasts on empty dread,
>
> fulfilling triumphs of the festal year.

The death of romantic and Christian art fits into a larger pattern of destruction and reconstruction. "Lachrimae's" pavans reenact this rhythm and thereby make it tolerable. Hill states that "we are possibly shaken out of our self-containment, our passionate attachment to those forms of hermetic mastery which must be so rebuked by life. But Romantic art is thoroughly familiar with the reproaches of life. Accusation, self-accusation, are the very life-blood of its most assured rhetoric" (*LL*, p. 3).

It is characteristic of Hill to speak of triumphant ends and climactic failures in the penultimate section and then, in the final section, to prophesy a new beginning: "At this dark solstice filled with frost and fire / your passion's ancient wounds must bleed anew." Hill's final colloquy questions the motives for final colloquy and reverses the traditional structure of meditation with its apocalyptic marriage at the end. "Lachrimae Amantis" (the tears of a lover) is a monologue which again affirms the poet's baffled attraction to Christ and his desire for communion, which pushes against his reservations but never overcomes them:

> What is there in my heart that you should sue
> so fiercely for its love? What kind of care
> brings you as though a stranger to my door
> through the long night and in the icy dew
>
> seeking the heart that will not harbour you,
> that keeps itself religiously secure?

Always critical of comforting angels and drowsy elixirs, Hill remains religiously secure from religious commitment and consolation to the end.

Although critics have welcomed Hill as a spokesman for "the spiritual chaos of the twentieth century,"[34] Hill disappoints them by speaking for the chaos of all centuries. His sense of estrangement from religious order is as intense as his expressed need for such order. More quizzical than Donne, he possesses some of the earlier poet's stormy desire for divinity:

> Batter my heart, three person'd God; for, you
> As yet but knocke, breathe, shine, and seeke to mend;
> That I may rise, and stand, o'erthrow mee, 'and bend
> Your force, to break, blowe, burn and make me new.
> I, like an usurpt town, to'another due,
> Labour to'admit you, but Oh, to no end . . .

Conjoining Donne's apocalyptic exclamations with Lope de Vega's less vociferous perplexities, Hill succeeds in creating a meditational poetry of his own that is at once dependent on the assumptions, expectations, and styles of past meditational poetry as well as critical of them. He recreates the form with such insight that it has all the vibrations of novelty.

Recreation and Decreation

Hill's second, third, and fifth sonnets ("The Masque of Blackness," "Martyrium," and "Pavana Dolorosa") renew Christian themes but explore their relations to the ambiguities in artistic creation. At the same time, however, they suggest that creation *is* crucifixion, the redemptive word nailed and twisted into significant shape. Hill sees the artist's sacrificial withdrawal from the world as "decreation" and its goal as "recreation." The artist-god creates "only by hiding himself," Simone Weil wrote. "We participate in the creation of the world by decreating ourselves."[35] Wallace Stevens, elaborating on Weil's distinction between decreation and destruction in *The Necessary Angel*, concluded that "modern reality is a reality of decreation, in which our revelations are not the revelations of belief, but the precious portents of our own powers."[36] For Hill, decreation and destruction are more closely aligned. The uncreated void, or what he calls "the chaos of the dark," arises from imaginative renunciation as well as from physical destruction. Revelations portend poetic powers as often as they portend political ones.

If the mystic celebrates delicious wounds, Hill, like Roland Barthes, recognizes the *jouissance* aroused by the gap in the decreated text, which resembles emotions stimulated by the rent in a woman's garment or the break in a musical harmony. Hill says of the artist:

> Self-wounding martyrdom, what joys you have,
> true-torn among this fictive consonance,
> music's creation of the moveless dance,
> the decreation to which all must move.

If decreation is a wounding, it is also integral to the rhythm of the "moveless dance," which proceeds by contrary stresses and releases, as do "Ash-Wednesday feasts, ascetic opulence, / the wincing lute, so real in its pretence, / itself a passion amorous of love." Hill's imaginary gardens, like Marianne Moore's, have real toads in them. His sombre fasts contain opulent feasts, his tenebrous silences ecstatic cries, and his chaotic darknesses magnificent splendors:

> Your silence is an ecstasy of sound
>
> and your nocturnals blaze upon the day.
> I founder in desire for things unfound.
> I stay amid the things that will not stay.

Torn by contrary forces, trapped in a dance of endless tears and tearings, urged on by a music of vibrant consonance and dissonance, Hill stands outside (in "ex-stasis") and contemplates the rhythm of life's "mournful melodies."

Without a decreative swerve from reality, Hill suggests in *The Masque of Blacknesse*, the artist would be destroyed by the sun's brilliance. He must erect artifice to absorb and reflect it:

> Splendour of life so splendidly contained,
> brilliance made bearable. It is the east
> light's embodiment, fit to be caressed,
> the god Amor with his eyes of diamond . . . .

Humankind can love life's splendors only when both wear masks.

But Hill is not always content with art's recreated world. It can be an unpalatable paradise of dainty devices for the man who wants real flesh and blood. He ponders, movingly and ambiguously, the

> celestial worldliness on which has dawned
> intelligence of angels, Midas' feast,
> the stony hunger of the dispossessed
> locked into Eden by their own demand.

Midas, the angelic genius or artist, wants to turn everything into gold but finds that his lust for artificial perfection locks him into a barren Eden. Hill wonders why he creates such a paradise since it offends the natural instincts and quickly comes to ruin. His dubious muse,

> Self-love, the slavish master of this trade,
> conquistador of fashion and remark,
> models new heavens in his masquerade,
>
> its images intense with starry work,
> until he tires and all that he has made
> vanishes in the chaos of the dark.

The title and motifs of Hill's poem come from Jonson's *Masque of Blacknesse* (1605). An opulent, costly affair, it was the form in which Jonson and Inigo Jones displayed their lavish theatrical schemes and flattered James I (and Elizabeth before him). In England, at the turn of the sixteenth century, capitalists controlled the theatres and the actors' companies. Entrepreneurs launched expeditions to America to take gold and other commodities from the Indians and trade in slaves. The conquistadors had ravaged the Aztecs a century earlier. Hill alludes obliquely to the historical milieu of Jonson's *Masque* to emphasize art's roots in impure motives. Art can be a "masquerade," a pretentious show confected out of self-love, just as easily as it can be a splendid embodiment of "the god Amor." It may do more harm than good, especially when, as Niger explains to Oceanus in Jonson's *Masque*,

> the fabulous voices of some few
> Poor brain-sicke men, stil'd *Poets*, here with you,
> Haue, with such enuie of their graces, sung
> The painted *Beauties*, other *Empires* sprung;
> Letting their loose, and winged fictions flie
> To infect all clymates . . . .

In "Lachrimae," Hill decreates myths of beauty and empire as well, but he also "models new heavens in his masquerade."

Faced by time's erosion, Hill is the raucous comedian of decreation as much as its gloomy disciple. With Yeats, Hill mocks the "masterful images" because the world from which they grow is so shockingly different. He mocks, for his romantic foolishness, the poet who martyrs himself to innocence, ceremony, and beauty. He looks both ways, at art's spirit world and at the world of carnal waste. He imitates both Jesus and Janus:

> The Jesus-faced man walking crowned with flies
> who swats the roadside grass or glances up
> at the streaked gibbet with its birds that swoop,
> who scans his breviary while the sweat dries,
>
> fades, now, among the fading tapestries,
> brooches of crimson tears where no eyes weep,

> a mouth unstitched into a rimless cup,
> torn clouds the cauldrons of the martyrs' cries.

The eyes and mouths of living and dead artists, once finely-tuned, are caught in a grotesque attrition of natural decay.

Although tempted to despair, Hill ends his "Martyrium" with a passionate declaration of the transfiguring power of love. The amorous poet may be confused by his "clamorous love," but he suffers it and transforms it into exquisite images. Like Christ, he submits to crucifixion, so humanity (his readers) can know that they do not suffer alone. Hill describes this process in a cryptic, allusive way: "Viaticum transfigures earth's desire / in rising vernicles of summer air." Viaticum is the Eucharist given to a dying person or one in danger of dying, and vernicles are pictures resembling St. Veronica's handkerchief, which held an impression of Christ's face. Rather fancifully, Hill imagines that Christ's spirit rises like summer air (like the *spiritus*, the breath of god) and uplifts the spirits of earthly lovers who are suffering or dying.

Few poets scrutinize their poetic motives with Hill's kind of self-consciousness and then write poems that criticize poetry as a gross act of self-wounding and self-seeking. Hill's poems are self-reflexive, even to the point of reflecting on their self-reflexiveness. Hill presents the imagination at war with itself, battling against romantic and Christian tenements it half loves in order to build new ones. But Hill does not accept the roles of poetic anarchist, Christian soldier, or bellicose romantic easily. His reservations are obvious in his essay, "Poetry as 'Menace' and 'Atonement' ":

> It is a not unfamiliar modernist theory which "requires art to be destructive," which "takes the violence of novelty as essential to success." I may choose to ignore this theory, but I can't seem to be ignorant of it. I have to say, therefore, that the "menace" to which I propose to refer is not that species of anti-bourgeois terrorism with which the names of Baudelaire, the Surrealists and Antonin Artaud have been indiscriminately linked. (*LL*, p. 4)

Tenebrae

The menace which Hill fights against is the anarchy and inevitable attrition of artistic tradition, its entropic decline into dead images and clichés. The repeated striving to perfect and enliven language, to cut away the dead wood to let the new shoots grow, is his self-appointed task. His stately music of inevitable failures and partial successes is accompanied by dolorous and joyful weeping. The meditator weeps over his failures, but he does not drown (or drown his melancholy) in them. He remains a swimmer in the harrowing, lachrymose waters.

"An Apology for the Revival of Christian Architecture in England"

In this long sequence of sonnets in the middle of *Tenebrae*, Hill shifts his focus from personal dilemmas explored in "The Pentecost Castle" and "Lachrimae" to tenebrous aspects of political and social life. No longer a narrative "I" but a communal "we" speaks in the poems, and for the whole culture. The sequence investigates nineteenth-century Britain, its romantic idealism, industrialism, and rural squirearchies with a characteristic blend of sceptical enchantment and incendiary wit. If historians tend to applaud the nineteenth century for its humanitarian achievements, its stability in foreign affairs, and improvements in living and working conditions, Hill tends to see the century in a larger context of renaissance, decadence, and the expansion of empire.

Hill's "Apology" has a clarity and crispness distinct from earlier sequences. He speaks in his first sonnet of "Linnaean pentecosts," as if now he wants to adopt the precise, orderly style of the great Swedish botanist Linnaeus, who originated the system of taxonomic classification to gather all species into one great, intelligible order. Hill goes to Keats for similar reasons. He alludes to "Ode on a Grecian Urn," "The Eve of St. Mark," and "Ode to a Nightingale" and finds in Keats's autumnal atmospheres of keen sounds, pungent smells, and sharp sights models for imitation. If the rhetoric of *For the Unfallen*, *King Log*, and *Mercian Hymns* seems clotted and baroque, the sonnets in

"An Apology" seem comparatively relaxed and lyrical. Instead of the organ's reverberating boom, Hill now plays clear notes on harpsichord or lute. "An Apology" abounds with ringing bells, bird songs, clear whispers, chiming clocks, carols, resonant calls, and cries. As the leaves fall, Hill notes with ironic joy that he can now see the fundamental architecture of things. Summer's blinding vegetation dispersed, the poet takes a new look at reality:

> Autumn resumes the land, ruffles the woods
> with smoky wings, entangles them. Trees shine
> out from their leaves . . . .

The preceding sonnet, "Vocations," ends with a similar chiaroscuro of light and dark, in which the aging poet, reminded of death, finds the sounds and sights around him all the more pungent:

> The twittering pipistrelle, so strange and close,
>
> plucks its curt flight through the moist eventide;
> the children thread among old avenues
> of snowberries, clear-calling as they fade.

If "An Apology" is, like Pugin's, a defense of Christianity rather than an embarrassed apology, the "architecture" it finds congenial belongs to Newman and his disciples, who saw an apprehensible structure underlying all being. Hill sides, at least tentatively, with the Gothic revival of the nineteenth century, in which Catholics like Pugin (the poem's title comes from his architectural treatise) looked to rural feudalism and the religious order of medieval times as an alternative to the sooty chaos of industrial Britain. Hill's poem praises the Gothic revival's "new-burgeoned spires that sprung / crisp-leaved as though from dropping-wells." It attempts to embody the same natural crispness in its lines.

If there is one thing that unifies the many writers invoked in Hill's sequence, it is their social idealism. The nineteenth century experienced the famous reform bills, Christian socialists, trade unions, and legislation to alleviate grievances of blacks, women, children, workers, and students. Respectful of utopian reformers, Hill cannot resist upbraiding "wild-eyed" schemes for human betterment. His epigraph from Coleridge's *Anima Poetae* introduces a chord that will be struck many times throughout, and whose purpose it is to conjure up "the spiritual, Platonic old England . . . ." Although one might expect that this England corresponds to the "Christian Architecture" of Pugin, Coleridge actually envisioned something quite different. He said in his notebook:

Let me not confound the discriminating character and genius of a nation with the conflux of its individuals in cities and reviews. Let England be Sir Philip Sidney, Shakespeare, Milton, Bacon, Harrington, Swift, Wordsworth; and never let the names of Darwin, Johnson, Hume, *fur* it over. If these, too, must be England let them be another England; or, rather, let the first be old England, the spiritual, Platonic old England, and the second, with Locke at the head of the philosophers and Pope of the poets, together with the long list of Priestleys, Paleys, Hayleys, Darwins, Mr. Pitts, Dundassess, &c., &c., be the representatives of commercial Great Britain.[37]

Like Pugin, Coleridge denounced contemporary industrialism, but he sought an antidote in Renaissance humanism rather than in medieval Catholicism. To Pugin, the Renaissance was the "fatal mistake" that created the "miserable confusion" in contemporary architecture. Apologizing for his 1843 "Apology," Pugin declared that "the object of this tract is . . . to place Christian architecture in its true position,—to exhibit the claims it possesses on our veneration and obedience, as the only correct expression of the faith, wants, and climate of our country."[38] Hill, Pugin, and Coleridge all seek to find and renew the fundamental lineaments of English culture, just as Plato sought the ideal beneath multiple appearances.

In order to give all parties equal time, Hill allows the nineteenth-century industrialist, condemned by Pugin and Coleridge, to speak in an epigraph taken from Disraeli's novel

Coningsby. The industrialist, Hill suggests, also serves an *anima poetae* in building an ideal city of factories and smokestacks. Christian spiritualism and Platonic idealism, in fact, may contribute to the industrialist's apocalyptic vision of nature converted to artifice. The three sonnets comprising "A Short History of British India" describe how capitalists and imperialists, in their "refusal . . . to submit to or be ruled by any of the exigencies of the created natural order," effectively ruin a nation's culture and natural environment. Another sonnet describes how the modern technological world, by chasing after supernatural ideals of power, gradually engineers its doom. Hill examines the architecture of nuclear power plants and missile silos, "the half-built ruins of the new estate, / warheads of mushrooms round the filter-pond." In defining the virtues of a Platonic, Christian England existing somewhere in the imagined past (and perhaps nowhere), Hill also finds it imperative to apologize for the faults it has either fostered or contributed to. His poem is an "Apology" in a double sense, a justification and a lament for past ideals.

In spite of all his reservations and caustic attacks, Hill opens "An Apology" by ceremoniously speaking for the spirits of nineteenth-century idealists rising from their graves. He hopes that their pentecostal utterance will not be "tongued with fire beyond the language of the living," but vigorously contemporaneous:

> And, after all, it is to them we return.
> Their triumph is to rise and be our hosts:
> lords of unquiet or of quiet sojourn,
> those muddy-hued and midge-tormented ghosts.

These are not rarefied, Christian ghosts but secular ghosts of heroes who slogged "knee deep in the salt marsh, heaving a cutlass, / bitten by flies." Hill's ghosts, unlike Eliot's Gerontion, who decays pathetically in his windy house, have suffered the torments of the "unquiet" life of political action (Disraeli, Oastler) and the travail of the "quiet" contemplative life (Coleridge, Wordsworth). History may be a deceptive labyrinth of "cunning passages, contrived corridors," but in Hill's "Quaint Mazes," the dead "speak a word" and do so with pentecostal vehemence. One of the dead who speaks is Titania, queen of the fairies in *A Midsummer Night's Dream*. She laments the death of the cultivated ground and the spiritual malaise which has imprisoned her people in a labyrinth.

> The fold stands empty in the drownèd field,
> And crows are fatted with the murrion flock;
> And nine men's morris is filled up with mud;
> And the quaint mazes in the wanton green
> For lack of tread are indistinguishable.
> (*MND* II, i, 96–100)

To carve out of the social wilderness a well-pruned, distinguishable garden, Hill imagines "Linnaean pentecosts" descending with a generative formality that is both sexual and artistic. Linnaeus was famous in his early years for his fanciful descriptions of the sexuality of plants. For Hill, he is a symbol of the naturalist who can rejuvenate civilization:

> On blustery lilac-bush and terrace-urn
> bedaubed with bloom Linnaean pentecosts
> put their pronged light; the chilly fountains burn.

As often in Hill, the ghosts appear more alive than the living. Their purpose is to descend on the quaint country estate and instruct the clipping of excrescent growths with pronged shears.

To strip away quaint fancies of nineteenth-century evangelists and utopians, Hill declares, the intellect should move closer to nature rather than further away from it. His religion takes for its domain the passions of the heart:

> Religion of the heart, with trysts and quests
>
> and pangs of consolation, its hawk's hood
> twitched off for sweet carnality, again
> rejoices in old hymns of servitude,

> haunting the sacred well, the hidden shrine.
> It is the ravage of the heron wood;
> it is the rood blazing upon the green.

Unlike Keats, who once said he was "certain of nothing but of the holiness of the Heart's affections and the truth of Imagination—What the imagination seizes as beauty must be truth,"[39] Hill shares with his contemporary Ted Hughes a belief in the heart's predatory desire "for sweet carnality." Hill, in fact, countermands Keats throughout the sequence. His "chilly" ravagings in the quiet garden (ornamented with a terrace urn) recall similar mad pursuits in Keats's "Ode on a Grecian Urn," but Hill's terrace urn, like the rest of his poem, is more susceptible to the entanglements of earth and vegetation (as the Latin root, *terra*, implies) than Keats's urn. Keats's Grecian urn is eternal; it will remain "when old age shall this generation waste." Hill's urn is fixed in time, "bedaubed with bloom" and already decaying. The sexual light and phallic hosts from the past have scratched and scarred it (with pronged tools and didactic pens). Keats's urn, on the other hand, has evaded ordinary sexuality and natural violence. It stands apart, innocent, quiet, like an "unravished bride."

Hill takes the first line of Keats's fourth stanza, "Who are these coming to the sacrifice?" for the title of his third sonnet but uses it only to set off an avalanche of contrasts. Keats describes a procession of townspeople towards a place of sacrifice, from which they will never return. Like Yeats's golden bird, they are "gathered into the artifice of eternity" forever. This notion of a transcendent realm of eternal beauty and truth is part of the Platonic "high idealism" endemic to nineteenth-century romantics and philosophers. T. H. Green, who liked to quote Keats's "Ode on a Grecian Urn," believed in similar sacrifices and similar heavens. Hill claims that "Green gave to his readers crucial ideas of self-sacrifice" (*LL*, p. 118), but he ridicules both the "high" praise given to such idealists and their "high" idealism. He imagines them in a church of their own making and, like Coleridge, often "high" on opiates. He begins his sonnet "Who are these coming to the Sacrifice?" with the "high voices in domestic chapels" but then presents a hilarious account of a holy ceremony (the sacrament of matrimony) turned on end. It echoes Carlyle's description of pealing tocsin and rushing carriages in Paris just before the September massacres in *The French Revolution* (part III, book 1, chap. iv). Hill writes:

> What an elopement that was: the hired chaise
> tore through the fir-grove, scattered kinsmen flung
> buckshot and bridles, and the tocsin swung
> from the tarred bellcote dappled with dove-smears.

The poem finishes, not with an affirmation of art's immortal marriage of beauty and truth, but with a recognition of vows perpetually broken and spoiled ("dappled with dove-smears").

Hill looks at all nineteenth-century ideals of social conscience and evangelical faith like the spider in his room of discarded bric-a-brac. If anything is permanent, it is the impermanence of things. What remains is not the perfected romantic image, "the unravished bride," but the sexual desire for new loves and the artistic desire for new icons. But ideals remain to be cherished:

> Be moved by faith, obedience without fault,
> the flawless hubris of heroic guilt,
> the grace of visitation; and be stirred
>
> by all her god-quests, her idolatries,
> in conclave of abiding injuries,
> sated upon the stillness of the bride.

Although "her" refers to India, Hill speaks generally, and he does so in a way Keats would find strange. His dense, ironic meditation concentrates on the artist's heroic, flawless commitment to conscience in a society of many idolatries and crimes. His "Apology" is not a "flowery tale," sweetly told, or a "cold pastoral," but a tough and often sad acknowledgment of political betrayals, artistic ugliness, and personal pain.

East and West

Following other twentieth-century writers, Hill journeys eastward to discover invigorating contrasts and correspondences with his own culture. Ezra Pound, in his search for poetic and philosophical wisdom, ransacked the literatures of China and Japan. T. S. Eliot found material for *The Waste Land* and *Four Quartets* in Sanskrit and Buddhism. Yeats studied Indian and Japanese literature to find ceremonious models for his poetry and evidence for his theory that Asia and Europe represented contrary gyres. Hill travels to India not so much to procure poetic techniques or religious wisdom but rather, like Forster, "to depict lyrically the consequences of old betrayals . . . in the governance of Empire."[40]

Hill's attitude towards the destruction of Indian civilization by the nineteenth-century empire builders, however, is not as clear-cut as might be anticipated. Being committed to the idea that a culture, like a person, is determined by the images it pursues, Hill rebukes India and England alike for chasing invidious ends. Hill wants to affirm the human similarities between the two cultures as well as their differences.

He begins his tripartite "A Short History of British India" with moral directives:

> Make miniatures of the once-monstrous theme:
> the red-coat devotees, mêlées of wheels,
> Jagannath's lovers. With indifferent aim
> unleash the rutting cannon at the walls
>
> of forts and palaces; pollute the wells.
> Impound the memoirs for their bankrupt shame,
> fantasies of true destiny that kills
> 'under the sanction of the English name'.

The metaphor of destructive sexuality (the rutting cannon), as opposed to creative sexuality (exemplified by ripe mangoes in the next sonnet), underscores the perversity in Indian and British relations. The British murder the Indians, but, Hill points out, the Indians also murder themselves. Indian devotees annually threw themselves to be crushed under the enormous car wheels of Jagannath (an avatar of Krishna, whose name meant "lord of the world") as it careered through the street of Puri in Orissa. More sardonically than Keats, Hill imagines the destiny of the two cultures not as gyres but as cannon wheels colliding with each other, not to create but to kill. The "red-coat devotees" could be either the English soldiers shooting phallic cannons at the Indians (rutting means roaring and copulating) or the Indian devotees hurling themselves suicidally beneath their divine image. If the Indians are submissive, the English are aggressive, but both violate life to the same effect.

Hill's conception of India is riven with paradoxes. Its culture exemplifies innocence, self-abnegation, submissiveness, and fatalism but also—in contradistinction—naturalness, patient self-sacrifice, principled devotion, and passive resistance. Hill imagines India, in a fanciful burst of irony, as waiting thirty centuries (the length of its civilization) so that Britain can either destroy itself or India or both: "Suppose they sweltered here three thousand years / patient for our destruction." "Destiny is the great thing," Hill retorts, as he contemplates millennial fictions. In a flurry of gorgeous images depicting native fruitfulness and sexual marriages, Hill elegizes what Britain overrules in its frenzy of empire building:

> The mango is the bride-bed of light. Spring
> jostles the flame-tree. But new mandates bring
> new images of faith, good subahdars!
>
> The flittering candles of the wayside shrines
> melt into dawn. The sun surmounts the dust.
> Krishna from Radha lovingly untwines.

> Lugging the earth, the oxen bow their heads.
> The alien conscience of our days is lost
> among the ruins and on endless roads.

The death of conscience and the death of culture occur simultaneously. The English governors in India, the subahdars, by haughtily ignoring the natural conditions and culture around them or by actively uprooting them, poison the native soil.

The third and last sonnet in Hill's "Short History" outlines Britain's "alien conscience" and the effects of its loss. He catalogs exemplary statesmen who affirmed policies that were sympathetic to Indian culture and who tried to adjust foreign codes of behavior to indigenous ones. Hill summarizes the general, humanist sensibility that has died with them:

> Malcolm and Frere, Colebrooke and Elphinstone,
> the life of empire like the life of the mind
> 'simple, sensuous, passionate', attuned
> to the clear theme of justice and order, gone.

The British statesmen who governed India during the nineteenth century exemplified the kind of Christian humanism set forth in Milton's *Of Education*. There, Milton argued that education should enable a person "to perform justly, skilfully and magnanimously all the offices both private and publike of peace and war."[41] Poetry, as opposed to rhetoric, in "being lesse suttle and fine, but more simple, sensuous and passionate," should teach the future rulers the rudiments of moral feeling. "What glorious and magnificent use," Milton exclaimed, "might be made of Poetry both in divine and humane things."[42]

Hill contends that politicians should think and feel like poets and that poets should think and feel like politicians. Elphinstone, who wrote books about Indian history, did not want to implant "a vague simulacrum of British society" on Indian soil but "conserve traditional institutions."[43] Malcolm, in his *Political History*, advocated abandoning "all arrogant pretensions arising from the presumed superiority of our own knowledge, and seek the accomplishment of the great ends we have in view by the means which are the best suited to the peculiar nature of the objects."[44] The just emperor, like Linnaeus, is a naturalist who expertly cultivates the native soil and the traditions of those who live on it.

Much of India's traditional culture is dying, according to Hill, because the mind's "simple, sensuous and passionate" nature is out of tune with ideals of "justice and order." Although decay fertilizes the soil for new cultures, the new renaissance may be merely a renewal of an old decadence. The tawdry vestiges of once vital arts litter India's landscape and tourist shops.

> Gone the ascetic pastimes, the Persian
> scholarship, the wild boar run to ground,
> the watercolours of the sun and wind.
> Names rise like outcrops on the rich terrain,
>
> like carapaces of the Mughal tombs
> lop-sided in the rice-fields, boarded-up
> near railway-sidings and small aerodromes.
>
> 'India's a peacock-shrine next to a shop
> selling mangola, sitars, lucky charms,
> heavenly Buddhas smiling in their sleep.'

Ironically, it was Europe that descended as a formless, injudicious darkness to vex Asia to stony nightmare. According to the art historian Ernst Gombrich, "the illustrating of romances, histories and fables done in Persia from the fourteenth century onwards and later also in India under Mohammedan (Mogul) rulers, shows how much the artists of these lands had learned from the discipline which had confined them to the designing of patterns."[45] With the Persian arts and the Mughal emperors dead, or reduced to mass-produced commodities, India has become a grotesque parody of her splendid past.

Throughout "An Apology," Hill maps the topographical curves of cultures, as they rise and fall. "Destiny is the great thing, / true lord of annexation and arrears," he says, focusing on the teleological drives of nations. Where Hegel recommends fatal submission to destiny, however, Hill encourages judgment and active revolt. Hegel wrote: "to resist these world-historical individuals is a futile undertaking, for they are irresistably driven on to fulfill their task."[46] Hill sees resistance, whether passive or violent, as imperative in the struggle against noxious imperialists and cultural decline. To Spengler, who claimed, that "world history is the history of the great Cultures, and peoples are but the symbolic forms and vessels in which the men of these Cultures fulfil their Destinies,"[47] Hill would exclaim that if a culture regards human beings as vessels, their destruction is inevitable.

In "An Apology," Hill writes as often about the decline of the East as about the decline of the West. Like Spengler, he regards decadence as seasonal, as natural as the falling of leaves after a golden summer, but he abhors those who tear off the leaves and uproot the culture in defiance of natural laws. He mocks the fatalists who accept man's criminal assault on nature as "destiny" and the culture heroes, East or West, who build their renaissances on inhuman and unnatural practices. Although geographically and historically remote, Eastern and Western cultures share common rules, which they either subvert, manipulate, transcend, or obey. The desire to achieve "unity of being," to reconcile the exigencies of the native soil with the ethical precepts of revelation, Hill believes, unifies the two cultures in a common pursuit.

Autumnal Elegies

"An Apology" is a patchwork of deaths and resurrections in which one culture's renaissance arises from another's decadence. Renaissance, Hill points out, often is decadence disguised. When the dead come back to invigorate the living, they often convince the living, as well as themselves, that they are truly dead. In the sonnets about past splendors decaying, Hill borrows devices from the traditional pastoral elegy, as he did in earlier poems, but then turns them upside down. Rather than project despair for the deceased onto a whole society or landscape, linking the death of one to the death of all, Hill diagnoses the erosion of culture like an ecologist. He resurrects the dead, but rather than apotheosize them, he harangues them for their blunders. In several elegiac sonnets, he does not mourn the seasonal dying and falling of vegetation but heralds it as a cleansing that will reveal the fundamental bones beneath. His elegies turn into visionary poems about dying into more candid perception or withering into "the desolation of reality."

While Renaissance humanism came back with the Linnaean ghosts in "Quaint Mazes," the ghosts quickly lapse into wintry darkness in the next sonnet, "Damon's Lament for his Clorinda, Yorkshire 1654." The time is November and the end of the English Renaissance. In September 1654, the first Protectorate parliament met, and in the same year, Milton wrote his *Second Defence of the English People*, which denigrated royalists and kings (Hill alluded to it in *Mercian Hymns*). Several years earlier, in 1649, Charles I was beheaded and several years later, in 1660, Charles II regained the throne and began the Restoration. Is the death of the Renaissance due to the death of royalty and aristocratic values and to the revival of democratic sentiments? Or is its death simply a moment in an inevitable rhythm, as natural as leaf fall? In a poem which imitates a sonnet from Spain's golden age, by Lupercia Argensola,[48] Hill speaks of the winds which batter and bring to ground all golden renaissances:

> November rips gold foil from the oak ridges.
> Dour folk huddle in High Hoyland, Penistone.
> The tributaries of the Sheaf and Don
> bulge their dull spate, cramming the poor bridges.
>
> The North Sea batters our shepherds' cottages
> from sixty miles.

Spengler in his seasonal forecast of renaissance and decadence claimed that "we cannot help it if we are born as men of the early winter of full Civilization, instead of on the golden summit of a ripe Culture. . . . Each Culture has its own new possibilities of self-expression which arise, ripen, decay, and never return. . . . We have to reckon with the hard cold facts of a *late* life."⁴⁹ As if to counterpoise Spengler's twentieth-century gloom, Hill observes that, in 1654, Western civilization was encountering the cold facts of winter and decadence as well. The imagination, as Stevens said, is always at the end of its era.

Like Stevens, Hill finds a bitter kind of consolation in "the stale grandeur of annihilation," just as he finds use for the stock figures from forgotten elegies (Damon, a musician memorialized in Plato's *Republic*, appears in Milton and Marlowe; Clorinda is the deceased shepherd's sister who mourns the death of Sir Philip Sidney in Spenser's "Astrophel"; both appear in Marvell's "Clorinda and Damon.") Hill, paradoxically, elegizes the elegiac tradition and consoles himself as well as he can, like Magdalen in "Lachrimae," weeping over its vestiges:

> No sooner has the sun
> swung clear above earth's rim than it is gone.
> We live like gleaners of its vestiges
>
> knowing we flourish, though each year a child
> with the set face of a tomb-weeper is put down
> for ever and ever.

If Hill remembers Milton's "Epitaphium Damonis," in which time deals cruelly with another child (it "snatches him, and leaves loss infinite / For ever and for ever"), he does not share Milton's enthusiasm for "the madness and ecstasy of Heaven." The poet doffs his mask at the poem's end and through rhetorical questions acknowledges the void beneath all elegiac pretensions:

> Why does the air grow cold
>
> in the region of mirrors? And who is this clown
> doffing his mask at the masked threshold
> to selfless raptures that are all his own?

When renaissance images are stripped off (like those at a court Masque), the actor once again is left alone to his solipsistic reveries.

The decay of imagery and the effect it has on culture are obsessions of twentieth-century poets. In justifying his elegiac tone in "An Apology," Hill told John Haffenden: "There are . . . good political and sociological reasons for the floating of nostalgia: there's been an elegiac tinge to the air of this country ever since the end of the Great War" (*VP*, p. 93). Several of Hill's elegies in "An Apology," however, remember periods very different from the Great War, or even the Elizabethan and Jacobean renaissance. "The spiritual, Platonic old England" is also the eighteenth-century England when the landed gentry, surrounded by country houses, quaint gardens, and lush estates, exerted a powerful influence on local and national government, only to be gradually replaced by the rising industrialists. Although Hill finds the wealthy, agrarian, Christian gentry a healthy antidote to rampant industrialists, he is not blind to their faults:

I think the sad serenity and elegance of the eighteenth-century country house landscape was bought at a price: not only the sufferings of English labourers but also of Indian peasants. Again, critics who think I've succumbed to nostalgia for that landscape cannot have looked with sufficient closeness to the texture of the sequence. The celebration of the inherited beauties of the English landscape is bound, in the texture of the sequence, with an equal sense of the oppression of tenantry. (*VP*, p. 93)

The England of country houses parodies rather than emulates a Platonic ideal of civilization. The squires, like the industrialists after them, condemn multitudes to live like barbarians.

Hill looks at the mold and ice beneath "the great structure" of Platonic England with the candor and eschatological resignation of Stevens. In "The Laurel Axe," he praises autumn because it allows him to see the complex motives and original sins at the root of all creation:

> Trees shine
> out from their leaves, rocks mildew to moss-green;
> the avenues are spread with brittle floods.
>
> Platonic England, house of solitudes,
> rests in its laurels and its injured stone,
> replete with complex fortunes that are gone,
> beset by dynasties of moods and clouds.
>
> It stands, as though at ease with its own world,
> the mannerly extortions, languid praise,
> all that devotion long since bought and sold,
>
> the rooms of cedar and soft-thudding baize,
> tremulous boudoirs where the crystals kissed
> in cabinets of amethyst and frost.

Hill shrinks England, in a progression of synecdoches, to a country house, game room, boudoir, cabinet, and finally to a crystal of stone or ice. In its ruins, the house mimes England's injuries and oppressions more accurately than when elegantly decorated and inhabited. The house of England, which is also a particular country house, grows symbolically "at ease" or "at-one" with its surrounding misfortunes. Hill treats its crystalline perfection with the iconoclasm of Blake, who wrote in his "Crystal Cabinet":

> I strove to seize the inmost Form
> With ardor fierce & hands of flame,
> But burst the Crystal Cabinet . . . .

Hill bursts the crystals by showing that England's laurels of achievement are wedded to her axes of oppression.

In "Loss and Gain," through a clever series of metaphors, in which bells signify solitary scholars (or the "learned class" that Hill, following Coleridge, calls the "clerisy") and fuchsia-hedges signify historians guarding the dead, Hill traces a path of perception into the graveyard of history. Menaced by the grit of air pollution and the thrum of industrial noise, the clerisy overlooks the shallows of the rabblement, symbolized by the sea, and guides wanderers.

> Pitched high above the shallows of the sea
> lone bells in gritty belfries do not ring
> but coil a far and inward echoing
> out of the air that thrums. Enduringly,
>
> fuchsia-hedges fend between cliff and sky;
> brown stumps of headstones tamp into the ling
> the ruined and the ruinously strong.
> Platonic England grasps its tenantry
>
> where wild-eyed poppies raddle tawny farms
> and wild swans root in lily-clouded lakes.

In the "war between the mind / And sky," as Stevens called it, the fuchsia-hedges protect history. The headstones press the dead into the heather (ling), and also into language (*lingua*), which, paradoxically, must be kept alive and orderly to remember the dead and disorderly. If the fuchsia-hedges guard a Platonic or romantic zone of memory, they also bear witness to the "wild-eyed" visions, opiated debauchery, and muddle-headed innocence of Platonists and romantics alike.

Hill portrays poets as hawks, spiders, mangoes, bells, headstones, bats, pigeons, fuchsia-hedges, and deciduous trees in his "Apology" and traces the movements of their *anima poetae* as they construct, or fall victim to, the Christian architecture of sin and redemption. In "Idylls of the King," a title borrowed from Tennyson's sequence of Arthurian legends, a pigeon again traces the spirit's flight towards greater clarity amid autumnal dilapidation. Like Percival, Hill searches the dark wood for a chapel and grail, but, like Eliot in *The Waste Land*, he finds an insubstantial chapel, "goldgrimy shafts and pillars of the sun." He says in one of his most resonant lines: "Weightless magnificence upholds the past." The past is held aloft by its transcendent splendor (it is seemingly weightless like the ceiling of a Gothic cathedral), but it is also held up by deceptive, nostalgic illusions. The will to splendor, for Hill, rises out of a mire of impure motives. Hill is the dark prophet of Tennyson's *Idylls of the King*:

> And spake I not too truly, O my knights?
> Was I too dark a prophet when I said
> To those who went upon the Holy Quest
> That most of them would follow wandering fires,
> Lost in the quagmire?
> ("The Holy Grail," lines 884–888)

Contemporary questers, Hill points out, seek will-o'-the-wisps of nuclear power rather than sunlit columns of sacred temples (the "warheads of mushrooms round the filter-pond"). Hill elegizes the chivalric ideals of grace and beauty, betrayed not only by England's landed gentry but by modern war hawks as well.

Perhaps the best example of Hill's elegiac method comes in the last sonnet, "The Herefordshire Carol," which serves as the sequence's coda. Once again, Hill bears witness to promises betrayed and civilization in decline. He now expands the elegiac device of correlating the death of a beloved with the seasonal death of vegetation to include the death of artifacts as well. Again, he focuses on a moment of intense perception, made possible by wintry purification. The poem borrows imagery from Eliot's "Little Gidding," but, unlike Eliot, Hill insists that his "midwinter spring" and pentecostal fire descending "in the dark time of the year" occur in "time's covenant," rather than outside it. Eliot, surveying the ruins of the seventeenth-century Anglican community, found in "the crowned knot of fire" in which "the fire and the rose are one" a symbol of contraries unified. Hill finds in working girls braiding and knotting their hair with mundane proficiency and the sun striking a rose window with unsanctimonious violence contraries not so much unified as conflicting in suspension.

From the start his carol is steeped in worldly disillusionment. Determined to find something to praise in past and present, he is persistently rebuffed. In a world of decay and disfigurement, however, viridian growths herald new life:

> So to celebrate that kingdom: it grows
> greener in winter, essence of the year;
> the apple-branches musty with green fur.
> In the viridian darkness of its yews
>
> it is an enclave of perpetual vows
> broken in time. Its truth shows disrepair,
> disfigured shrines, their stones of gossamer,
> Old Moore's astrology, all hallows,
>
> the squire's effigy bewigged with frost,
> and hobnails cracking puddles before dawn.

The decay of squirearchies, the advent of labor movements (the marching hobnail boots on spring ice) map a worldly rhythm of breakings, mendings, and transfusions of power as common as the cottage girls rising from their beds by candlelight to "mend their ruined braids."

Hill finishes his poem with a brilliant climax, which is also a shattering denouement: "Touched by the cry of the iconoclast, / how the rose-window blossoms with the sun!" Hill's impassioned touch and cry, like Lawrence's pentecostal tortoise-shout, express dualities in all creation. "The Herefordshire Carol," which is an actual carol, offers a Christian pattern for the artist's creative and destructive energies:

> Now to him that is ascended
>   Let all our praises be;
> May we his steps then follow,
>   And he our pattern be;
> So when our lives are ended,
>   We all may hear him call—
> 'Love, souls, receive the kingdom,
>   Prepared for you all.'

A Christian pattern of descent and ascent guides the passionate man into love's kingdom.

Privacies

Although "An Apology" forsakes the narrative "I," several of the sonnets shift attention from the poet's public concerns to more private ones. The poet speaks of friends and family, his vocation as a poet, his Christian upbringing, and frequently with comic severity. If his tone is softer, his ironies are still sharp. Often, he adopts the pose of a soliloquist speaking to himself or to someone close, half-smiling at the absurdity of what he recollects. Playing psychoanalyst, he traces current agonies back to childhood relationships with parents, vicarious religious parents (Christ, Mary), godmothers, cousins, literary forbears, and ministers. At the same time, he makes a joke of psychoanalysis. In his early family romance, the child does not indulge in fantasies of Oedipal marriages with mother so much as mystical marriages with Christ, the Father. He wants to bring mother and father back to life and gently heckle them. To Hill's insubordinate mind, Christ is a welfare official in a socialist state, handing out grace as if it were dole money. The child's mother appears as a tough-nerved capitalist. She is a patriarchal reverend and rigorous ascetic who can draw sustenance from rocks. "The familiar ministrants" and "distant cousins, virgin till they died" embody a family penchant for asceticism.

In "Fidelities," Hill recalls his religious heritage, with characteristic wit:

> Remember how, at seven years, the decrees
> were brought home: child-soul must register
> for Christ's dole, be allotted its first Easter,
> blanch-white and empty, chilled by the lilies,
>
> betrothed among the well-wishers and spies.
> Reverend Mother, breakfastless, could feast her

> constraint on terracotta and alabaster
> and brimstone and the sweets of paradise.

If the poet's mother is a strange amalgam of constraint and indulgence, of hellish and heavenly moods, of devouring appetites and stony renunciations, her legacy has affected her son and driven him, not to Freud, but to the scholastic theologians. He says, half-jokingly:

> Theology makes good bedside reading. Some
> who are lost covet scholastic proof,
> subsistence of probation, modest balm.
>
> The wooden wings of justice borne aloof,
> we close our eyes to Anselm and lie calm.
> All night the cisterns whisper in the roof.

With the toilet's cistern whispering in the background, the poet observes his family's religious penchant through a septic rather than antiseptic eye (as he does in "The Eve of St. Mark," gazing over the family photographs preserved "in sepia waterglass").

Hill's fidelities are not to family eccentricities, however, but to a poetry which redeems them. In "Vocations," the poet appears at his writing desk or "escritoire," faithfully honoring his covenant with his muse (as in *Mercian Hymns* where he communes with the muse of History), scouting the literary scene for competitors. The poet puts on the mask of a Christian martyr and soldier whose church of high priests unites the great writers of tradition. The heretics in this church are writers who abandon art's demands for less enervating tasks. A heretic in one church, Hill is a passionate disciple in another. He judges lapsed artists like a grand inquisitor:

> While friends defected, you stayed and were sure,
> fervent in reason, watchful of each name:
> a signet-seal's unostentatious gem
> gleams against walnut on the escritoire,

> focus of reckoning and judicious prayer.
> This is the durable covenant, a room
> quietly furnished with stuff of martyrdom,
> lit by the flowers and moths from your own shire,
>
> by silvery vistas frothed with convolvulus—
> radiance of dreams hardly to be denied.

Sequestered in this imaginary museum of dead moths and flowers, surrounded by a dream vista of convoluted vines, Hill ends his poem with a melancholy valediction that transcends what at first seemed to be self-congratulatory back slapping. Twittering bats and clear-calling children fade into the evening dew. His former militant enthusiasms have worn thin as an old tapestry.

As shadows descend on the poet, his song grows quieter but sharper, like Keats's "plaintive anthem" fading at the end of his "Ode to a Nightingale." Immortal birds and forlorn bells toll both Hill and Keats back from death to their solitary selves and, in Hill's case, to his family and English heritage. In "The Eve of St. Mark," a title borrowed from one of Keats's unpublished poems, Hill imagines himself fading into a Keatsian twilight of whispers, glimmering lights, and faint music. He stoops over the photograph album of his family, conjures up familiar spirits and talismans:

> Stroke the small silk with your whispering hands,
> godmother; nod and nod from the half-gloom;
> broochlight intermittent between the fronds,
> the owl immortal in its crystal dome.

The immortal owl offsets the more pressing world of clockwork time and family history:

> Along the mantelpiece veined lustres trill,
> the clock discounts us with a telling chime.
> Familiar ministrants, clerks-of-appeal,
> burnish upon the threshold of the dream.

As the time gets later and night's darkness falls, Hill's mentors flare briefly over the fireplace, like the stars in Stevens's "Auroras of Autumn," which "flash / Like a great shadow's last embellishment." Hill's "stars," however, constitute a clerisy: the body of writers and scholars originally formulated by Coleridge, devoted to traditional excellence (clerisy and clerk suggest this, coming from *klerikos*, which means "belonging to inheritance"). Hill's heritage includes "churchwardens in wing-collars bearing scrolls / of copyhold well-tinctured and well-tied." All of these, in one way or another, "serve" (*famulus* means servant, *ministrare* means to serve, and clerks serve by keeping records in offices).

In Keats's poem "The Eve of St. Mark," Bertha, like Hill's godmother, presides over a separate service in which Christian iconography is scrutinized by a laborious, devoted, sceptical intellect. Christian symbols pale in the darkening twilight, but Bertha retrieves them in the lamplight of her study. Isolated from the ordinary Christian community that commemorates St. Mark in traditional rituals, she honors "the sanctity of the intellect" in her persistent, puzzled inspection of the patched book of icons. In this way, she acts as a synecdoche for Hill's "Apology." She restores Christian architecture in the same perplexed way that he does. Like Hill and most of the characters who personify the *anima poetae* in "An Apology," Bertha does her work among a growing awareness of tenebrous gloom, which is lit only intermittently and faintly by her lamp.

"Tenebrae"

At first glance, Hill's "Tenebrae," which gathers together eight short poems at the end of the book, has nothing to do with vigils in dark churches and Easter candle lighting. Most of the individual sections, including the two sonnets, recall Petrarchan themes of tortured love. In fact, they lament the poet's estrangement from the symbolic ritual of Tenebrae. The poem's epigraph states this matter-of-factly: "He was so tired that he was scarcely able to hear a note of the songs: he felt imprisoned in a cold region where his brain was numb and his spirit was isolated." This terrible isolation may bring the poet closer to Christ's agony but, too, it separates him from the church ritual which attempts to portray it.

The poem grinds on this crux. If Christ's crucifixion is an apt metaphor for all sacrificial suffering, why is there not "atonement"? Hill, as before, denies Christian atonement that presupposes a timeless, otherworldly zone where anxieties evaporate. Christian ritual, for Hill, must operate on earth or nowhere. In his third section, he depicts Christ's consolations fading into the empyrean:

> Veni Redemptor, but not in our time. [50]
> Christus Resurgens, quite out of this world. [51]
> 'Ave' we cry; the echoes are returned.
> Amor Carnalis is our dwelling-place.

Hill uses his Latin for double effect. He puts on a scholarly display only to assure us that we dwell in an unscholarly place of carnal love.

Because Hill finds "amor carnalis" an exasperating maze, his love poems in "Tenebrae," to mirror it, become equally complex. The passionate lover appears as the passionate Christ, carrying his cross through the shadows and winding avenues of hell. Hill begins with a request for the angel, traditional symbol of the intelligence, to descend to the sacrificial body from which it arose. He addresses the holy ghost which rose from Christ on the cross and, with mock seriousness, orders it to return to the body's wounds. He might be addressing Plato's angel of love, whose wings supposedly grew from the body's amorous sweat and flew to the beloved:

> Requite this angel whose
> flushed and thirsting face
> stoops to the sacrifice

out of which it arose.
This is the lord Eros
of grief who pities
no one; it is
Lazarus with his sores.

In this communion between angel and sacrifice, the angel welcomes Christ (who *is* Eros), grieving but pitiless, and Lazarus, the poor man with his sores licked by dogs.

The angel's redemptive message achieves its fullest and most complicated expression in the two Petrarchan sonnets which make up sections two and five. The angel, perched over the lover's body, ventriloquizes his incriminations, confessions, and anguished cries. For him, falling in love is comparable to falling off a cliff. Before his "fall," he is a lost somnambulist; afterwards, he is a lost fiend, possessed by dread, self-loathing, guilt. He addresses his beloved:

> And you, who with your soft but searching voice
> drew me out of the sleep where I was lost,
> who held me near your heart that I might rest
> confiding in the darkness of your choice:
> possessed by you I chose to have no choice,
> fulfilled in you I sought no further quest.
> You keep me, now, in dread that quenches trust,
> in desolation where my sins rejoice.
> As I am passionate so you with pain
> turn my desire; as you seem passionless
> so I recoil from all that I would gain,
> wounding myself upon forgetfulness,
> false ecstasies, which you in truth sustain
> as you sustain each item of your cross.

As in "The Pentecost Castle," Hill teases out the various implications of Yeats's assertion that both desire and the fulfilment of desire are terrible. His sonnet is a gothic romance portraying love as an imprisoning, at times ecstatic, seduction.

Interestingly, the sonnet can be read as the agonized protest of a Christian against spiritual marriage as well as a protest of a secular man against carnal love. The second sonnet in "Tenebrae" is more explicitly about imagined love, with its succubae and dream images, and serves as a qualified response to the first. It remembers many of Petrarch's posthumous dialogues with his sublimated Laura and his mood of resignation before pain and rapture:

> Stupefying images of grief-in-dream,
> succubae to my natural grief of heart,
> cling to me, then; you who will not desert
> your love nor lose him in some blank of time.

But the image of a suffering, feminine Christ does not attract Hill for long:

> You come with all the licence of her name
> to tell me you are mine. But you are not
> and she is not.

Hill then wonders if all this agony hurts his "breath," his poetic spirit, and in a rather turgid, discursive finale affirms that it does:

>   Can my own breath be hurt
> by breathless shadows groaning in their game?
> It can. The best societies of hell
> acknowledge this, aroused by what they know:
> consummate rage recaptured there in full
> as faithfulness demands it, blow for blow,
> and rectitude that mimics its own fall
> reeling with sensual abstinence and woe.

Spiritual love, for Hill, is also a communion with the "breathless shadows" of past lovers who, like Christ, descend into a tenebrous hell because of their passion. Hill compares it to shadowboxing, which he intends to comment on, blow by blow.

After the baroque elaborations and the clichés of tormented love, Hill finishes his poem with a litany of allusive but limpid descriptions of events, places, and personalities in an imagined church. He assumes the role of tour guide, pointing out rituals and unritualized emotions like Kathe in Joyce's "museyroom." His litany traces in oblique fashion events in Holy Week, from the ashes of Palm Sunday (used on Ash Wednesday) to the praise for Christ's resurrection on Easter. He then offers another descriptive litany of the Passion and regards a poetic Christ and his martyrdom to love with dubious reverence:

> He wounds with ecstasy. All
> the wounds are his own.
> He wears the martyr's crown.
> He is the Lord of Misrule.
> He is the Master of the Leaping Figures,
> the motley factions.
> Revelling in auguries
> he is the Weeper of the Valedictions.

The Lord of Misrule was the peace keeper at Renaissance plays, the Master of Leaping Figures an official connected with the Winchester School of medieval artists (and probably intended to recall the "Master of the Revels" or theatre director of Shakespeare's time). The Weeper of Valedictions is an imaginary figure compiled from titles of Crashaw's and Donne's poems. Although Hill is probably thinking of Southwell and the Catholic martyrs during the reign of Elizabeth I, he speaks for all who suffer trials of passion and struggle to control them.

If Hill's ritual, tenebrous artifice establishes consonance between emotion and symbol with great mastery, it does so at a great cost. He finishes "Tenebrae" with his favorite analogy between the perfect work of art and the harmonious music of the spheres but asserts that harmonies are fictions which disintegrate as soon as humans accost and examine them. The world of "real cries" brings them crashing to earth. Ruskin's Athene or "Angel of Tones" is Hill's ambiguous muse, who, like Christ, no longer seems to communicate with the earth:

> Music survives, composing her own sphere,
> Angel of Tones, Medusa, Queen of the Air,
> and when we would accost her with real cries
> silver on silver thrills itself to ice.

In contrast to the end of "An Apology for the Revival of Christian Architecture," where an iconoclastic cry imitates sunlight by making a rose window "blossom," the cry here threatens to turn all living artifice to ice. The cry comes like a blast of air "thrilling" through the metal strings of a finely-tuned instrument or the vocal chords of the poet. The windy *spiritus*, the afflatus of inspiration, kills rather than invigorates. "The harp hangs silent from the windless tree," as in "An Ark on the Flood," written two decades earlier. The sky is untuned, the pantheon of artist-gods (the medusas) destroyed. Rather than a resurrection or transfiguration, which would traditionally end the Tenebrae ritual, Hill envisions a new descent, endless and indestructible, into an inferno of ice.

Throughout *Tenebrae*, Hill remembers and celebrates the monumental splendors of the artistic and religious past. The book is, in a way, an extended hymn and elegy for the English and Spanish Renaissances. It borrows the ballad and sonnet forms popular at the time. It alludes to Renaissance court masques, lute music, and meditational exercises, and then to chorale preludes, Pre-Raphaelite paintings, Gauguin and his Pont-Aven School, and to Florentine artists during Dante's time. Again and again, Hill stands back from his craftsmanship and the great works of tradition and reflects, either gloomily or elatedly, on their deliquescence and renewal. All of his poetry, in one sense, is ritualistic: it attempts to bring both writer and audience into closer contact with universal rhythms in art, society, and nature. Although Hill rarely escalates to a state of "tragic joy," there is "a single voice of purest praise" audible within the cries of sarcasm and pain.

6 / SPIRITUAL BIOGRAPHY
The Mystery of the Charity of Charles Péguy

That Geoffrey Hill should choose to write a poem of one hundred quatrains about the life and death of Charles Péguy and find a title in Péguy's little-known verse drama *Le Mystère de la Charité de Jeanne D'Arc* will strike many readers as extraordinary. In Péguy's life, however, which began among peasants in La Beauce, the region surrounding Orléans, and which ended in 1914 after years of financial and domestic hardship at the Battle of the Marne, Hill finds a moving example of a man comically and tragically at odds with both his age and his ideals. "A man of the most exact and exacting probity, accurate practicality, in personal and business relations" (MC, p. 30), Péguy was also implicated in the assassination of the great socialist leader Jean Jaurès and was prepared to murder an officer in the French army because he suspected, on completely unfounded evidence, that the man had mistreated (and thereby killed) his friend Marcel Baudoin. Péguy's otherworldiness, and the chivalric values engendered by it, made for heroic crimes. He was a saintly felon and a felonous saint, whose vices were entangled in his virtues. A "great soul" (MC, p. 31), he was capable of the atrocities "great souls" commit. In his *Mystery*, Hill succeeds brilliantly in resurrecting from the past a hero whose charitable acts and gross misdeeds offer directives to the present.

In earlier poems, such as "The Songbook of Sebastian Arrurruz" and *Mercian Hymns*, Hill conferred upon fictitious characters the motives and actions of real men; in *The Mystery*, he does the opposite. A historical figure, whose life is well-documented, is made mythical. Although Hill takes details, phrases, and even whole lines from Péguy's biographers,[1] they become part of a new pattern. But why choose Péguy, whose life and art are so different from Hill's? The most obvious reason is that Hill, fascinated by a tortuous stance towards Catholicism and political conservatism, finds in Péguy an instructive ally and opponent. Hill has described his poetry as "a heretic's dream of salvation expressed in the images of the orthodoxy from which he is excommunicate" (*VP*, p. 98), and Péguy's life bears an obvious resemblance. "Estranged from the Church for a number of years, first by his militant socialist principles, then by the consequences of a secular marriage, he had, in 1908, rediscovered the solitary ardours of faith but not the consolations of religious practice. He remained self-excommunicate but adoring. . . . "(*MC*, p. 31). Péguy joins Hill's army of martyrs, whose devotions are noble as well as vicious and whose acts of faith are as condemnable as they are commendable. But if Jeanne d'Arc provides Péguy with a paradigm of self-sacrifice and charity, Péguy provides Hill with a model that remains, after much communing, deliberately elusive. Although Hill longs to talk with Péguy's ghost, he never gets beyond dramatic monologue, interspersed with salutations, denunciations, and repeated qualifications. As mystic and martyr, Péguy offers symptoms to diagnose as well as heroic acts to enthrone.

Le mystère and *la charité* for Péguy, as for Hill, have specific rather than vague connotations. For Péguy, *le mystère* is the secret impulse behind a moral act. The goal to which *le mystère* is directed is *la mystique*. In his life, Péguy identified la mystique with Dreyfusism, Republicanism, Socialism, and Catholicism. "The essence of mysticism," Péguy declared, "is . . . an invincible anxiety"[2]; for Hill, "an anxiety about *faux pas*, the perpetration of 'howlers', grammatical solecisms, misstatements of fact, misquotations, improper attributions" (*LL*, p. 7) is the generative impulse of poetry. For Péguy, *la charité* was "the spiritual, temporal and constant communion with the poor, the weak and the oppressed."³ Socialism, based on charity, was "a mystic socialism . . . profoundly related to Christianity" and "no less than a religion of temporal salvation."⁴ It was the socialism of St. Francis rather than Marx.

Hill's poem meditates on the mystery of Péguy's Christian charity but only offers momentary glimpses of requital. Charity is continually a possibility envisaged, like utopia, rather than something concretely accomplished. Sublime fulfilment is tantalizingly out of reach. In "The Modern World," the essay from which Hill takes his epigraph, Péguy declares that "everything begins in mysticism and ends in politics."⁵ Hill's poem maps *la mystique* and *la politique*, as one is betrayed or corrupted by the other, and as they shift back and forth dialectically between sublimity and banality. "The charge and counter-charge," as Hill calls it, is a structural principle of his poem as well as of the world it portrays. Its origins may be mysterious; its path, as his poem demonstrates with great finesse, is eminently traceable.

Behind Hill's examples of charity, or "the divine love," as he calls it in "Ovid in the Third Reich," the presence of Christ repeatedly asserts itself. For Hill, Christ embodies perfect selfless devotion, but while He invites imitation, He judges and damns whoever tries to abide by His example. In "Lachrimae," Hill summarizes the situation in which Christ is imminent but always beyond the communicant—a conscience divided against itself. Péguy, as Hill portrays him, is similarly divided. "We are one with the eternally damned,"⁶ Péguy said in his early days. Hill places him among "the damned in the brazen Invalides of Heaven" with good reason.

In pursuit of salvation, Péguy sinks his roots into the "terre charnelle," which, for Hill, is the mystery of sin, anxiety, and death. He reincorporates the energies of earth to imitate earth's will to give—her charity. As in the Eleusinian mystery cult of ancient Greece, Hill's *Mystery* reenacts the descent of a vegetation god, a Christ-like Demeter, through wintry death towards the center of the earth (Jules Verne is mentioned in section 6) and his subsequent efflorescence in spring. We must "turn away and contemplate the working / of the radical soul," Hill says in his fifth section, emphasizing the "rootedness" of "radical." Although numerous mediating presences appear in *The Mystery* (Jeanne d'Arc, Dreyfus, Bergson, Foch, Charles George Gordon, Emile Zola, Jules Verne, Christ), Péguy predominates and guides the meditation, not towards transcendental paradise but towards a recognition and articulation of "the 'specific gravity of human nature' " (*LL*, p. 15). "It is at the heart of this 'heaviness'," Hill has written, "that poetry must do its atoning work" (*LL*, p. 15). At "the heart / of the mystère," the poet, like Lucifer fallen into hell, gathers together his powers and materials for his palace.

Three years after translating Ibsen's *Brand*, Hill told an interviewer that working on it had widened the scope of his "art in a quite unexpected way" and that it had given him "self-confidence and the means to write fluently" (*VP*, p. 97). What is immediately noticeable in *The Mystery* is a new fluency; the poem moves from the casual to the elegiac, the fiercely declarative to the interrogative, and from ecstatic revelation to sarcastic gloom with an ease unattained in many of the earlier poems. The liability of this style is prosiness, but Hill guards against it by tightening his lines into loosely-metered iambic pentameters and half-rhymed quatrains. He divides his poem into ten sections, whose movements and countermovements, as in sections four and five, overlap. Hill's style is "antiphonal," as he explains that term in "Redeeming the Time." It enacts "the drama of reason" (*LL*, p. 93); it considers many positions from different angles and struggles towards decision and action. "Its structure is a recognition and a resistance; it is parenthetical, antiphonal, it turns upon itself" (*LL*, p. 94). Rather than follow the traditional linear plot of a dramatic story, Hill's poem traces the mind's brilliant leaps, rapid associations, and spiraling moods. What is lost in narrative sweep is gained in lyrical intensity. It is a discursive meditation and an impassioned argument, broken up by attacks and graced with eloquent praise.

Hill begins his poem with the pistol shot of an athletic race. His beginning has all the startling clamor of Yeat's "Leda and the Swan," and perhaps even imitates it. But the crime is political rather than mythical—the assassination of Jaurès:

> Crack of a starting-pistol. Jean Jaurès
> dies in a wine-puddle. Who or what stares
> through the café-window crêped in powder-smoke?
> The bill for the new farce reads *Sleepers Awake*.

Yeats wrote his poem out of a conviction that a violent annunciation was needed to invigorate a culture's sterile soil and also to show what the consequences of such a violent annunciation might be. Like Yeats, Hill depicts the public, historical consequences of a private crime. From Zeus's rape came Helen and Clytemnestra, the Trojan War, and the death of Agamemnon. From Péguy's reckless denunciation of Jaurès came the death of a great political leader. Yeats focuses on sexual crimes, Hill on verbal ones, but both to indict misguided power.

The starting pistol is a brilliant choice by Hill, not only because it starts the poem with a bang, but because it suggests many of the paradoxical attributes of "the word" and its "annunciation." Language's ability to compel great numbers of people to commit atrocities, as well as bear witness to them, is a central theme in Hill's poem, and his starting pistol cleverly embraces both the innocent and invidious powers of the word. A starting pistol only fires blanks (symbols or signs), but Hill points out that these have a "murderous innocence." In "The Man and the Echo," Yeats wondered: "Did that play of mine send out / Certain men the English shot?" For Hill, as for Yeats, the word kills as well as heals. It is "the starting cry of a race," as at the beginning of *Mercian Hymns*—not the race of Offa's Anglo-Saxon England, however, but of the unholy, cartoonlike stampede of modern times.

In Hill's opening scenes, Péguy is villain as well as hero. Just before the First World War, Péguy attacked his old friend Jaurès for holding pacifist views. "I am a good republican, I am an old revolutionary. In war time, there is only one policy, and that is the policy of the National Convention. But we must realise that the policy of the National Convention means Jaurès in a tumbril and that great voice drowned in the beating of drums."[7] Hill alludes to this at the end of his fourth section:

> Jaurès was killed blindly, yet with reason:
> 'let us have drums to beat down his great voice.'
> So you spoke to the blood.

On 13 July 1914, two months before Péguy himself was to die, a young man drew back the curtains of the Café du Croissant in Paris and shot Jaurès in the head. Seeking to revoke or at least assuage this memory, Hill recalls the Advent Hymn, which praises the coming birth of Christ and His eventual spiritual marriage in a new heaven and new earth:

> Sleepers, wake! The watch-cry pealeth
> While slumber deep each eyelid sealeth:
>   Awake, Jerusalem, awake.

Historical assassinations and world wars, however, have reduced these Christian expectations to rubble. Annunciations become denunciations. Christian births precipitate political deaths. The Word, which unifies and redeems through communion, is the word which divides and kills. Starting pistols are loaded revolvers. The old hymn "Sleepers Awake" is the "new farce." The poem's beginning is a rehearsal of its ending.

The idea that history and politics are often a farcical and tragic parody of justice is as central to Péguy as to Hill. History's repetitions are dress rehearsals, full of mistakes, for a final performance or apocalypse that never comes. Hill personifies history as a murderous clown, arousing laughter and horror as he frolics on the stage:

> History commands the stage wielding a toy gun,
> rehearsing another scene. It has raged so before,
> countless times; and will do, countless times more,
> in the guise of supreme clown, dire tragedian.
>
> In Brutus' name martyr and mountebank
> ghost Caesar's ghost, his wounds of air and ink
> painlessly spouting. Jaurès' blood lies stiff
> on menu-card, shirt-front and handkerchief.

In these first stanzas, Péguy is a type of Brutus—an essentially honorable person who kills for his republican ideals but who sacrifices his moral integrity in doing so. The martyrs and mountebanks, Hill suggests, misrepresent the Caesars and Jaurèses of the world by transforming them into inhuman symbols or ghosts, which they then murder. Hill condemns ghostly or "spiritual warfare" because of its murderous opposition to human blood and refers to Brutus's debate in *Julius Caesar* over Caesar, the spirit, versus Caesar, the man:

> Let's be sacrificers, but not butchers, Caius.
> We all stand up against the spirit of Caesar,
> And in the spirit of men there is no blood.
> O that we then could come by Caesar's spirit
> And not dismember Caesar! But, alas,
> Caesar must bleed for it. And, gentle friends,
> Let's kill him boldly . . .
>   (II, i, 166–172)

After the murder, Caesar's ghost pursues Brutus to the battlefield of Philippi and finally drives him to suicide. He exclaims:

> O Julius Caesar, thou art mighty yet!
> Thy spirit walks abroad and turns our swords
> In our own proper entrails.
>   (V, iii, 94–96)

Péguy, after the murder of Jaurès and on another battlefield, also elects a suicidal form of death. He refuses to lie down as the German machine-guns commence firing.

Hill surveys "modern times" sardonically and reenacts them as Charlie Chaplin might have. The poem moves quickly to an examination of silent movies and political cartoons. The flickering gestures of Chaplin and of the films he appeared in are an apt *mimesis* of the times themselves. The medium, for Hill, is part of the message and is at once funny, sad, and deplorable:

> Violent contrariety of men and days; calm
> juddery bombardment of a silent film
> showing such things: its canvas slashed with rain
> and St Elmo's fire. Victory of the machine!
>
> The brisk celluloid clatters through the gate;
> the cortège of the century dances in the street;
> and over and over the jolly cartoon
> armies of France go reeling towards Verdun.

Hill may be recalling Hart Crane's overture to *The Bridge*:

> I think of cinemas, panoramic sleights
> With multitudes bent towards some flashing scene
> Never disclosed, but hastened to again
> Foretold to other eyes on the same screen . . .

Hill also imagines a flashing scene in which knowledge is revealed to a select few but concealed from the multitude. He compares an illuminated cinema screen to a slashed canvas on an old battle ship (lit with "St Elmo's fire"—a flamelike appearance occurring in stormy weather on prominent points of a ship, attributed to the patron saint of sailors, Elmo, and mentioned in the film *Moby Dick*). Hill, however, describes a nefarious cause and effect relationship between projected image and murderous fact. The cartoonlike battles of the First World War, "reeling" (as if drunk) through the film projector's "gate," are not enchanting but terrifyingly real.

After scrutinizing the instruments of communication as instruments of destruction (and implicating his own words and strategies), Hill begins to fill out Péguy's character. Péguy the mystic and martyr, as Hill portrays him, is an innocent child but also a bullish, irascible man, hermetically sealed behind his stacks of unsold books. He revels in his own style of class and trench warfare, pitting "stratagems of the out-manoeuvred man" against his adversaries:

> braving an entrenched class
> of fools and scoundrels, children of the world,
> his eyes caged and hostile behind glass. . . .

His struggle, Hill wittily remarks, is a kind of children's crusade, in which fallen and unfallen children clash to prevent defeat rather than to win unconditional victory.

Hill succeeds brilliantly in creating a pastoral, fairy-tale atmosphere to envelop Péguy's ruins. His poem, like Péguy's *Le Mystère de la Charité de Jeanne d'Arc*, is partly about an "improved infancy" of militant innocence and justice, but Hill sets out to distinguish the child from the man, not to judge his virtues against his vices. For Péguy, the child symbolizes hope, the impulse behind moral aspiration. In the sixth stanza, Hill alludes to Péguy's *Mystery of the Holy Innocents*, in which Madame Gervaise says:

> Faith is a loyal wife.
> Charity is a fervent mother.
> But hope is a very little girl.

Hill, less sentimental, in a lyrical vignette eulogizes the example of Jeanne d'Arc, in which innocent vision is complemented by political tenacity, but also voices qualifications:

> On the hard-won
> high places the old soldiers of old France
> crowd like good children wrapped in obedience
>
> and sleep, and ready to be taken home.
> Whatever that vision, it is not a child's;
> it is what a child's vision can become.

On the slopes of this Elysium, Hill's "golden codgers" relive their ordeals and deaths in dreams. They preserve their childlike selves but purged of childhood's sins. They are soldierly martyrs who, after pitching off their burdens, are perpetuated in the minds that remember them.

Hill harrows the past for examples of moral and artistic excellence. He assumes the role of a dour farmer, a grim reaper, a forager of graveyards, a cultivator of corpses, a trustee of legacies, and an inveterate funeral goer. He is fascinated and appalled by the fact that culture, agriculture, and indeed all organic life lives by killing and digesting other life. Tradition, for Hill, is a graveyard or field where the dead are plowed into the ground to insure future fertility. Tradition in *The Mystery* assumes the form of beetroot fields by the Marne where Péguy died. Here the heroic innocents (and criminals too) are transformed into life-giving crops. Of the benefits Hill observes:

> Memory, Imagination, harvesters of those fields,
>
> our gifts are spoils, our virtues epitaphs,
> our substance is the grass upon the graves.
> 'Du calme, mon vieux, du calme.' How studiously
> one cultivates the sugars of decay,
>
> pâtisserie-tinklings of angels . . . .

With an aside to Hobbes, who, in the *Leviathan*, stated that "*Imagination* and *Memory* are but one thing"—the "*decaying sense,*"[8] Hill affirms the physicality of imagination and memory as they consume and convert raw material (like a stomach) into new sustenance. Péguy used to exclaim to his friends: "Ah, les mots, mon vieux, les mots!"[9] Hill alters Péguy's line to "du calme, mon vieux, du calme" and elevates metamorphosis into a narrative technique of his poem.

In the third section, after his graveyard meditation subsides, Hill reveals Péguy in the role of Joseph of Arimathea. A cedar tree "uprears its lawns of black cirrus," throwing up its cloud and clothlike boughs and perhaps uprooting a lawn as well, all in symbolic anticipation of the bodily uprooting of the resurrection. Hill envisions the resurrection on many planes, all related. Like a farmer tabulating expenditures against profits, Hill assures Péguy: "You have found / hundred-fold return." Vegetal and economic compensations, in this case, are poetic as well. Through death, Péguy has discovered a mystic paradise—in the splendors of both his native landscape and Hill's one hundred quatrains. The poem recreates and finds for Péguy (just as Joseph found for Christ a tomb after His Crucifixion) the ideal kingdom of *l'ancienne France* that Péguy, during his life, regarded as his birthright. This is his "lost kingdom of innocence and original justice," to which both Hill and Péguy play Joseph of Arimathea:

> You are Joseph the Provider;
>
> and in the fable this is your proper home;
> three sides of a courtyard where the bees thrum
> in the crimped hedges and the pigeons flirt
> and paddle, and sunlight pierces the heart—
>
> shaped shutter-patterns in the afternoon,
> shadows of fleurs-de-lys on the stone floors.
> Here life is labour and pastime and orison
> like something from a simple book of hours;
>
> and immortality, your measured task,
> inscribes its antique scars on the new desk
> among your relics. . . .

On this significant soil, where prayer is valid, the poet lives a stately, contemplative life, a "death-in-life" as Yeats called it in "Byzantium," in communion with his dead ancestors and mentors. As with Eliot's ancestral house at East Coker and the religious community of Little Gidding, its antique beauty seems "past time."

During his life, Péguy was haunted by a vision of lost paradise. He declared that "in my Paradise, there won't only be souls, there will be things too,"[10] and specified that his paradise would contain France's tools along with its cathedrals. In response to this, Hill generously provides Péguy with Chartres, Château de Trie, ancient towns like Colombey-les-deux-Eglises (where De Gaulle retired to write his memoirs), Domrémy (the village in whose church Jeanne d'Arc received her missionary call), military academies like St. Cyr, and assorted workshops and manoirs. In a poem about charity, Hill is eminently charitable, delivering to Péguy his "dream of France," along with the peasants, teachers, and soldiers needed to establish it. Hill, however, redefines Péguy's *cité harmonieuse*, the socialist utopia which he designed with his university friend Marcel Baudoin as both a private dream and an ideal shared by many:

> Yours is their dream of France, militant-pastoral:
> musky red gillyvors, the wicker bark
> of clematis braided across old brick
> and the slow chain that cranks into the well
>
> morning and evening. It is Domrémy
> restored; the mystic strategy of Foch
> and Bergson with its time-scent, dour panache
> deserving of martyrdom. It is an army
>
> of poets, converts, vine-dressers, men skilled
> in wood or metal, peasants from the Beauce,
> terse teachers of Latin and those unschooled
> in all but the hard rudiments of grace.
>
> Such dreams portend, the dreamer prophesies . . . .

In this apostrophe to Péguy's ghost, Hill acts as benefactor of his will. He surveys the landscape of L'Île de France, as he surveyed the landscape of "the spiritual, Platonic old England" in "An Apology for the Revival of Christian Architecture in England," and presents it to the living for edification and imitation.

Charles Péguy

But Hill never allows the didactic thrust of his poem to lapse into pedantry or dreamy nostalgia. Much time is devoted to marking the sharp and often comic lines between Péguy's utopian enthusiasms and the hard facts of his workaday life:

> This world is different, belongs to them—
> the lords of limit and of contumely . . . .
>
> This is no old Beauce manoir that you keep
> but the rue de la Sorbonne, the cramped shop,
> its unsold *Cahiers* built like barricades,
> its fierce disciples, disciplines and feuds . . . .

Péguy's "wolfish" zealotry reasserts itself now, and the poem returns to indict Péguy for collusion in the murder of Jaurès. How can the man of unbending principles act in the world without attacking everyone around him or abandoning his beliefs?

Only in death, which Péguy so excitedly embraced, does he attain unity between mysticism and politics. Hill's puzzlement and shock at such a rapprochement provokes a pause, a moment of reckoning. He declares:

>   we are constrained
> to leave you sleeping and to step aside
> from the fleshed bayonets, the fusillade
> of red-rimmed smoke like stubble being burned;
>
> to turn away and contemplate the working
> of the radical soul . . . .

What is shocking about the rooted, "radical soul" ("instinct, intelligence, / memory, call it what you will") is its gravitational urge towards destruction. If the baptism in earth is a purgatory— and Hill offers images of Péguy's pilgrimage from Paris to Chartres in 1912 and 1913 to suggest that it is—its outcome is ambiguous. On the one hand, it is a necessary prelude to redemption, like the journey of Christ through hell; on the other, it is bodily dissolution.

Hill sketches Péguy's mystical kingdom, which is simply his home ground of La Beauce lyrically evoked, as a dreamscape of sun falling on kalefields, grass leafing from chalk pits, village workshops standing by sunflower fields, "walled gardens espaliered with angels", where hedgers and ditchers work alongside "curés de campagne." Here "images / of earth and grace" are divinely married. But to attain this paradisal harmony, Péguy must die. Hill's Christian ritual traces the crucial passage as a simple biological and seasonal change. With "strange Christian hope," Péguy goes down, paradoxically,

> into the darkness of resurrection,
>
> into sap, ragwort, melancholy thistle,
> almondy meadowsweet, the freshet-brook
> rising and running through small wilds of oak . . . .

In this earthly paradise, grace is dispensed in the form of sun and sap. In "Quaint Mazes" ("An Apology . . ."), Hill conferred empirical proof and sanctity on this animating *élan vital* by calling it a "Linnaean pentecost." Now he depicts Pentecost as he did in his early Oxford poem "Pentecost," as a hawthorn tree blooming in sunlight. Magi transport gifts of grace to this Christ-like tree in the form of seasonal rain. They are "cloud-shadows of seasons" irrigating the growing fields. They are also mythical "rois-mages," whose spring pilgrimages aim to restore France's wintry kingdoms to vernal abundance.

Hill views Christian events of crucifixion, resurrection, and apocalyptic marriage both with and through a physiological eye. Christian events in *The Mystery* are metaphors for natural processes. His empiricism brings with it bitterness and dread but also gives "strange Christian hope." As in Eliot's myth of wasteland and fisher-king, Hill's deracinated protagonist revives only after he sinks his roots into earth and draws from his old culture and body new energy. Hill affirmed in "Pentecost":

> The sudden putting-on of grace
> Though fresh, new-nerved, is all the more

> Dependent on its neutral base
> That, root-secure though commonplace,
> Has stood the test of strength before.

Hill now recalls the refrain from Péguy's *Eve*, "Heureux ceux qui sont morts pour la terre charnelle," in order to describe Péguy's euphoria as he stood above the beetroots at the Battle of the Marne. Hill writes:

> Happy are they who, under the gaze of God,
> die for the 'terre charnelle', marry her blood
> to theirs . . . .
>
> Here the lost are blest, the scarred most sacred. . . .

For its enrichment, Hill clinically observes, the earth welcomes sacrifices and corpses. The earth is one of the main characters in Hill's *Mystery*—indeed, it *is* the mystery, the "Androgynous Muse" with whom Péguy consummates his "blood marriage."

What is Hill's attitude to Péguy's Christian and patriotic sacrifice, then, if it requires death? A psychological aberration born out of anxiety or a noble act of devotion to God and country? In the middle of the poem, he imagines Péguy prepared

> for early mass from which you stood aside
>
> to find salvation, your novena cleaving
> brusquely against the grain of its own myth,
> its truth and justice, to a kind of truth,
> a justice hard to justify.

As with Yeats, Péguy holds together truth and justice in a myth of his own making, which is also dubious and hard to justify. His novena—his "blood marriage" through death—is his interpretation of the church's rite of devotion consisting of special prayers or services delivered on nine consecutive days. Hill reenacts it with ambivalence. He juxtaposes Péguy's self-styled crucifixion, as well as Jaurè's, against Dreyfus's to show how Péguy is both crucified and crucifier, campaigner for victims of injustice and injudicious victimizer. To vindicate Dreyfus (he was twenty-four when Dreyfus was falsely convicted of passing government secrets to the Germans), Péguy published articles in his *Cahiers* and engaged in street fights against the anti-Dreyfusards. For five years, he devoted himself "to right the wrong which Dreyfus had suffered and to restore the good name of French justice."[11] Hill recalls the rallying cry of the militant Dreyfusards who battled against *Les camelots du Roi*, a royalist organization supporting the government against Dreyfus ("the camelot-cry of 'sticks!' "). Péguy's militancy is a severe judgment of all those, past and present, who shy away from direct confrontation. Hill synchronizes Dreyfus's court-martial and public humiliation with Christ ("nailed at Golgotha") in a general indictment of the innocent bystander.

> Drumrap and fife
> hit the right note: 'A mort le Juif! Le Juif
> à la lanterne!' Serenely the mob howls,
> its silent mouthings hammered into scrolls

> torn from *Apocalypse*.

This travesty of St. John's Revelation, for Hill, may be "a concretion . . . a *mimesis*, of the way in which things ultimately are" (*LL*, p. 3). For Hill, human and cosmic natures are amoral. To submit to them without resistance, however, is not only immoral, it is criminal. Hill speaks in an act of atonement for the mob that makes shreds of Apocalypse and its envisioned Judgment.

In his interrogation, he is unsparing in his depiction of the man who passively condones injustice. "But who are 'we', since history is law," he asks, and replies:

> 'We' are crucified Pilate, Caiaphas
> in his thin soutane and Judas with the face
> of a man who has drunk wormwood. We come
> back empty-handed from Jerusalem

> counting our blessings, honestly admire
> the wrath of the peacemakers, for example
> Christ driving the money-changers from the temple,
> applaud the Roman steadiness under fire.

Although Pilate, the efficient governor, washed his hands of the sin committed against Christ, according to legend he later committed suicide. Caiaphas actively conspired against Christ. Judas, after his betrayal, repented and then hanged himself. Hill casts his and Péguy's lot with these famous betrayers as they reveal themselves in the agony of self-judgment:

> We are the occasional just men who sit
> in gaunt self-judgment on their self-defeat,
> the élite hermits, secret orators
> of an old faith devoted to new wars.
>
> We are 'embusqués', having no wounds to show
> save from the thorns, ecstatic at such pain.
> Once more the truth advances; and again
> the metaphors of blood begin to flow.

Embusqués are soldiers who avoid front-line combat. Hill's "embusqués," however, are not complacent cowards. They are martyrs who, unlike Péguy, persist in their personal struggles rather than rush to the battlefield. Having no war wounds, they take perverse pleasure in displaying self-inflicted wounds. Unbloodied, they satisfy their enthusiasm for war through "metaphors of blood."

As the spokesman for the "embusqués," Hill's attitudes vacillate. He damns them, but also salutes their militant spirituality, exclaiming:

> Salute us all, Christus with your iron
> garlands of poppies and ripe carrion.

Hill's Christ is very much of this world, a symbolic embodiment of the embattled earth, and specifically of the poppy fields and grave markers of the First World War. But as the immensity of

Christ's sacrifice impresses itself, Hill looks for a humbler representative or "witness" for the "embusqués." He says to Christ:

> No, sleep where you stand; let some boy-officer
> take up your vigil with your dungfork spear.

After this grotesque humbling of Christ into a farm-boy for whom the dead are manure to be dug into the earth, Hill worries:

> What vigil is this, then, among the polled
> willows, cart-shafts uptilted against skies,
> translucent rain at jutting calvaries;
> on paths that are rutted and broken-walled?
>
> What is this relic fumbled with such care
> by mittened fingers in dugout or bomb-
> tattered, jangling estaminet's upper room?
> The incense from a treasured tabatière,
>
> > you watchmen at the Passion.

This pilgrimage to war relics traces, in brief scenario, the poet's quest for metaphors or icons to embody his own passion. It resembles but does not equal such quests as Percival's for relics of Christ's Passion. His model may be Keith Douglas in his war poems. Hill once observed that "Douglas poses the dead in such a way that they become icons of a somewhat-ornate sense of doom and loss. . . . It would seem that he possessed the kind of creative imagination that approached an idea again and again in terms of metaphor, changing position slightly, seeking the most precise hold."[12] Hill both depicts the dead as icons and invokes the dead, in an act of secular communion, to judge the icons as well as those witnesses who represent them.

The Mystery is as much a meditation on writing and metaphors as on Péguy's life. The fact that Péguy wrote of war only because he had never fought in one is a paradox which Hill intends to resolve. Péguy's writing ("Heureux ceux qui sont morts") propelled him towards death. In an essay, Hill recalls that "Julian Green is 'somewhat of the opinion' that the poet Charles Péguy 'was providentially influenced by his own work' " (LL, p. 16). His tragedy was that he failed to find "the evident signs of grace in his own work" (LL, p. 16) life-furthering. Hill celebrates the poet's vision that "set[s] at one the piercing insight [of man's unmoral nature] and the carnal blundering" (LL, p. 16) and thus achieves tentative grace. His poem, similarly, strives to set at one Péguy's blindness and persipience. After scenes of pilgrimage among bomb-shattered walls and cratered battlefields, it offers a fable of the poet's quest for visionary "at-one-ment":

> Drawn on the past
> these presences endure; they have not ceased
> to act, suffer, crouching into the hail
> like labourers of their own memorial
>
> or those who worship at its marble rote,
> their many names one name, the common 'dur'
> built into duration, the endurance of war;
> blind Vigil herself, helpless and obdurate.

Hill alludes to Bergson's definition of duration to give a metaphysical dimension to what is brutally physical. Bergson said of duration that "it cannot be represented by images. . . . there is only one unique duration, which carries everything with it—a bottomless river, which flows without assignable force in a direction which could not be defined."[13] Hill, however, proposes to erect as many images as he can to catch its flux.

He achieves this *mimesis* in the rhythms of his lines and many allusions to past stories of blindness and recovered vision. Péguy's blindness is compared to Saul's in Acts (9. 3). Saul is blinded by a light from heaven which eventually purifies his sight and fills him with the Holy Ghost. Hill also compares Péguy to the two apostles who encounter Christ on the road to Emmaus. Their "eyes were holden that they should not know him" (Luke,

24. 16) but later opened so that they should. These conversion experiences are given added support by the fourteenth-century mystical text *The Cloud of Unknowing*, which describes a darkness between soul and God and a "cloud of forgetting"[14] between soul and creation in preparation for final illumination and "at-one-ment." Péguy's mysticism, however, is also a mockery of mysticism, a blindness which destroys without recreating. Hill accounts for it:

> And yet what sights: Saul groping in the dust
> for his broken glasses, or the men far-gone
> on the road to Emmaus who saw the ghost.
> Commit all this to memory. The line
>
> falters, reforms, vanishes into the smoke
> of its own unknowing; mother, dad,
> gone in that shell-burst, with the other dead,
> 'pour la patrie', according to the book.

Everything is reversed to highlight Péguy's blundering. Mystical quests are debauched "trips," in which military lines are blown up. Sacrificial acts of patriotism (Péguy's early book *Notre Patrie* was a "stream-of-consciousness" meditation on his country) culminate in familial killings.

Hill follows his inventory of the blind and dead with salutations addressed to the afflicted, who, strangely, act as guardians of the living. Although they die into the shadows, they act as instructive witnesses "of what is past, or passing, or to come." Hill begins his address:

> Dear lords of life, stump-toothed, with ragged breath,
> throng after throng cast out upon the earth,
> flesh into dust, who slowly come to use
> dreams of oblivion in lieu of paradise,
>
> push on, push on!—through struggle, exhaustion,
> indignities of all kinds . . . .

In this *danse macabre*, the dead awaken from Lethe to the sounds of a drill sergeant—"push on, push on!" and are honored in a memorial service which doubles as an awards ceremony:

> every heroic commonplace, 'Amor',
> 'Fidelitas', polished like old armour,
> stamped forever into the featureless mud.

But beneath this recompense is gloom:

> The blaze of death goes out, the mind leaps
> for its salvation, is at once extinct;
> its last thoughts tetter the furrows, distinct
> in dawn twilight, caught on the barbed loops.

This is literally "tragedy wrought to its uttermost," as Yeats described it in "Lapus Lazuli," the "black out" and "heaven blazing into the head" of the mind *in extremis*. For Hill, however, it is the final spasm before mental extinction.

Against this background of death and sickness ("tetter" is any herpiform eruption), Hill paints Péguy's mystical communities with the floral ebullience of the impressionists (some of whom were Péguy's contemporaries). The politics of these utopias are radically conservative and conservationist, as Péguy dictated. They are devoted to fertilizing the present with what is best from the past:

> There is an ancient landscape of green branches—
> true tempérament de droite, you have your wish—
> crosshatching twigs and light, goldfinches
> among the peppery lilac, the small fish
>
> pencilled into the stream. Ah, such a land
> the Ile de France once was. Virelai and horn
> wind through the meadows, the dawn-masses sound
> fresh triumphs for our Saviour . . . .

The phrase "tempérament de droite" is from Jacques Maritain, one of Péguy's friends. In the biography of the Catholic novelist

George Bernanos, Robert Speaight uses it to describe Bernanos's antidemocratic sentiments. "Bernanos was never to go back on his original faith in the French monarchy. . . . He remained to the end of his days a *tempérament de droite*—although no one castigated the droite more ferociously than he."[15] Péguy also felt nostalgia for the aristocratic *droite* of France and also battered its most precious assumptions, as did Hill's favorite nineteenth-century radical Tory, Richard Oastler, in another context. The great house, where "marshals of porte-cochère and carriage-drive" could impose a ceremonious order, was a desirable alternative to a world of war and dissipation (although Péguy never lived in such a house).

Hill's coda centers on Péguy's death and burial at Villeroy and gathers together motifs of betrayal ("A rooster wails"), cartoonlike massacres (Mr. Punch attending), crucifying earthly "at-one-ments" (Péguy's corpse "smeared by fraternal root-crops and at one / with the fritillary and the veined stone"), and natural laws clashing with laws of grace. Hill employs, as an emblem of perfection and its demise, Péguy's scrupulously correct copybooks ("At Villeroy the copybook lines of men / rise up and are erased"). He ends with a meditation on writers, soldiers, martyrs, and their vain attempts to act as the consciences of their race. Péguy's sacrifice (to win "love in the form of recognition and 'absolution' "), at the end, consumes both body and artifice. His body, indeed, is his artifice:

> the body's prayer,
> the tribute of his true passion, for Chartres
> steadfastly cleaving to the Beauce, for her,
> the Virgin of innumerable charities.

But if Péguy experiences any sort of judicious, consoling "last rites of truth," they are mockeries of the church's rite of Extreme Unction. Péguy is not judged or redeemed by God; he is conjured up and judged by Hill and his readers. As in Auden's elegy for Yeats, the dead poet (and the living poet who memorializes him) are "punished under a foreign code of conscience." They are judged by their audience:

> having composed his great work, his small body,
>
> for the last rites of truth, whatever they are,
> or the Last Judgment which is much the same,
> or Mercy, even, with her tears and fire,
> he commends us to nothing, leaves a name
>
> for the burial-detail to gather up
> with rank and number, personal effects,
> the next-of-kin and a few other facts . . . .

Péguy's position in death, as in prayer, imitates and also parodies devotion. Although Péguy's prayers may "commend us to nothing," being entirely for himself, his family, God, or France, Hill resurrects him and commends him.

Péguy's sacrifice, at the end, has some of the predictability of Christ's, but little of its apocalyptic grandeur. Biblical notions of law and grace, prophecy and fulfilment, clash with harsh facts:

> Whatever is fulfilled is now the law
>
> where law is grace, that grace won by inches,
> inched years. The men of sorrows do their stint,
> whose golgothas are the moon's trenches,
> the sun's blear flare over the salient.

But grace here, as it comes after death, is dispensed only by the earth and Hill's poem, not by God in an extraterrestrial paradise, and it is won with the sacrificial diligence of those soldiers during the Great War who pushed the "salient" forward inch by inch.

Hill's perplexity over death, final judgment, and grace is reflected in the more immediate technical problems of bringing his poem to a just and graceful conclusion. At the end of *The*

Mystery, as at the end of his earlier "An Apology," he utters an iconoclastic cry against his cathedral of well-built images, as well as against the world of "quotidian shapelessness and imperfection." Hill dispels the tempting "sense of pure fulfilment which might too easily and too subjectively be misconstrued as the attainment of objective perfection" (*LL*, p. 2) in a final, clarion protest against the complacency that such completion instills. He echoes Zola's famous denunciation of the French government for maltreating Dreyfus:

> J'accuse! j'accuse!—making the silver prance
> and curvet, and the dust-motes jig to war
> across the shaky vistas of old France,
> the gilt-edged maps of Strasbourg and the Saar.

The dust of old wars, for Hill, is never completely settled. Unlike Eliot, Hill refuses to accept tradition or history as a completed whole. If Eliot strived to find purpose in "disturbing the dust on a bowl of rose-leaves," Hill proposes to raise a dust storm from the grave. As his documentary on Péguy approaches its end, he reverses the chronological progression of the poem, reviews old battles, old tragedies and farces, and indicates, wittily, that the dance of dust motes in the film projector's beam is an apt metaphor for the events themselves.

Faced with history's motley troop of mountebanks, cartoon characters, guignols, and Mr. Punches, Hill, in his last stanzas, searches for an image of exemplary conduct. He finds a tentative one in a graveyard mourner who bellows his salutations "with hoarse dignity into the wind." But this ideal fades into the shadows. What is left besides the vacillations of "douloureux et doux," bitterness and euphoria, "éloge and elegy / . . . moving on the scene"? To countervail the destructive words and deaths of his beginning, Hill offers at the end creative words and a birth. "In memory of those things," he says of Péguy's acts of pilgrimage and devotion, "these words were born." Although Hill's poem shows rituals of devotion continually breaking beneath private misfortune and public disaster, and charity turning into bitterness and hatred, it also shows the strength of rituals to combat and order the darker side of experience. Memory and imagination, in the end, triumph over misfortune and death. Hill resurrects Péguy's virtues, along with his sins, and shapes them into an act of love and devotion, which is the marvelous poem itself. Hill's *Mystery* is a song to charity, not always mellifluous, which praises and warns against charity's zealous devotees. It is a powerful testament to a mind, both practical and principled, politically cognizant and mystically tensed, which is able to transform recalcitrant material into brilliant verse. Although Péguy's infelicities are never condoned or excused, his mystical ideal of charity, in the very care of Hill's craftsmanship, is faithfully served.

Notes
Selected Bibliography
Index

NOTES

1. Journeys, Meditations, and Elegies

1. Geoffrey Hill, "Letter from Oxford," *The London Magazine* 1, no. 4 (May 1954): 73.
2. Ibid., p. 72.
3. Hill, "Robert Lowell: 'Contrasts and Repetitions'," *Essays in Criticism* 13, no. 2 (April 1963): 191.
4. Hill, "A Writer's Craft—5," *The Isis* (17 February 1954): 14.
5. William Butler Yeats, *Letters on Poetry from W. B. Yeats to Dorothy Wellesley* (New York: Oxford Univ. Pr., 1940), p. 94.
6. Thomas Hobbes, *Leviathan* (London: Dent, 1973), p. 367.
7. John Keats, Letter to George and Thomas Keats, December 21, 27, (?), 1817, *The Letters of John Keats*, ed. Hyder Edward Rollins (Cambridge: Harvard Univ. Pr., 1958), p. 193.
8. St. John of the Cross, *The Dark Night, The Collected Works*, trans. Kieran Kavanaugh and Otilio Rodriguez (Washington: Institute of Carmelite Studies, 1973), p. 361.
9. T. S. Eliot, "Tradition and the Individual Talent," *Selected Prose*, ed. Frank Kermode (London: Faber and Faber, 1975), pp. 38–39.
10. Hill, "Letter from Oxford," p. 74.
11. Ibid., p. 73.
12. Such as Philip Larkin, Thom Gunn, Donald Davie, Anthony Thwaite, Donald Hall, Adrienne Rich, George Steiner.
13. Hill, "Under Judgment," *New Statesman* (8 February 1980): 214.

2. The Embattled Poet and His Tradition

1. Hill, "The Conscious Mind's Intelligible Structure—A Debate," *Agenda*, nos. 4–1 (1971–72): 21.
2. Hill, "The Conscious Mind," p. 15.
3. Hill, "The Conscious Mind," pp. 15–16.

4. Hill, "The Conscious Mind," p. 14.
5. Allen Tate, *Essays of Four Decades* (London: Oxford Univ. Pr., 1970), p. 599.
6. Kavanaugh and Rodriguez, trans., *The Collected Works of St. John of the Cross* (Washington: Institute of Carmelite Studies, 1973), p. 362.
7. Donald Davie, *Articulate Energy* (London: Routledge & Kegan Paul, 1955), p. 165.
8. William Wordsworth, "Preface to *Lyrical Ballads* (1802)," *Norton Anthology of English Literature* (New York: W. W. Norton, 1979), p. 162.
9. James Joyce, *Selected Letters*, ed. Ellmann (New York: Viking Pr., 1966), p. 318.
10. Hill, "The Conscious Mind," p. 23.
11. Hill, "Under Judgment," p. 213.
12. Frank Kermode, *The Sense of an Ending* (Oxford: Oxford Univ. Pr., 1966), pp. 107, 109.
13. Ibid., p. 38.
14. Hill, "Under Judgment," p. 213.
15. Christopher Ricks, *Geoffrey Hill and 'The Tongue's Atrocities'* (Llandysul: Gomer Pr., 1978), pp. 9–10.
16. The "gross error" may also refer to sodomy, allegedly committed by the crew.
17. B. Jowett, trans., *Passages from Plato* (Oxford: Clarendon Pr., 1895), pp. 21–22.
18. Yvor Winters, *On Modern Poets* (New York: World Publishing Co., 1943), p. 143.
19. William Empson, *Some Versions of Pastoral* (London: Chatto & Windus, 1935), p. 11.
20. Hill " 'I in Another Place.' Homage to Keith Douglas," *Stand*, no. 4 (1964): 7.
21. D. H. Lawrence, *Apocalypse* (London: Heinemann, 1931), pp. 103.
22. Michael Hamburger, *Reason and Energy* (London: Weidenfeld & Nicholson, 1970), p. 12, quoted from Hölderlin's *Works* (Grosse Stuttgarter Ausgabe), 5: 201.
23. Stéphane Mallarmé, *Selected Prose Poems, Essays, & Letters*, trans. Bradford Cook (Baltimore: Johns Hopkins Pr., 1956), pp. 11, 12.
24. Henry Adams, *The Education of Henry Adams* (Boston: Houghton Mifflin, 1918), p. 389.
25. Hill, *The Illustrated London News*, 20 August 1966, p. 25.
26. T. E. Hulme, *Speculations* (London: Routledge & Kegan Paul, 1914), p. 132.
27. Davie, *Purity of Diction* (London: Routledge & Kegan Paul, 1952), p. 99.

28. Adorno, as quoted by George Steiner, *Language and Silence* (New York: Atheneum, 1976), p. 53.
29. Hill, "The Poetry of Allen Tate," pp. 8-9.
30. E. M. Forster, as quoted in Henry James, *The Ambassadors* (New York: Bantam Books, 1969), p. 516.

3. Power and Authority

1. A. Alvarez, "Enter a Myth-Maker," *The Observer*, 25 October 1959, p. 23.
2. John Wain, *Preliminary Essays* (London: Macmillan, 1957), p. 179.
3. Robert Lowell, as quoted by Hugh Staples, *The First Twenty Years* (London: Faber and Faber, 1962), p. 13.
4. Hill, "The Poetry of Allen Tate," p. 9.
5. *Fables of Aesop*, trans. S. A. Handford (Harmondsworth, England: Penguin, 1954), p. 44.
6. Arthur Rimbaud, *Complete Works*, trans. Paul Schmidt (New York: Harper & Row, 1967), p. 102.
7. Harold Bloom, "The Survival of Strong Poetry," *Somewhere is Such a Kingdom* (Boston: Houghton Mifflin, 1975), p.. xvi.
8. Hill, "The Conscious Mind," p. 21.
9. Kenneth Allott, *Penguin Book of Contemporary Verse* (Harmondsworth, England: Penguin, 1962), p. 391.
10. Bloom, *Somewhere is Such a Kingdom*, p. xvii.
11. Allott, *Penguin Book*, pp. 391–92.
12. Hill refers to the obsolete definition of excrement as "outgrowth" and implies that the outer husk of both word and body need cleansing.
13. Allott, *Penguin Book*, pp. 392–93.
14. Bloom, *Somewhere is Such a Kingdom*, p. xxv.
15. Paul Valéry, *Monsieur Teste*, trans. Jackson Mathews (London: Owen, 1951), p. 32.
16. Ibid., p. 4.
17. Oscar Wilde, "The Critic as Artist," *The Portable Oscar Wilde* (New York: The Viking Pr., 1946), p. 118.
18. James Joyce, *Ulysses* (New York: Random House, 1961), p. 32.
19. Ibid., p. 34.
20. Jon Silkin, "The Poetry of Geoffrey Hill," *British Poetry Since 1960*, ed. Schmidt and Lindop (Manchester: Carcanet Pr., 1972), p. 149.
21. Yvor Winters, *On Modern Poets*, p. 132.
22. Alexis de Tocqueville, as quoted by Carl Sandburg, *Abraham Lincoln, The Prairie Years* (New York: Harcourt, Brace, 1962), p. 73.

23. Edmund Burke, *A Philosophical Enquiry into the Origin of our Ideas of the Sublime and Beautiful* (London: Routledge & Kegan Paul, 1958), p. 133.
24. Ricks, "Cliché as 'Responsible Speech': Geoffrey Hill," *London Magazine*, no. 8 (1964): 96.
25. Yeats, as quoted by Ellmann, *Yeats, the Man and the Masks* (Oxford: Oxford Univ. Pr., 1979), p. 285.
26. Thomas Mann, *Dr. Faustus*, trans. H. T. Lowe-Parker (Harmondsworth, England: Penguin, 1949), p. 235.
27. Hill, "Under Judgment," p. 214.
28. Mann, *Dr. Faustus*, p. 236.
29. Bloom, *The Anxiety of Influence* (Oxford: Oxford Univ. Pr., 1973), p. 10.
30. F. E. Halliday, *Shakespeare in his Age* (London: Duckworth, 1971), p. 2.
31. R. L. Storey, *The End of the House of Lancaster* (London: Barrie & Rockliff, 1966), p. 5.
32. Ibid., p. 7.
33. Joachim Fest, *The Face of the Third Reich* (Harmondsworth, England: Penguin, 1979), p. 17.
34. Eliot, "Tradition and the Individual Talent," *Selected Prose*, p. 38.
35. Wilfred Owen, *Poems* (London: Chatto & Windus, 1920), p. vii.
36. R. O. Jones, *A Literary History of Spain, The Golden Age* (London: Benn, 1971), p. 30.
37. Hill, "Robert Lowell: 'Contrasts and Repetitions,'" p. 188.
38. Valéry, *Monsieur Teste*, p. 4.
39. Hill, "Robert Lowell: 'Contrasts and Repetitions,'" pp. 193–94.

4. The Anglo-Saxon Heritage

1. Jessie Weston, *From Ritual to Romance* (Cambridge: Cambridge Univ. Pr., 1920), p. 21.
2. David Jones, *The Anathemata* (London: Faber and Faber, 1952), p. 10.
3. St. John Perse, *Anabasis*, trans. Eliot (London: Faber and Faber, 1930), p. 8.
4. Frederick Brittain, *Penguin Book of Latin Verse* (Harmondsworth, England: Penguin, 1962), p. xvi.
5. Ibid., p. xvii.
6. Hill, "Letter from Oxford," p. 75.
7. W. F. Bolton, *A History of Anglo-Latin Literature* (Princeton: Princeton Univ. Pr., 1967), p. 191.
8. Mathew Arnold, "Culture and Anarchy," *English Prose of the Victorian Era*, eds. Charles Frederick Harrold and William D. Templeman (New York: Oxford Univ. Pr., 1938), p. 1119.

9. Eliot, *Notes Towards a Definition of Culture* (New York: Harcourt, Brace, 1949), pp. 27, 56, 124.
10. Ibid., pp. 57, 58.
11. Ibid., p. 17.
12. Joyce, *Finnegans Wake*, (New York: The Viking Pr., 1939), p. 10.
13. Charles Oman, *England Before the Norman Conquest* (London: Methuen, 1910), p. 343.
14. Sir Thomas Malory, *King Arthur and His Knights*, ed. Eugene Vinaver (Oxford: Oxford Univ. Pr., 1956), p. 106.
15. Sayers, trans., *The Song of Roland* (Harmondsworth, England: Penguin, 1957), p. 37.
16. F. Stenton, *Anglo-Saxon England* (Oxford: Oxford Univ. Pr., 1943), p. 202.
17. Ezra Pound, *Guide to Kulchur* (London: Owen, 1938), p. 42.
18. Michael Alexander, *The Earliest English Poems* (Harmondsworth, England: Penguin, 1966), pp. 11–12.
19. Eliot, "Tradition and the Individual Talent," *Selected Prose*, p. 38.
20. Doris Stenton, ed., *Preparatory to Anglo-Saxon England* (Oxford: Oxford Univ. Pr., 1970), p. 378.
21. R. H. M. Dolley, *Anglo-Saxon Coins* (London: Methuen, 1961), p. 41.
22. Walter J. Ong, *Darwin's Vision and Christian Perspectives* (1960), pp. 134–5.
23. Aristotle, "Nicomachean Ethics," in *Introduction to Aristotle*, ed. Richard McKeon (New York: Random House, 1947), p. 308.
24. Originally in C. H. Sisson's privately-printed *Essays*.
25. Hill, "The Conscious Mind," p. 23.
26. John Ruskin, *Collected Works* (London: George Allen, 1903), 13:29.
27. F. Stenton, *Anglo-Saxon England*, p. 210.
28. Oman, *England Before the Norman Conquest*, p. 341.
29. Edward Gibbon, *The Decline and Fall of the Roman Empire* (London: Dent, 1977), 4:143–44.

5. Passion Ritualized

1. Hill, "Under Judgment," p. 213.
2. Yeats, *Dramatis Personae* (London: Macmillan, 1936), p. 13. Found originally in Aristotle.
3. Pound, *The Spirit of Romance* (London: Owen, 1910), p. 97.
4. Ibid., p. 97.
5. Richard Ellmann, *The Identity of Yeats*, p. 170.
6. W. H. Auden, "Poetry as Rite," *The Modern Tradition* (New York: Oxford Univ. Pr., 1965), p. 215.

7. Jones, *A Literary History of Spain. The Golden Age,*), pp. 87–88.
8. Hill, *Agenda,* nos. 4–1 (1972–73), p. 68.
9. St. Teresa, *The Interior Castle,* ed. Hugh Martin (London: SCM Press, 1958), p. 74.
10. St. John of the Cross, *Collected Works,* p. 716.
11. Hill, "Under Judgment," p. 212.
12. St. John of the Cross, *Collected Works,* p. 712.
13. J. M. Cohen, ed., *The Penguin Book of Spanish Verse* (Harmondsworth, England: Penguin, 1956), p. xxviii.
14. St. Teresa, *Interior Castle,* p. 81.
15. Cohen, *The Penguin Book,* p. 114.
16. St. Teresa, *Interior Castle,* p. 112.
17. St. John of the Cross, *Collected Works,* p. 715.
18. Richard Whitford, trans., *The Imitation of Christ* (New York: Harper, 1941), p. 161.
19. Ibid., p. 219. From St. John, 6:56.
20. Etienne Gilson, *The Mystical Theology of St. Bernard* (London: Sheed & Ward, 1940), p. 39.
21. Eliot, "Baudelaire," *Selected Prose,* p. 235.
22. Hill, "Under Judgment," p. 212.
23. Cohen, *The Penguin Book,* p. 163.
24. Ibid., p. 247.
25. St. Robert Southwell, *Mary Magdalen's Funeral Tears* (London: Havilard, 1823), p. 59.
26. Ibid., p. vii.
27. John Peck, "Geoffrey Hill's *Tenebrae,*" *Agenda* 1 (1979): 21.
28. Lorenzo Scupoli, *Unseen Warfare, the Spiritual Combat and Path to Paradise,* trans. E. Kadloubouski (London: Mowbras, 1978), p. 77.
29. Louis Martz, *The Poetry of Meditation* (New Haven: Yale Univ. Pr., 1954), p. 38.
30. Ibid., p. 183.
31. Southwell, *Mary Magdalen,* p. 201.
32. Hill, "The Conscious Mind," p. 16.
33. Pound, *Selected Prose,* p. 72.
34. William Milne, " 'Decreation' in Geoffrey Hill's 'Lachrimae'," *Agenda* 1 (1979): 68.
35. Weil, as quoted by Milne, pp. 62–63.
36. Wallace Stevens, *The Necessary Angel* (New York: Vintage Books, 1942), pp. 174–75.
37. Samuel Taylor Coleridge, *Anima Poetae* (London: Heinemann, 1895), pp. 151–52.

38. A. Welby Pugin, *An Apology for the Revival of Christian Architecture in England* (Frome: Butler & Tanner, 1969), p. 4.
39. Keats, Letter to Benjamin Bailey, Nov. 22, 1817.
40. Hill, "Under Judgment," p. 213.
41. John Milton, "Of Education," *Complete Prose Works* (New Haven: Yale Univ. Pr., 1964), 2:378–79.
42. Ibid., pp. 403, 404-06.
43. Edwardes, *British India, 1772–1947* (London: Sidgwick & Jackson, 1967), p. 51.
44. Ibid., p. 52.
45. Ernst Gombrich, *The Story of Art* (London: Phaidon, 1950), p. 101.
46. Georg Wilhelm Friedrich Hegel, *Lectures on the Philosophy of World History*, trans. Hugh Barr Nisbet (Cambridge: Cambridge Univ. Pr., 1975), p. 84.
47. Spengler, *The Decline of the West*, ed. Helmut Werner (London: Allen & Unwin, 1961), p. 262.
48. Cohen, p. 202.
49. Spengler, *Decline*, pp. 56, 42, 53.
50. "Come Redeemer"—A Pentecost Hymn.
51. "Christ Resurrecting"—Sung as antiphon on Easter Day. "Ave" echoed could be heard as "Eve," who for Hill symbolizes carnal as opposed to spiritual love.

6. Spiritual Biography

1. Marjorie Villiers, Daniel Halévy, Hans Schmitt, Ann and Julian Green.
2. As quoted by Marjorie Villiers, *Charles Péguy, A Study in Integrity* (London: Collins, 1965), p. 235.
3. Charles Péguy, *Basic Verities*, trans. Ann and Julian Green (London: Kegan Paul, 1943), p. 169.
4. Ibid., p. 111.
5. Ibid., p. 169.
6. Péguy, as quoted by Daniel Halévy, *Péguy and Les Cahiers de la Quinzaine* (London: Dennis Dobson, 1946), p. 137.
7. Péguy, as quoted by Halévy, *Péguy*, p. 184.
8. Hobbes, *Leviathan*, p. 5.
9. Péguy, *Basic Verities*, p. 36.
10. Péguy, as quoted by Halévy, *Péguy*, p. 178.

11. Péguy, as quoted by Villiers, *A Study in Integrity,* p. 60.
12. Hill, " 'I in Another Place', Homage to Keith Douglas," p. 10.
13. Henri Bergson, from *An Introduction to Metaphysics* in *The Modern Tradition,* ed. Richard Ellmann and Charles Feidelson (New York, 1965), pp. 728–29.
14. *The Cloud of Unknowing,* anonymous, trans. Clifton Wolters (Harmondsworth, England: Penguin, 1961), p. 58.
15. Robert Speaight, *George Bernanos* (London: Collins and Harvill, 1973), p. 36.

SELECTED BIBLIOGRAPHY

Works by Geoffrey Hill

COLLECTED WORKS

The Fantasy Poets. (A Pamphlet. No. 11. Edited by Donald Hall). Swinford: The Fantasy Pr., 1952.
For the Unfallen: Poems 1952–1958. London: André Deutsch, 1959. Chester Springs, PA: Dufour Editions, 1960.
Preghiere. (A Pamphlet.) Leeds: Northern House Pamphlet Poets, 1964.
King Log. London: André Deutsch, 1968. Chester Springs, PA: Dufour Editions, 1968.
Mercian Hymns. London: André Deutsch, 1971.
Somewhere is Such a Kingdom. Boston: Houghton Mifflin, 1975.
Tenebrae. London: André Deutsch, 1978. Boston: Houghton Mifflin, 1979.
Brand. London: Heinemann, 1978. Minneapolis: Univ. of Minnesota Pr., 1981.
The Mystery of the Charity of Charles Péguy. London: André Deutsch, 1983. New York: Oxford Univ. Pr., 1984.
The Lords of Limit: Essays on Literature and Ideas. London: André Deutsch, 1984. New York: Oxford Univ. Pr., 1984.

UNCOLLECTED ESSAYS AND REVIEWS

"*Jerusalem*, by William Blake." *The Isis* 1198 (1953): 22.
"Richard Eberhart: *Undercliff, Poems 1946–1953.*" *The Isis* 1212 (1953): 31.
"*Fantasy Poets,* No. 13, by Michael Shanks." *Trio* 3 (1953): 23–24.
"Personal Choice–4" (on Housman). *The Isis* 1218 (1954): 31.
"A Writer's Craft–5." *The Isis* 1219 (1954): 14.
"Letter from Oxford." *London Magazine* 4 (1954): 71–75.
"Contemporary Novelists–4: Francois Mauriac." *The Isis* 1238 (1954): 22.
"The Poetry of Allen Tate." *Geste* 3 (1958): 8–12.
"Issac Rosenberg Exhibition, at Leeds University." *The New Statesman* 1473 (1959): 795.

SELECTED BIBLIOGRAPHY

"The Poetry of Jon Silkin." *Poetry and Audience* 12 (1962): 4–8.
"Robert Lowell: 'Contrasts and Repetitions.'" *Essays in Criticism* 2 (1963): 188–197.
"The Dream of Reason" (on Empson). *Essays in Criticism* 1 (1964): 91–101.
" 'I in Another Place.' Homage to Keith Douglas." *Stand* 4 (1964): 6–13.
"Allen Tate." *The Concise Encyclopedia of English and American Poets and Poetry*, edited by Stephen Spender and Donald Hall, 303. London: Hutchinson, 1970.
"Issac Rosenberg." *The Concise Encyclopedia of English and American Poets and Poetry*, edited by Stephen Spender and Donald Hall, 259–60. London: Hutchinson, 1970.
"Geoffrey Hill writes:" (about *Mercian Hymns*). *Poetry Book Society Bulletin* 69 (1971).
" 'The Conscious Mind's Intelligible Structure': A Debate." *Agenda* 4–1 (1971–72): 14–23.
"Geoffrey Hill writes:" (about *Tenebrae*). *Poetry Book Society Bulletin* 98 (1978).
Review of Edward Mendelson's *Early Auden*. *The Cambridge Review* 2267 (1982): 172.
"C. H. Sisson." *PN Review* 39 (1984): 11–15.
"Gurney's Hobby." *Essays in Criticism* 2 (1984): 97–128.
Review of John Haffenden's *Berryman* and Eileen Simpson's *Poets in Their Youth*. *Essays in Criticism* 3 (1984).

INTERVIEWS

"*Symposium*: a discussion between Alan Brownjohn, Alistair Elliot, Geoffrey Hill, and Jonathan Price, with Anthony Thwaite in the chair." *Trio* 3 (1953): 4–7.
With Michael Dempsey. "Literature Comes to Life . . ." *The Illustrated London News*, 20 August 1966, pp. 24-25.
In Leeds University magazine, quoted by *TLS* reviewer, 31 October 1968.
With Blake Morrison. *New Statesman* (8 February 1980): 212–14.
With John Haffendon. *Quarto* (March 1981): 19–22. Reprinted in *Viewpoints: Poets in Conversation*, 79–99. London: Faber and Faber, 1981.

SELECTED BIBLIOGRAPHY

Selected Criticism of Geoffrey Hill

BOOKS

Robinson, Peter, ed., *Geoffrey Hill, Essays on his Work.* Milton Keynes: Open Univ. Pr., 1984.

ESSAYS AND REVIEWS

Allot, Kenneth. *The Penguin Book of Contemporary Verse.* Harmondsworth, England: Penguin, 1962.
Alvarez, A. "Enter a Myth-Maker." *The Observer,* 25 October 1959.
Bedient, Calvin. "On Geoffrey Hill." *Critical Quarterly* 2 (1981): 17–26.
Bloom, Harold. "Geoffrey Hill: The Survival of Strong Poetry." Introduction to *Somewhere is Such a Kingdom.* Reprinted in *Figures of Capable Imagination,* 234–46. New York: Seabury Pr., 1976.
Brown, Merle. *Double Lyric: Divisiveness and Communal Creativity in Recent English Poetry.* London: Routledge & Kegan Paul, 1980.
Cookson, William, ed., *Agenda: Geoffrey Hill Special Issue* 1 (1979): 4–89.
Fraser, G. S. "Formal and Relaxed." *New Statesman,* 31 October 1959.
Haffenden, John. "From Ibsen to Hill." *PN Review* 9 (no. 1): 24–25.
Hall, Donald. "Naming the Devils." *Poetry* 5 (1980): 102–6.
Heaney, Seamus. "Artists on Art: Now and In England." *Critical Inquiry* 3 (1977): 471–88. Reprinted in *Preoccupations: Selected Prose, 1968–1978.* London: Faber and Faber, 1980.
"The Isis Idol." *The Isis* 1212 (18 November 1953): 17.
Levi, Peter. *The Noise Made by Poems.* Southampton, England: Camelot Pr., 1977.
Matthias, John. "Such a Kingdom." *Poetry* 4 (1976): 232–40.
Milne, William. "Geoffrey Hill's *Mercian Hymns.*" *Ariel* 1 (1979): 43–63.
Morgan, Robert. "The Reign of King Stork." *Parnassus, Poetry in Review* 2 (Spring, Summer, 1976): 31–48.
Needham, John. "The Idiom of 'Geoffrey Hill's *Mercian Hymns.*'" *English* 131 (Summer, 1979): 139–49.
Purkis, John. "Geoffrey Hill." *A Third Level Course: Twentieth Century Poetry, The Open University,* unit 31, pp. 47–64. Milton Keynes: The Open Univ. Pr., 1976.
Ricks, Christopher, "Cliché as 'Responsible Speech': Geoffrey Hill." *London Magazine* 8 (1964): 96–101.

SELECTED BIBLIOGRAPHY

———. "Geoffrey Hill and 'The tongue's atrocities.'" *TLS* (30 June 1978): 743–47. Reprinted by Univ. College of Swansea as the W. D. Thomas Memorial Lecture. Llandysul, Wales: Gomer Pr., 1978.

———. "Overload of the M5." *The Listener*, 26 August 1971, 274.

———. "Geoffrey Hill 1: 'The Tongue's Atrocities'" and "Geoffrey Hill 2: At-one-ment," *The Force of Poetry*, 285-355. Oxford: Clarendon Pr., 1984.

Schmidt, Michael. *An Introduction to 50 Modern British Poets*, 398–407. London: Pan, 1979.

Silkin, Jon. "The Poetry of Geoffrey Hill." *British Poetry Since 1960*, edited by Michael Schmidt and Grevel Lindop, 143–64. Manchester: Carcanet Pr., 1972.

Sisson, C. H. "Geoffrey Hill." *Agenda* 3 (1975): 23–28.

Thurley, Geoffrey. *The Ironic Harvest*, 154–57. London: Edward Arnold, 1974.

Thwaite, Anthony. *Twentieth Century English Poetry*. London: Heinemann, 1978.

Waterman, Andrew. "The Poetry of Geoffrey Hill." *British Poetry Since 1970: A Critical Survey*, edited by Michael Schmidt, 85-102. Manchester: Carcanet, 1980.

Webb, Igor. "Speaking of the Holocaust: The Poetry of Geoffrey Hill." *The Denver Quarterly* 1 (1977): 114–25.

INDEX

Adam (biblical), 5, 73, 105, 109, 119, 120, 137, 157, 167, 176, 179, 192, 200, 204
Adams, Henry: *The Education of Henry Adams*, 69
Adeimantus, 47
Adorno, Theodor W., 76
Aelfric's Homilies, 20
Aeneas, 49–50, 165, 190
Aeolian harp, 19
Aesop, 84, 178
Ahab, 6–7, 11, 16
Aiaia, 197
Albigensian wars, 205
Albion, 138
Alcyone, 146
Alexander, Michael, 173
Alfred the Great, 155, 178
Allot, Kenneth: *Penguin Book of Contemporary Verse*, 91–95
Alvarez, A., 81
Anchises, 49
Andersen, Hans Christian, 120
Andromeda, 74
Aneirin, 178
Anglican Church, vii–viii, 159, 187, 244
Anglo-Saxon Chronicles, The, 20
Annunciation, 70–72, 259–60. See also Hill, "Annunciations"
Anthony, St., 148
Apocrypha, The: Book of Tobit, 33
Aquinas, St., 134
Ararat, 9, 65–66, 142, 144, 148, 150, 213

Arc, Jean d', 256, 258, 263, 266
Arendt, Hannah, 104
Argensola, Lupercia, 239
Ariel, 14
Aristotle, 28, 63; *Nicomachean Ethics*, 180; *Poetics*, 20
Armageddon, 167
Armenia, 149–50
Arnold, Mathew: *Culture and Anarchy*, 165
Artaud, Antonin, 226
Arthur, King, 16, 23; legends, 243
Astronauts, 184
Auden, W. H.: elegy for Yeats, 93, 276–77; on finishing poems, 140; on rites/rituals, 196; "September 1, 1939," 201
Augustine, St., 194, 211
Auschwitz, 75–76
Averroes, 134–35
Aztecs, 225

Babel, 77
Bacon, Francis, 85, 229
Barth, Karl, 175
Barthes, Roland, 223
Baudelaire, Charles, 82, 212, 215, 226
Baudoin, Marcel, 255, 266
Bayeux tapestry, 184
Beatrice (Dante's), 95; in Middleton's *The Changeling*, 23
Beethoven, Ludwig van, x
Beowulf, 20, 155–56, 173–74
Bergson, Henri, 258, 266, 273

INDEX

Bernanos, George, 276
Bernard, St., 211
Berryman, John, 141
Bethlehem, 9
Beulah, 4
Bible, 28, 54–56, 58, 62, 88, 277; Acts, 273–74; Apocalypse, 59, 270; Corinthians, 78; Epistles (Paul), 194; Exodus, 19; Genesis, 3, 5, 9, 119; Isaiah, 202; Jeremiah, 194; Job, 5; John, 9; Luke, 273–74; Matthew, 83, 106; Psalms, 3, 194; Revelation, 15, 40–41, 46, 105, 270; Song of Solomon, 201
Binyon, Lawrence: "For the Fallen," 84
Blackstone, William, 180–81
Blake, William, 8, 37, 51, 106, 137–38, 150; "Crystal Cabinet," 242; *Jerusalem, The Songs of Innocence, The Songs of Experience*, 3
Bloom, Harold, 90, 92, 96–97, 123
Boethius, Anicius M. S.: *The Consolation of Philosophy*, 155, 189
Bolton, W. F., 162
Bonhoeffer, Dietrich, viii
Boscán, 206
Botticelli, Sandro, 66
Brand (Ibsen), 258
Brittain, Frederick, 157
Bromsgrove, 154, 160
Brown, Merle, 210
Brutus, 261
Buchenwald, 43
Burke, Edmund, 111

Caiaphas, 270–71
Calvary, 213
Calvinists, 105
Cambridge University, vii
Campanella, Tommasso, 111–13
Cancioneros, 140–41
Canterbury, 155
Capricorn, 6–7

Carlyle, Thomas: *The French Revolution*, 233
Catholicism, 31, 113, 126–28, 129, 189, 200, 205, 215, 217, 220, 228, 229, 253, 256, 275
Catraeth: battle site, 179
Ceolred, 171
Cernunnos, 166, 177
Ceyx, 146
Chaplin, Charlie, 262
Charlemagne, 154, 162, 184, 188–89, 190
Charles I, King, 179, 239
Chartres, 266–67, 276
Chaucer, 20
Christ and Christianity, *passim*
Church Fathers, 114
Churchill, Sir Winston, 190
Church of England. *See* Anglican Church
Civil War (American), 107–8
Civil War (Spanish), 113
Clemenceau, Georges, 70
Cliché, 43, 46, 93, 116, 152, 163, 205, 220, 227, 252
Cloud of Unknowing, The, 274
Cohen, J. M.: *Penguin Book of Spanish Verse*, 195, 205
Coleridge, S. T., 230, 233; *Anima Poetae*, 229; clerisy, 242, 249; "Kubla Khan," 96; primary and secondary imaginations, 9, 54; "Rime of the Ancient Mariner," 5–6
Communion, *passim*
Compostela, 183–84, 205
Confessional poets, 52, 101, 160
Conrad, Joseph, 78
Conservatism, 159–60, 182, 256
Crane, Hart, 48, 63, 69; "The Bridge," 262; "Passage," 106
Crashaw, Richard, 253; "To his (Supposed) Mistresse," 83; "Sancta Maria Dolorum," 218
Creeley, Robert, x
Cromwell, Oliver, 179

296

INDEX

Croyland Abbey, 132
Cumae, 49, 190
Cuthbert, St., 12–13. See also Hill, "Saint Cuthbert on Farne Island"
Cythera, 197

Danelaw, 178
Dante Alighieri, 63, 94–95, 165, 254
Davie, Donald, 73, 76; *Articulate Energy*, 27–28, 35; and *Movement*, 26; *Purity of Diction*, 28
de Cabezón, Antonio, 195
Dedalus, Stephen, 102–3, 141, 147
de Gaulle, Charles, 266
de la Pole, William, 129
de la Vega, Garcilaso, 206
Delphic Oracle, 64. See also Yeats, "News for the Delphic Oracle"
Demeter, 7, 257
de Quevedo, Francisco, 214
Desnos, Robert, 114
de Toqueville, Alexis, 107
de Vega, Lope, 195, 199–200, 214–15, 222
de Victoria, Tomás Luis: "Tenebrae Responsories," 200
Dionysus, 7
Disraeli, Benjamin: *Coningsby*, 229–30
Dolley, R. H. M.: *Anglo-Saxon Coins*, 176
Domrémy, 266
Donne, John, 17, 81, 98, 222, 253; "The Calme," 7; "The Crosse," 218; "Holy Sonnets," 23; "Riding Westward," 133–34
Douglas, Keith, 41, 272
Dowland, John, 215, 217
Drake, Sir Francis, 67
Dreyfus, Alfred, 256, 258, 269–70, 278
Dulles, John Foster, 95
Dunbar, William, 16

Easter, 166–67, 202, 246, 249, 253
Eberhart, Richard: "The Fury of Aerial Bombardment," 32; "The Groundhog," 21; "If I could only live at the Pitch that is near Madness," 10
Eden, 3, 51, 71, 105, 137–38, 167, 177, 200, 208, 224
Eichmann, Adolf, 104
Eleusinian mystery cult, 257
Eliot, George, 159
Eliot, T. S., 62, 110, 115, 125, 129–31, 142, 154–55, 173, 218, 234, 268, 278; anti-Shelley, 73; on Baudelaire, 212; East Coker, 265; on Middleton, 123; mind of Europe, 71; pentecostal tongues, 116; on Perse, 157; timeless moments, 128
—Works: *Ash-Wednesday*, 29, 218; "Burnt Norton," 87, 185; "Coriolan," 167; "Dry Salvages," 212–13; *Four Quartets*, 11, 83, 93, 126, 129, 139, 234; "Gerontion," 72, 230; *The Hollow Men*, 37–38; "Little Gidding," 4, 40, 244, 265; "The Love Song of J. Alfred Prufrock," 37, 117, 141; *Notes towards a Definition of Culture*, 165; "Tradition and the Individual Talent," 16, 31; *The Waste Land*, 11, 15, 70, 141, 147, 149, 153–54, 234, 243
Elizabeth I, Queen, 217, 225, 241, 253
Elphinstone, Mountstuart, 236
Embusqués, 271–72
Emerson, Ralph Waldo, 106
Emmaus, 273–74
Empire, British, 126, 194, 234, 235
Empson, William, 20, 51, 63, 81
Ethandune (battle site), 178
Ethelbert, 155, 187

INDEX

Eurydice, 29
Eve, 70, 120, 200

Fisher King, 154, 268
Foch, Ferdinand, 258, 266
Fors Clavigera (Ruskin), 185–86
Forster, E. M., 78, 234
Forsyth, P. T., 97
Francis, St., 257
Franco, Francisco, 113
Frazer, James, 162
Freud, Sigmund, 124, 171, 247
Frost, Robert, x; "The Lesson for Today," 103; "The Most of It," 65; "An Old Man's Winter Night," 96
Furies, 89, 99–100

Gabriel (Annunciation), 91
Galicians, 205
Gauguin, 254
Gea Mater, 147
George, Lloyd, 70
Gibbon, Edward, 189
Gideon, 14–15
Gilgamesh, x
Gilson, Etienne, 211
Goebbels, Joseph Paul, 136
Golgotha, 167, 271
Gombrich, Ernst, 236
Gordon, Charles George, 258
Gorgon, 19
Gothic revival, 228
Gower, John, 20
Grant, Ulysses S., 107
Green, Julian, 273
Green, T. H., 97, 102, 232
Grotowski, J., 54
Gurney, Ivor, 41

Hadrian, Pope, 163, 168
Haffenden, John, 110, 141, 191, 208, 217, 241
Haggard, H. Rider: *King Solomon's Mines*, 29

Halleck, General, 107
Hamartia, 164
Hamburger, Michael, 60
Hardy, Thomas, 78, 114
Harpies, 121
Heaney, Seamus, ix; "Glanmore Sonnets," 175
Hegel, Georg Wilhelm, 97, 108, 118, 238
Henry I, King, 46
Henry VI, King, 85, 130–31, 134, 138
Hermod, 197
Hernandez, Miguel, 114–15
Herod, 110
Hill, Geoffrey: "After Cumae," 49–50; "Annunciations," 90–96; 220; "An Apology for the Revival of Christian Architecture in England," 227–49, 254, 266, 268, 278; "An Ark on the Flood," 1, 6–9, 11–12, 17–20, 25, 254; "Asmodeus," 25, 32–34, 143; "The Bibliographers," 123–24; "The Bidden Guest," 11, 13–14; "Canticle for Good Friday," 57, 81; "Captain Richard Fraser, Aged 24 Years," 22–24; "Of Commerce and Society," 58, 62, 69–80, 86; "The Distant Fury of Battle," 22, 25, 29–32; "Doctor Faustus," 118–23; "Elegiac Stanzas," 34–40, 85; Fantasy Poets pamphlet, vii; "Four Poems Regarding the Endurance of Poets," 86, 111–16; "Funeral Music," 85, 126–40, 198; "Genesis," 2–6, 8–9, 20, 86, 120; "Gideon at the Well," 7, 14–15; "God's Little Mountain," 19–20, 25, 30–31; "Good Friday," 9–10; "The Guardians," 47–48; "History as Poetry," 115–18; "The Imaginative Life," 86–89, 96; "For Isaac Rosenberg," 20–24; *King Log*, vii, 81–152,

INDEX

227; "Lachrimae," 194, 212–27, 240, 257; "Little Apocalypse," 59–61; "Locust Songs," 104–9; *Lords of Limit, passim*; "In Memory of Jane Fraser," 22–23; *Mercian Hymns*, vii–viii, 20, 153–92, 194, 227, 247, 255, 259; "Merlin," 22–24; "Metamorphoses," 62–69, 80–86; *The Mystery of the Charity of Charles Péguy*, vii, 1, 255–79; "In Piam Memoriam," 61–62; "Old Poet with Distant Admirers," 86; "An Order of Service," 96–97; "Orpheus and Eurydice," viii; "Ovid in the Third Reich," 103–4, 257; "A Pastoral," 51–53; "Pentecost," 11–12, 16, 268; "The Pentecost Castle," 194–212, 214, 227, 251; "Picture of a Nativity," 55–56, 81, 86–87; *Preghiere*, 115; "Prospero and Ariel," 7, 14–15, 20; "Requiem for the Plantagenet Kings," 45–46; "The Revelation," 7, 15–16; "Saint Cuthbert on Farne Island," 7, 12–13; "September Song," 110–11; "Solomon's Mines," 25–26, 28–29, 30, 32, 117; *Somewhere is Such a Kingdom*, vii; "The Songbook of Sebastian Arrurruz," 85, 140–52, 195, 255; "To the (Supposed) Patron," 81–84; *Tenebrae*, vii, 193–254; "Tenebrae," 194, 249–54; "Three Baroque Meditations," 85, 98–102; "The Tower Window," 22–23; "Two Formal Elegies," 41–44, 129; *For the Unfallen*, vii, 25–80, 81–86, 119, 227; "The White Ship," 46–48; "To William Dunbar," 7, 12; "Wreaths," 48–49
Hitler, Adolf, viii, 60, 70, 110, 136–37, 181

Hobbes, Thomas, 12, 264
Hoffa, Jimmy, 163
Hölderlin, Friedrich, 59–60
Holocaust (of WW II), 41–44, 71, 73, 75–77, 103, 110
Homer, 175; *The Iliad*, 42
Hopkins, Gerard Manley, x, 58, 81
Horeb, 19
Hughes, Ted, 4, 115, 232; *Hawk in the Rain*, 99
Hulme, T. E., 35, 71, 76

Icarus, 120
Illustrated London News, The, 70
Imitation of Christ, 210
India, 230, 241. *See also* Hill, "A Short History of British India," 233–37
Indians (American), 105, 115, 142, 225
Ine of Wessex, 155
Inquisition, 111, 115
Ishmael, 6–7, 16

Jacob (biblical), 158–59
Jagannath, 235
James, Henry, 78–79, 122
James, St. (of Compostela), 184, 204–5
James I, King, 225, 241
Janus, 59, 225
Jaurès, Jean, 255, 259–61, 267, 269
Jefferson, Thomas, 107
Jehovah, 5, 43, 76–77, 104, 109–10, 153
Jerome, St., 148
Jesse tree, 202
Jews, 41–43, 110–11; Jewish demonology, 33
John, St., 46, 59, 132. *See also* Bible: Apocalypse, Revelation
John of the Cross, St., 142, 198, 200, 205–6; *The Dark Night*, 15,

INDEX

John of the Cross, St. (cont.) 34; "The Dark Night," 201; "The Spiritual Canticle," 207
Johnson, Samuel, 169, 229
Johnston, General, 107
Jones, David, 53; *The Anathemata, In Parenthesis*, 157
Jones, Inigo, 224
Jones, R. O., 141, 197–98
Jonson, Ben: *Masque of Blacknesse*, 215, 224–25
Joseph of Arimathea, 264–65
Joyce, James, 53, 142, 163, 166, 191, 253; diction, 28; Earwicker, 72, 177, 190; *Finnegans Wake*, 39, 153; "history's nightmare," 102–3; *Ulysses*, 141
Judas, 70, 194, 270–71
Jung, C. G., 124

Keats, John, 13, 227; "The Eve of St. Mark," 248–49; "Ode on a Grecian Urn," 232–34; "Ode to a Nightingale," 248
Keble College, vii, 1
Kermode, Frank: *The Sense of an Ending*, 41, 43
Keyes, Sidney, 197
Kipling, Rudyard, 44
Krishna, 235

La Beauce, 254, 266–68
Lancaster (in Wars of the Roses), 127, 132
Langland, William, 20
Larkin, Philip, 57, 61; "Church Going," 58
Last Judgment, 5, 19, 105, 270, 277; final judgment, 59
Lawrence, D. H., 41, 60, 245
Lazarus: in Gospel of John, 116–18; in Gospel of Luke, 251
Leda, 75. *See also* Yeats, "Leda and the Swan"
Leechdom, 171–72

Leeds University, vii, 1, 55
Leopardi, Giacomo, 152
Les camelots du Roi, 270
Lethe, 14
Leverkühn, Adrian, 119
Leviathan (biblical), 5, 85
Lincoln, Abraham, 107
Linnaeus, Carolus, 227, 231, 237, 239
Logres, 22
London, 128–30
London Magazine, 1
Lorca, Federico García, 199
Lord of Misrule, 253
Lowell, Robert, 2, 17, 20, 51, 63, 101, 109; "Children of Light," 71, 108; *Imitations*, 142, 152; "At the Indian Killer's Grave," 105; *Land of Unlikeness*, 211; "Quaker Graveyard in Nantucket," 17, 108; on raw and well-cooked poetry, 82, 124; "Winter in Dunbarton," 94
Loyola, St. Ignatius: *The Spiritual Exercises*, 189, 213, 217
Lucifer, 14, 79, 119, 121, 123–24

Machado, Antonio, 141
Magdalen, Mary, 58, 199, 215, 217, 240
Magi, 56, 87–88. *See also* Yeats, "The Magi"
Malcolm, Sir John: *Political History*, 236
Mallarmé, Stéphane, 64
Malory, Sir Thomas, 170
Malvern, 181
Mandelshtam, Osip, 114, 150
Mann, Thomas: *Doctor Faustus*, 118–19, 121–22
Margaret of Anjou, Queen, 132
Maritain, Jacques, 27, 275
Marlowe, Christopher, 240; *Dr. Faustus*, 118–19, 121–22
Marne, battle of, 255, 264, 269

INDEX

Martyrs, vii, 10, 41, 55, 59, 76, 85, 95, 100, 110, 208–9, 218, 225, 261, 264, 271, 276; Arrurruz as martyr, 141–42; Boethius as martyr, 189; Catholic martyrs under Elizabeth 1, 217; Christian martyrdom, 212, 247; "The Martyrdom of St. Sebastian," 78; "Martyrium," 226; Péguy as martyr, 256, 263
Martz, Louis, 216
Marvell, Andrew, 240
Marx, Karl, 257
Mary, the Virgin, 58, 205, 218, 246, 276
Master of the Leaping Figures, 253
Medina, 199–200
Mediterranean, 44, 50
Medusa, 74
Mellor, Oscar, 20
Melville, 17; Ahab and Ishmael, 16; *Moby-Dick*, 7, 16, 18
Mephistophilis, 121
Mercia, vii. *See also* Hill, *Mercian Hymns*
Merlin, 16, 23. *See also* Hill, "Merlin"
Merovingian kings, 190
Midas, 224
Middle English, 20
Middleton, Thomas, 123
Midlands (England), 44, 155, 159
Milton, John, 20, 229; *Defence of the English People*, 179; *Of Education*, 236; "Epitaphium Damonis," 240; "grand style," 18; "Lycidas," 17–19; *Paradise Lost*, 108–9; *Second Defence of the English People*, 239
Minerva, 98–99
Mnemosyne, 118, 187
Moby Dick (film), 262
Modernism, 28, 34, 36, 62–80
Moore, Marianne, 223
Mormons, 107
Morpheus, 146

Morrison, Blake, 40, 194
Moses, 2, 19, 42, 65, 158
Movement, The, 26, 28, 33, 52, 81
Mughal, 237
Muir, Edwin: "The Absent," 109
Mwynfawr, 179
Mystical experience: Hill's views on, 208

Narcissus, 182
National Convention (French), 260
Nazis, 43, 110–11
Nero, 186
Neville, Richard, 129
Newbolt, Henry: "Drake's Drum," 67
Newman, John Henry Cardinal, 39, 228
Newton, Sir Isaac, 184
Nicetas, St., 157
Nietzsche, Friedrich, 130
Noah, 65, 213
Norman Conquest, 184, 188
Novena, 269

Oastler, Richard, 160, 230, 276
Oedipus, 123
Offa, King, 20, 59, 153–92 *passim*, 259
Old English, viii
Old Testament, 41, 108
Olson, Charles: *Maximus Poems*, 153–54
Oman, Charles, 168, 188
Orlando, Vittorio, 70
Orpheus, 29. *See also* Hill, "Orpheus and Eurydice"
Ovid, 104; *Amores*, 103; *Metamorphoses*, 63, 146. *See also* Hill, "Ovid in the Third Reich"
Owen, Wilfred, 41, 51, 131, 140
Oxford (England), 1, 9, 17, 20, 24–26, 40, 42, 49, 62, 154, 159–60, 268

INDEX

Palestine, 108
Pandemonium, 14, 121
Pandora's box, 100
Pangloss, 43
Parnassus, 64
Peck, John, 216
Péguy, Charles, 255–79 passim; Eve, 269; "The Modern World," 258; Le Mystère de la Charité de Jeanne d'Arc, 255, 263; The Mystery of the Holy Innocents, 263; Notre Patrie, 274
Pengwern, 179
Pentecost, 11–15, 19, 116, 129, 136, 245, 268. See also Hill, "The Pentecost Castle"
Percival, 170, 243, 272
Perse, St.-John: Anabasis, 157
Perseus, 74, 138
Persia, 237
Peter's Pence, 163, 168
Petrarch, 143, 145, 196, 206, 210, 214–15, 249, 251–52
Philips, Peter, 215
Phineus, 121
Phoenix, 6, 72
Piers Plowman, 149
Pilate, Pontius, 270–71
Pilgrim Fathers, 104–5
Plantagenet kings, 45, 59, 127. See also Hill, "Requiem for the Plantagenet Kings"
Plath, Sylvia, 101; "Lady Lazarus," 65
Plato, 34, 130, 140, 229; allegory of the cave, 16, 50, 128, 130, ideas and idealism, 182–83, 230, 232; Ion, 125; love, 250; Platonic forms, 8; "Platonic old England," 241, 243, 266; The Republic, 47, 50, 240; vision, 18
Pomfret, 128
Pound, Ezra, ix, 62, 142, 154, 169, 185, 234; anti-Shelley, 73; The Cantos, 70, 153; Christian and romantic love, 220; economics, 168; Guide to Kulchur, 172; "Hugh Selwyn Mauberley," 141, 150; "ideogrammatic method," 80; Offa, 176; Spirit of Romance, 196
Powys, Princes of, 179
Pre-Raphaelite painters, 254
Prometheus, 33
Prose poems, 155–59
Prospero, 14–15
Protectorate parliament, 238
Protestant, 105, 107–8, 127, 178, 220
Provençal, 196, 205
Psalter: Jewish, 158; Roman, 155, 158
Pugin, A. Welby, 228–29
Punch, Mr., 276, 278
Puyana, Rafael, 195

Quixote, Don, 206

Radical Tories, 160, 276
Renaissance (English), 124, 127, 132, 214–15, 217, 229, 238–39, 253–54
Renaissance (Spanish), 140–42, 195, 214, 239, 254
Republicanism (French), 256, 260
Richard II, King, 128
Ricks, Christopher, ix, 44, 116
Rimbaud, Arthur, 88–89, 215
Roethke, Theodore: The Far Field, 203
Romanticism, 73, 92, 104, 106, 152, 198, 211, 220–21, 225–27, 232, 243; Baudelaire's romanticism, 212; romantic tradition, 25–40
Rome, 49, 161, 187, 189–90, 196, 217, 271; Roman Britain, 168;

INDEX

Roman Empire, 189; Roman Europe, viii
Rosenberg, Isaac, 16, 41. *See also* Hill, "For Isaac Rosenberg"
Rosetti, Dante Gabriel: "The White Ship," 46
Ruskin, John, 169, 185–86, 253

Sagar, Keith, 33
St. Cyr, 266
St. Elmo's fire, 262
Salmasius, 179
Sassoon, Siegfried, 41
Saul (Acts), 273–74
Scott, Sir Walter, 127
Scupoli, Lorenzo: *Unseen Warfare*, 216
Scyld Shefing, 156
Sebastian, St., viii, 78, 122, 142, 144
Shakespeare, William, 20, 45, 130, 229, 231, 253; *Cymbeline*, 164; *Hamlet*, 16, 21; *Henry IV*, 174; *Henry VI*, 127–28, 132, 137; *Julius Caesar*, 261; *King Lear*, 43; *The Tempest*, 14–46
Shelley, Percy Bysshe, 17, 73–75
Shiloh, 107–8
Sibyl, 20, 49–50, 190
Sidney, Sir Philip, 229, 240
Silkin, Jon, 104
Sirens, 17
Sisson, C. H., viii, 180–81
Sisyphus, 167
Smart, Christopher, 3
Socrates, 47
Solomon, King. *See* Hill, "Solomon's Mines"
Somerset (in *Henry VI*), 127
Song of Roland, The, 170–71, 184
Southwell, St. Robert, vii, 217, 253; *Mary Magdalen's Funeral Tears*, 213, 215–16
Speaight, Robert, 276

Spengler, Oswald, 178, 238–40
Spenser, Edmund, 20, 240
Stalin, Joseph, 114
Steiner, George, 76
Stenton, F., 186
Stevens, Wallace, 54, 215, 240–41, 243; "Adagia," 87; "Asides on the Oboe," 61; "Auroras of Autumn," 249; "Lebensweisheitspielerei," 97; "The Man on the Dump," 93; "Of Modern Poetry," 95; *The Necessary Angel*, 222–23; "An Ordinary Evening in New Haven," 86; "The Snow Man," 96; "Sunday Morning," 99
Storey, R. L., 127
Stork, King, 84
Suffragans, 88–89
Surrealists, 226
Sutton Hoo, 173
Sweet's Anglo-Saxon Reader, 20, 155, 158
Swift, Jonathan, 17, 58, 81, 182, 229
Symbolism. *See* Symbolist
Symbolist, 36, 53, 64–65, 87, 92, 102, 197, 214–15
Symons, Arthur, 87

Tamworth, 162
Tantalus, 2
Tate, Allen, 20, 24, 63, 77, 106; "More Sonnets at Christmas," 58, 70; "The Oath," 31; "Ode to our Young Pro-Consuls of the Air," 70; "Ode to the Confederate Dead," 30, 32, 45, 74, 108; "Seasons of the Soul," 67; "The Swimmers," 212
"Te Deum," 157–58
Tenebrae (ritual), 193–94, 202, 249, 254
Tennyson, Alfred, 44, 243–44

INDEX

Teresa, St., 142, 198, 205–6; *The Interior Castle*, 14, 207
Terezin camp, 114
Teste, Monsieur and Emilie, 101, 144
Tewkesbury, 131–32
Theodoric, 189
Third Reich, 110, 136
Thomas (doubting Thomas), 49–51, 57–58, 81, 91
Thomas, Dylan, 118; "The force that through the green fuse . . .," 21–22
Thor, 192
Tiber, 49
Tiptoft, John, 129
"Titanic, The," 77–78
Towton (battle of), 127, 131–32, 137
Troilus, 12
Troubadour, 195, 205
Troy, 49
Tusser, Thomas, 105

Ulysses, 17, 197
USSR, 115
University of Michigan, 91
Uranus, 68

Valéry, Paul, 101, 144
Venus, 65–68
Verdun, 262
Verne, Jules, 258
Veronica, St., 226
Versailles, 70, 73
Viaticum, 226
Villeroy, 276
Virgil, 17; *The Aeneid*, 20, 49, 190
Voltaire, 43
Vosges, 189

Wain, John, 81
Wakefield (battle site), 131–32
Wars of the Roses, The, 85, 115, 126–40 *passim*

Weil, Simone, 27–28, 219, 222; *The Need for Roots*, 27
Wergild, 169, 187
Westminster Abbey, 17, 128
Weston, Jessie: *From Ritual to Romance*, 154
Whiggery, 160
Whitman, Walt, 106, 154
Whittaker, Nancy, 25
Wilde, Oscar, 100, 102
Williams, William Carlos, 64; *Paterson*, 153–54
Wilson, Woodrow, 70
Wimsatt, W. K., 185
Winters, Yvor, 48, 106
Woodville, Anthony, 129
Worcestershire, vii, 12, 154, 160–61, 163, 186, 191–92
Wordsworth, William, 39, 137–38, 170, 229, 230; diction 28; "Elegiac Stanzas," 35–38; "Intimations of Immortality," 14, 36–37; "Preface to *Lyrical Ballads*," 38; "Prospectus," 66–67
World War I (The Great War), 67, 70–71, 84, 142, 150, 189, 241, 260, 263
World War II, 4, 41, 43, 60, 70, 75, 114, 130, 153, 168, 197, 271

Yeats, William Butler, 26–28, 51, 54, 93, 118, 148, 166, 170, 188, 200, 225, 232, 234, 251, 269, 276; ballads, 195; "Byzantium," 6, 11, 43, 265; on civilization, 183; "A Dialogue of Self and Soul," 133; dramatic lyrics, 63; "Easter 1916," 39–40, 42; gyres, 132; language, 91; "Lapus Lazuli," 275; later poetry, 73; "Leda and the Swan," 259; "The Magi," 56, 87–88; "The Man and the Echo," 259; "Meditations in Time of Civil

War," 152; "News for the Delphic Oracle," 67, 104, 122; "Sailing to Byzantium," 16; "Among Schoolchildren," 213; "The Second Coming," 85, 87; "terrible beauty," 66; "Vacillation," 68

York (in Wars of the Roses), 127, 132

Zeus, 75, 84–85, 259
Zola, Emilie, 258, 278
Zyklon, 110

Henry Hart received the D.Phil. degree from Oxford University in 1983 and is currently Professor of English at The Citadel. His previous work on Geoffrey Hill has appeared in *Essays in Criticism, Critical Survey of Poetry* (1982), and *Geoffrey Hill: Essays on His Work* (1984). He is coeditor of *Verse*, an international literary magazine, and has received a number of awards for his own poetry, including third prize in England's National Poetry Competition (1983).

Northern Michigan University

3 1854 003 708 271

EZNO
PR6015 I4735 Z68 1986
The poetry of Geoffrey Hill

DATE DUE

WITHDRAWN

DEMCO 38-297